*Meaning, Reference and Necessity*

# Meaning, Reference and Necessity

## NEW STUDIES IN SEMANTICS

EDITED BY

## SIMON BLACKBURN

Fellow of Pembroke College, Oxford

## CAMBRIDGE UNIVERSITY PRESS

CAMBRIDGE

LONDON · NEW YORK · MELBOURNE

Published by the Syndics of the Cambridge University Press
The Pitt Building, Trumpington Street, Cambridge CB2 1RP
Bentley House, 200 Euston Road, London NW1 2DB
32 East 57th Street, New York, NY 10022, USA
296 Beaconsfield Parade, Middle Park, Melbourne 3206, Australia

© Cambridge University Press 1975

Library of Congress Catalogue Card Number: 74–31785

ISBN: 0 521 20720 7

First published in 1975

Printed in Great Britain by
Western Printing Services Ltd, Bristol

# Contents

v

# Introduction

These essays represent work by some young British philosophers on the theory of meaning. It seemed useful to put them together to form one volume, for a number of reasons. Mainly, they are each concerned with some aspect of the problem of individuating meaning and meaning change, so that although the detailed problems discussed are various, philosophers interested in one are likely to be interested in the rest. Furthermore none of the essays presupposes a great deal of technical ability, so that all should be within the reach of students who have mastered the syntax and semantics of elementary logic, and some might form an introduction to the area for students who have not even done that. Finally the essays have a certain unity of approach, for each is basically optimistic about the solubility of problems associated with meaning, although each is also aware of the difficulties such optimism faces. In the last analysis, of course, the justification for a collection lies in the quality of the pieces, but this is something for an editor to believe in rather than assert.

The first essays in the collection explore the relation between necessary truth and meaning. Neither of them finds the connection nearly as straightforward as recent philosophers have suggested. E. J. Craig carefully displays the precise way in which both Conventionalism and Quinean theories of necessity fail to give a satisfactory explanation of the inexorability of necessary truths: the slogan that these are "true in virtue of meaning" is left entirely valueless. Susan Haack supports Craig from another direction, by showing that there is no straight veto from the theory of translatability, forbidding us from interpreting people as holding alternative logical truths to the ones we have adopted. What forces us to believe necessary truths is therefore a good deal more complicated than anything theories of meaning have so far envisaged, and is even, if Craig is right, to be sought wholly outside the scope of the theory of meaning.

Necessity is also one of the topics of Thomas Baldwin's paper, but here it is the interpretation of referential devices and quantifiers in sentences using modal and propositional attitude constructions which provides the problem. The importance of such contexts is twofold: until we know how to construe them we cannot be said to understand the sense of even the most basic items of communication —names, predicates, and quantifiers. And, as Quine has emphasised, unless we can be satisfied that such contexts are logically proper we should not rely on their occurrence in natural language as itself legitimising intensional notions. It might be the part of prudence to eschew such contexts, or give at best a pallid reconstruction of them. Baldwin argues that the problems of interpretation are soluble, but that the solution must involve acceptance, in a basically Fregean way, of a strong equivalence between sentences: analyticity. In the course of his discussion he defends and relies on a basically Kripkean account of the contribution of proper names, which is further discussed and illuminated in Christopher Peacocke's paper following.

If the technical problems of interpreting indirect contexts demand acceptance of analyticity then we are confronted squarely by the argument that no empiricist can make sense of the notion. Ralph Walker shows some of the difficulty which arises with any attempt to construct a precise distinction between the content of an assertion on the one hand and implications it may have but which do not belong to its content, on the other. This indeed threatens us with some degree of indeterminacy in the concept of the sense of the single sentence, but not the massive indeterminacy which Quine and others have detected. It is part of the purpose of my own paper to show that this pessimism at least is ungrounded, although I also believe that the notion of meaning which epistemology licenses will not have many of the properties traditionally claimed for it, particularly by writers in the tradition of Frege.

This is a brief indication of the topics of the essays. The issues are among those most discussed, some might say over-discussed, in contemporary philosophy. But they have more than purely parochial popularity. The whole course of philosophy over the last three hundred years witnesses that without a basic clarity about meaning we can gain no basic clarity about anything else, and without a fundamental understanding of meaning we can hope for a fundamental understanding of nothing else. Again and again issues in the philosophy of mind, in ethics, in the whole sphere of epistemology, have been found to turn on some crux in the notion of meaning. So if the theory of meaning should, eventually, be just a tool in the construction of higher and wider philosophies, we must still remember that it is a necessary tool; as yet it waits to be fashioned.

*Pembroke College,*                                    SIMON BLACKBURN
*Oxford*

# I

# The problem of necessary truth

E. J. CRAIG

Of the things which we hold to be true there are some which are not only true but could not thinkably have been false. So, at least, it appears, and the appearance is persistent enough to be troublesome. And it is likely to be particularly troublesome when the prevailing mood in philosophy is broadly empiricist, since even if we have put behind us, as either solved or non-existent, problems about how the senses can inform us as to what is the case, it remains unclear how they can provide the basis of our apparent knowledge that certain things could not be otherwise. One response to this has been the rise to popularity of the view that necessary truths are not forced upon us by the nature of the world, but are rather some type of convention.

This popularity can hardly be due to any immediate plausibility or intuitive appeal. Far from it: there is *prima facie* an element of paradox about Conventionalism, since the truths in question seem to be anything but conventional, and attract attention precisely by their air of inexorability. It draws support by its supposed explanatory power, its power of making the existence of such truths, and our knowledge of them, non-problematic. So that if any form of Conventionalism is to recommend itself more than superficially, it really must have this explanatory property, and our first question must therefore be: what form of Conventionalism, if any, satisfies that condition?

It has often been said that necessary truth is truth by virtue of meaning, and I shall take this dictum as my starting point, but that does not mean that my paper will have nothing to say to any philosopher who rejects it. Its rejection is associated, in particular, with the name of Quine, who also doubts whether there are any propositions which are necessary, if that be taken to mean that they are absolutely "immune from revision". Readers who share his opinions may therefore feel, after two or three pages, that what is written here can be of little interest to them, being concerned solely with the consequences of an assumption which they reject. That would be mistaken—the argument does in fact throw light on a Quinean theory of necessity, and perhaps on other issues from the history of the problem. What light, it will be easier to see when the argument has been stated.

No question but words have the meanings they do have as a result of what is, in a perfectly acceptable sense, a convention, but this fact, even if we are allowed to combine it with the view that necessary truths are those in which truth is guaranteed by meaning, does not go very far as an *explanation* of necessary truth. Why it is necessary that one plus one is two may not be an easy question: but why it should be necessary that the meanings of "one", "plus", and the rest, when combined in just that way, should yield a true statement, is certainly no easier. So the crucial Conventionalist move is to shift attention from the individual words to the whole sentence. Necessity is regarded as having its source in some such corporate decision as that the sentence in question is to be held true whatever factual circumstances may arise or be imagined. Concentration on the whole sentence as the immediate object of the convention enables us to overcome the awkward problem about the way in which the various individual word-meanings fit together. There is no reason why we should not go on saying that the meanings of "one", "plus", etc., do so fit together that it is necessarily true that one plus one is two, but how this can be so will, if we adopt the Conventionalist suggestion, cease to be puzzling. For in legislating that the whole sentence cannot be false we are, in effect, legislating about the individual word-meanings too. The agreement that "One plus one is two" shall always be true is one of the factors which contribute to the meanings of "one", "plus", "two", and "is". The meanings dovetail because we make them dovetail by our stipulation, and the fact of their dovetailing can now itself appear as a convention.

The structure of this paper is, then, as follows: it is first argued that anyone who wishes to combine two plausible (and in fact widely accepted) assumptions about meaning with a conventionalist attitude to necessity will be forced, *via* the position which I have briefly sketched in the last paragraph, to certain other views about necessity; otherwise his Conventionalism will become trivial and completely non-explanatory. This part (sections I and II) therefore concerns the theory of necessary truth in general; but in section III we turn to the more specific subject matter of arithmetical necessity. Sections IV–VI contain the detailed argument for holding that the position into which the Conventionalist is driven is false in its application to arithmetic. This argument is such as to lead on to positive points about the form which an account of arithmetical truth has to take, and the paper ends with a section relating these points to the doctrines of Quine, and also suggesting some Kantian parallels.

<h1 style="text-align:center">I</h1>

A sentence is composed of certain words arranged in accordance with certain rules of syntax. The first of the two assumptions is:

(A) Given the meanings of the words and the syntax the meaning of the sentence is fixed.

A sentence can of course have more than one meaning. But, according to (A), that can only be so if either one of its constituent words has more than one meaning, or there is more than one syntactical way of reading it. The assumption is attractive. After all, what other factors could there be that are partially determinative of the meaning of a sentence? It is often said that one thing which can affect the meaning of a sentence is the context of utterance, and I do not wish to deny this. There are plenty of sentences which are plainly ambiguous, and when we hear or read such a sentence we decide which of the admissible meanings is actually intended by consideration of features of the context. But this need not be seen as conflicting with the principle that sentence-meaning is totally determined by word-meaning plus syntax. In the cases of context dependence which most quickly come to mind it is clear that what the context does is to decide the meanings of certain words within the sentence, or its syntactical construction, so that to use these cases to assault the principle (A) would be rather like attacking the statement that the shape of a house is wholly determined by the positions and shapes of its bricks by calling up the undeniable truth that the shapes of houses depend on builders. Admittedly there can be found examples in which two utterances of one sentence seem to have different significance, although the meaning of no word, or element of the syntax, has been changed by the variation in the context. The question "When did you last see your father?" is not always as sinister as it becomes in the well-known picture, though one would not wish to say that any word or the syntax had altered in meaning. But differences of this kind are best attributed, I think, to one's knowledge of the whole situation, in this case the probable consequences of the child's answering truthfully, rather than to any difference in the meaning of the sentence. That all such cases can plausibly be treated in this sort of way is to some extent an article of faith; but it may be backed up by the consideration that any theory of meaning which did not include it would be heading for appalling complexities over the notion of the meaning of a sentence, since it would turn out that a sentence scarcely ever had the same meaning twice. Nevertheless, it should be kept in mind that there is an element of stipulation, or perhaps rather of prediction of the form which a satisfactory theory of meaning will take, involved in acceptance of (A).

It is an easy step from here to the view that any property which a sentence has as a result of its meaning it has, in a more thorough analysis, as a result of the meanings of its syntax and its individual terms. Now the second of the two assumptions is:

(B) Necessary truths are precisely those whose meaning is logically sufficient for their truth.

Any sentence (identified phonologically or typographically rather than semantically) could come to express something false. For very many sentences, this could happen in either of two ways—there might be a change in the facts they describe, or their meanings might change as a result of change in linguistic practice. But, according to (B), such sentences as express necessary truths could express something false *only* if they came to express something else. This is widely accepted, and like (A), it is very attractive, especially when we have observed that it does not depend on the truth of the controversial (though also widely accepted) view that all necessary truths are analytic.[1] Suppose we find that from the statement that a given sentence, which happens to express a necessity, has the meaning it does, we cannot deduce that what it expresses is true without adding to our premises some further proposition. Thus if we con-

---

[1] Unless, that is, the view that all necessary truths are analytic is so understood as to make it identical with (B).

sider, for instance, someone who takes a broadly Kantian line about synthetic necessary truth, we find that he would, in certain cases, wish to include some statement about the deliverances of "pure intuition". This I give simply as an example, since it is quite immaterial what the additional premiss is said to be: for suppose we are given that

(1) The sentence S says that *p*,

and it is claimed that we need some further premiss

(2) *q*

in order to deduce the conclusion

(3) The sentence S says something true.

Now if *q* is a necessary truth, then given that (3) does follow from the conjunction of (1) and (2), (1) by itself is logically sufficient for (3), in the sense that it is logically impossible that (1) should be true and (3) false. If on the other hand *q* is contingent, and (3) cannot be reached without its help, that means that the truth of some contingent proposition is necessary for the truth of *p*, in which case *p* is itself contingent. So if what S expresses *is* necessary, that it means what it does is logically sufficient for its truth; and it scarcely needs arguing that if it is *not* necessary, something further is required for its truth. Which proves (B), and proves it independently of any particular theory about necessary truth. Those who deny, as does Quine, that there is such a thing as truth-guaranteed-by-meaning, also deny that there is such a thing as absolute necessity.

## II

On (A) and (B) is built one of the standard objections to Conventionalism: the meanings of the words of any sentence and the force of its syntax have been laid down by what is admittedly a convention, if in a somewhat extended sense. But once that has been done there is no scope for further, necessity-generating, conventions. For the conventions that govern the meanings of the words and the import of the syntax fully determine the meaning of the whole sentence, and then either the meaning is sufficient for truth, in which case we have a necessity, or it isn't, in which case we don't.

If this meant that the Conventionalist were compelled to deny either (A) or (B), it would constitute very strong, if not completely conclusive, grounds for rejecting Conventionalism. And at first sight it may well appear that it does mean this. To put the point slightly differently: the Conventionalist must say that the conventions he speaks of are conventions applying directly to *whole sentences*; if he says that the conventions apply in the first instance to individual words and syntactic arrangements, and then have *consequences* which concern whole sentences, he will have said nothing to distinguish himself from his opponents, since they also hold this. But now it seems that from (A) and (B) it follows that there is no room for any conventions which apply directly to entire sentences—not, at any rate, for conventions which can have anything to do with the origin of necessary truth—since word-and-syntax conventions decide meaning, and meaning decides necessity or contingency.

One thing that can make this seem to be so, however, is an unclarity in the meaning of such terms as "decide" or "determine". If it be said that whatever determines the meanings of words and syntax thereby determines the meaning of the sentence, this may simply mean that the former is logically sufficient for the latter, that it is logically impossible for sentence-meaning to be different without a difference in word- or syntax-meaning, and this is what the principle (A) asserts. But it may also be taken to mean that word- and syntax-meaning may be formed prior to and independently of any conventions about the uses of entire sentences in which they occur, and having been so formed, then determine the meanings of sentences, and this is a view which quite certainly goes beyond what is meant by (A) as I have explained it. For the truth of (A) is perfectly compatible with the view that certain words have the meanings they do *only because* various sentences, in which they occur, are treated, as a matter of direct convention, as expressing necessary truths.

An example may help to clarify this abstract presentation of the point. It might be said (I do not wish to suggest that it would be totally free of all difficulty or obscurity) that only a part, if perhaps a large part, of the meaning of such words as "square" and "round" is determined by the conventions which lay down what sensory experiences justify a speaker in applying the terms to objects, or, less technically, what square and round things look like and feel like. Other conventions which are further determinants of the meaning are, e.g., that "Nothing is both round and square" is to be held true no matter what. Essential to the view I am stating is that this is a *further* convention, that it is independent of the former set of conventions and not an obligatory consequence of them. The final meaning is to be seen as a product of these separate factors, so that (in the words of D. A. T. Gasking):

the "connections among what is meant" are determined by what propositions are necessary, and not vice-versa.

(Gasking [1939] p. 75)

That this should be true is not only compatible with the outcome of (A) and (B), namely that for any necessary truth, the meanings of the constituent words and syntax are sufficient for its necessity; it even offers an explanation of it. It tells us that the reason why the meanings of the components are sufficient for the truth of the whole is precisely that the truth of the whole is one of the factors which *gives* them those meanings. That the meanings generate a necessity is true, but there is no further problem as to how they generate it; that, on this view, is a triviality, and amounts to no more than that the fact that they do feature in this sentence is one of the things which makes them mean what they do.

This, then, is the Conventionalist's reply to the standard objection based on (A) and (B). It is, so far as I can see, his only possible reply, and, at first sight, it is one he can gladly give. It maintains the essential feature of his theory, namely that there is an *independent* necessity-generating convention which applies directly to the whole sentence; and it has the additional advantage just mentioned, that it accounts for the way in which word-meanings determine necessity, namely by so presenting the phenomenon that it can be seen to need no accounting for.

The second of these points is worth dwelling on, since it may be thought to give the Conventionalist an advantage over all rival theorists. They hold that the ultimate explanation of the necessity of a sentence is to be given in terms of the meanings of individual words and syntactical patterns, so that if they are asked to account for the truth of

(1) What the sentence S expresses is necessarily true,

their answer will take the form

(2) $W_1 \ldots W_n$ (the words of S) have such and such meanings and stand in such and such syntactical relationships in the sentence S.

In giving this as an answer they imply, of course, that if (2) then (1), and the question arises, what is the status of *that* proposition? How is it that these various items, specifiable according to them independently of the fact that S expresses a necessity, necessarily fit together in the way they do, i.e. so that a necessarily true sentence results? This looks to be a question of just the same form as the original one, except that its subject matter is one stage more obscure and less well understood. We have seen that the Conventionalist has an answer to it; but his competitors attract the suspicion that they have "solved" the problem by substituting for it one which is, perhaps, even more intractable.

Just what this Conventionalist theory is, in its essence, is a question which needs careful handling. It can too easily sound like something it must not be allowed to be confused with, that is a thesis of the genetic type, a commentary on the process by which a novice speaker in fact arrives at a complete grasp of word-meanings: first of all contact with examples, which permits the learning of much, though not the whole, of the meaning; after which there has to be further instruction, in the matter of which sentences containing the given word are necessary, to round the job off. It has to be insisted that this is no part of the Conventionalist view as I wish it to be understood. The crucial Conventionalist thesis is that among those various linguistic conventions which impart to words (and to syntactic conformations) the meanings they have, there are some conventions which take the form:

> The sentence S (which contains the given word, or is formed in accordance with the given syntactic construction) is to be held to express a truth whatever experiences may occur.

And further, it is crucial that these latter conventions are independent of the others in this sense: that a person who did not yet know them, but who already knew all the others, could not deduce from the conventions which he already knew to be in force, that these further conventions would also have to hold, however insightful he might be as a logician.

It is at once clear that this could be true even though the genetic form of the thesis, the one about how speakers in fact have to be taught, was false; and that it could be false even though the genetic form were true. In the first case, it might be that although the "whole-sentence" conventions were independent of the rest, human beings who had learnt the rest would, as a result of the operations of some unknown psychological mechanism, come to apply the "whole-sentence" conventions without further teaching. In the second case, it might be that although "whole-sentence" conventions were not independent, but followed from the others, all speakers had to be taught them just as if they were independent, since the insight required to reach them by deduction was in fact too much for any language-learner.

So much for the lack of relation between the genetic version and that version of the Conventionalist thesis on which I believe the emphasis should be placed. There is another caveat to be entered, this time against a misunderstanding suggested by the word "conventionalism" itself. It carries the implication that the sources of necessary truth are communal decisions made by groups of people who had other alternatives before their minds. But nothing of this sort is to be regarded as belonging to the doctrine which, following approximately the terminological tradition, I am now calling "Conventionalism". That doctrine is simply the asser-tion that the determinants of necessity are facts about our behaviour with respect to certain *whole sentences*, and that these facts are primary in the sense that I have tried to explain, that is, that they are not logical consequences of any of the *other facts* which determine the meanings of their constituent words and the import of their syntax. It contains no component about the social or psychological history of these facts. Quine once wrote:

In dropping the attributes of deliberateness and explicitness from the notion of linguistic convention we risk depriving the latter of any explana-tory force and reducing it to an idle label. We may wonder what one adds to the bare statement that the truths of logic and mathematics are *a priori*, or to the still barer statement that they are firmly accepted, when he characterizes them as true by convention in such a sense.

(Quine [1936] p. 99)

We do indeed take this risk. But the thesis which I am urging the reader to think of as the really important part of the Conventionalist theory of logical necessity certainly can survive the dropping of "the attributes of deliberateness and explicitness from the notion of... convention". For these features concern the history of the facts which underlie the phenomenon of necessary truth, and this history is quite irrelevant to the thesis which I have isolated.

## III

For all I have said so far it is still open to the Conventionalist to
deny that there are at least two independent sorts of convention
which together determine the meanings of words—he may still say
instead that the fact of a word's occurrence in various sentences
which are held to be true whatever happens in the *only thing* which
decides its meaning. But although my argument so far leaves this
open as a theoretical possibility, it is absolutely clear on other
grounds that it is unacceptable, and I am not aware that anyone
has ever tried to maintain it. One of its consequences would be that
all words had the same meaning. For if the meanings of words were
determined by nothing else than the fact that they occurred in various necessary sentences, then the only thing which could distinguish
one word from another in meaning would be the fact that they occurred respectively in sentences with different meanings. But for the
relevant sentences to have different meanings, something would
have to distinguish them other than the fact that they were used to
express necessary truths, which *ex hypothesi* is a feature of all of them,
and does not differentiate one from another. And then that other
factor, whatever it was, would also be a factor determining the
meanings of the constituent words, which contradicts the original
hypothesis. So that on that original hypothesis, nothing could distinguish one word from any other in point of meaning, a consequence
not likely to be swallowed even by those who so restrict the concept
of meaning as to make all necessary truths synonymous.

One differentiating feature which could be called upon would be
the position which a word or symbol occupies in the framework of
some formal system—this might seem obviously available in the
case of the numeral words, for example. But it is quite clear that there
is something very important which would still have been left entirely
out of account. To stay with the example of the numeral words
(since from this point on my interest will move away from necessary
truth in general and towards arithmetic as a special case of it), we
easily see that it would provide no information at all about their
*application*, and yet this is surely something which any complete
account of how they get their meaning must do, as F. P. Ramsey
once remarked in a famous passage (Ramsey [1925] p. 2). A person
who confined himself to telling us how numeral words function in
their purely formal aspect would have omitted to say that (let alone

*how*) they are used in the empirical counting of objects. No explanation of the meanings of the numerals can be complete that gives me
no help at all in deciding which one to apply to the number of my
fingers. This being so, I do not see how one can possibly avoid a
conclusion which many will be inclined to accept without argument
anyway: that at least some of the rules which go towards determining the meanings of numeral words are rules which lay down the
perceptual circumstances for their correct use, or, more precisely,
rules relating the perceptual conditions for applying the phrase
"*n* Xs" (where *n* is a numeral and X a general term) to those for
applying "an X". In other words, a part of knowing the meaning
of "two" is this: that if you know what counts as perceiving, for
instance, a man, then you also know what counts as perceiving two
men. This point is scarcely controversial, but it has quite definite
consequences for Conventionalism, in so far as Conventionalism is
supposed to provide a philosophical theory of arithmetic as well as
of other types of necessary truth.

These consequences were very well stated by Michael Dummett
in his paper "Wittgenstein's Philosophy of Mathematics" (Dummett
[1959b]), though he did not present them as arising out of the
acceptance of the principles (A) and (B):

the criterion we adopt in the first place for saying that there are *n* things of
a certain kind is to be explained by describing the procedure of counting.
But when we find that there are five boys and seven girls in a room, we say
that there are twelve children altogether, without counting them all
together. The fact that we are justified in doing this *is not, as it were, implicit
in the procedure of counting* itself; rather, we have chosen to adopt a *new* criterion for saying that there are twelve children, different from the criterion
of counting up all the children together. It would seem that, *if we have
genuinely distinct criteria for the same statement, they may clash.* But the necessity
of "5 + 7 = 12" consists just in this, that we do not count anything as a
clash; if we count the children all together and get eleven, we say, "We
must have miscounted".[2] (p. 329.)

This passage contains the essence of the Conventionalist theory.
The description of the procedure of counting gives us the purely
perceptual criteria for an ascription of number. There is then a
"new" criterion, not "implicit in" the former, but "genuinely
distinct" from it, and this is the arithmetical criterion. What
Dummett meant by these phrases is, I believe, that the two criteria

---

[2] My italics, except for "new" in line 6.

are logically independent of one another, and that interpretation is strongly supported when he says that if they are "genuinely distinct", they may clash. What is it exactly that may clash? It is not that one may "count correctly", but get a result not in accordance with some proposition of arithmetic. This is because the notion of counting correctly is governed not solely by perceptual criteria, but also by the requirement that the result reached should not be counter-arithmetical. What *is* possible, on the Conventionalist view, is that all the *perceptual* requirements for having counted correctly should be satisfied, that it should look, sound, feel just as if the counting had been done correctly, and that the result should clash with arithmetic.

Our method, therefore, must be to examine closely a proposition which states that on some occasion it seemed to all observers in every particular exactly as if certain counting operations had been quite correctly performed, when the combined result of these operations was counter-arithmetical. The Conventionalist must be able to maintain that such a proposition is contingent, even though it never actually happens. For if it should turn out on inspection to be necessarily false, that would mean that the perceptual criteria and the arithmetical criteria were not independent of each other; it would mean that if the number-concepts were *completely* circumscribed by the perceptual criteria for their application, that would *by itself* be sufficient to make various arithmetical statements relating the numbers to one another necessarily true. And this is just what the Conventionalist has to deny if he is to maintain, as he must, that the necessary truth of arithmetical propositions is independent of the perceptual criteria for the number-concepts, an optional extra for which we do in fact opt. The investigation of such a "purely perceptual" proposition does, I hope to show, give an insight into the sort of necessity which belongs to truths of arithmetic, and to this the following sections are devoted.

## IV

The proposition to be investigated I shall randomly call "(M)", and I shall express it as follows:

(M) There was the best possible perceptual evidence that someone counted a group of boys correctly and made the answer 5, that someone counted a group of girls correctly and made the answer 7, that someone counted the whole group of children correctly and made the answer 13, and that no child joined the groups, or simply appeared in them, during the counting operations.

This at once raises two questions. Firstly, what is to be understood, in general, by the idea of *the best possible perceptual evidence* for something? Secondly, what does having the best possible perceptual evidence actually amount to in the particular case of a *correctly performed counting* operation? It will be as well to attempt at this stage some preliminary answer to each question, although I hope that how they are to be understood will become apparent from the way they function in the argument of the coming pages.

The concept of having the best possible perceptual evidence that an event E has occurred is not to be equated with that of having had perceptions, all of which tell for the occurrence of E and none against it. The latter is quite compatible with one's having hardly any evidence for E at all, perhaps just that of a fleeting glance or a sound indistinctly heard. To have the best possible perceptual evidence, on the other hand, involves having carried out an exhaustive investigation and still to have found only positive and no negative evidence. It will be said that no such investigation can in fact be exhaustive; that however many tests have been applied and have been successful, there could always be others made which might fail. The point is familiar in the form of an objection to the phenomenalist claim that sense-datum statements can entail statements about physical objects. Whether it is true or not, it may for our present purposes be admitted. That would mean that the best possible perceptual evidence is something which no person or persons can ever actually have, but this does not obliterate the distinction between two ways of not being able to have it. Firstly, because one cannot complete the set of possible tests; secondly, because one will demonstrably be able to find contrary evidence in a finite time, or because there is some particular and crucial piece of evidence which one will never be able to get. The Conventionalist need not be ashamed of (M)'s being impossible for the first of these reasons— after all, it applies just as much to any conjunct of (M) taken separately as to the whole proposition, and establishes no difference between "Seven and five made thirteen" and "The cat is on the mat"

—but it would be quite otherwise if (M) were to turn out to be necessarily false for the second reason. When, from now on, I speak of the possibility and impossibility of (M), it will be the second, and only the second, which I have in mind.

Before we move on to the special case where the event E is a correct counting, some remarks should be made about something even more general, namely the concept of perceptual evidence. I shall assume that the statements which I discuss later, the statements which are involved in the assertion that counting went on and was done correctly, are the sort of statement for and against which there can be perceptual evidence; that is to say, those perceptual states of human beings which we often describe in phrases like "It sounded to him as if a dog was barking", "It looked to me as if the door was open", really do provide grounds for believing corresponding statements about the physical world. Were this an essay on the epistemology of perception the matter would have to be discussed; in this context, I merely assert the commonsense view. But a second point calls for more detailed inspection: if I see all the birds in the garden fly off at once, that is evidence that the cat is in the garden; but it does not seem, as evidence, quite on a par with its seeming to me as if I actually saw the cat. The former case I recognise as evidence only through the mediation of a general principle relating the behaviour of birds to the presence of cats, and I cannot be said to perceive the truth of this principle, even though I undoubtedly have perceptual grounds for my belief in it. So it is very doubtful whether one can properly speak of "purely perceptual" evidence in this case; the task of distinguishing accurately between perceptual evidence and *purely* perceptual evidence in the strict sense would be a very difficult business, and I am not even certain whether anything at all would turn out to be purely perceptual. Fortunately we have no need to employ this distinction. I shall forget about the "purely", and call everything "perceptual evidence" for a statement, *except* what would not be held to be evidence *without the prior acceptance of some part of arithmetic.*

The reason behind this proviso, and the sense in which it is to be taken, will be clear if we look at the proposition (M). Suppose that its first two clauses—those concerning the counts of the two separate groups—were satisfied. If, in deciding what this is perceptual evidence for, we make use of standard arithmetic, it will itself count as perceptual evidence that there were twelve children present; in other words, it would itself be perceptual evidence against thinking that any count which now yielded "thirteen children" could possibly be a *correct* count. Hence, by the definition of "the best possible perceptual evidence", there never could be the best possible perceptual evidence that a correct count of children had given the answer 13, and (M) would immediately appear as necessarily false. But to show by *this method* that (M) was necessarily false could have no bearing on Conventionalism. Conventionalism claims that the arithmetical criteria are only contingently connected with the perceptual criteria, so that to allow one's acceptance of arithmetic implicitly to determine what the perceptual criteria are is not to give it a fair trial. When, in the present context, we are delineating the concept of perceptual evidence for correctness of counting, we must stipulate that each counting operation is to be considered on its own. We are asking, in effect, whether the correlation between correct counting and obtaining results in accordance with our arithmetic *could* break down; therefore we must not so formulate the question that it gets a negative answer merely because the correlation has not (so far as we know) broken down yet. To avoid this we lay it down that the three counting operations mentioned in (M) are to be taken independently of one another, so that what has been perceived during the first two shall not be regarded as belonging to the perceptual evidence relevant to the third.

Finally, what is involved in being able to have the best possible perceptual evidence that a count has been carried out correctly? The first requirement is that the counting be done in the most open and explicit way. For one thing, the objects counted should be of a kind easily seen and distinguished from one another—this condition is satisfied by (M). Then, the counting should be done out loud and with unmistakeable gestures, and the objects counted should not move during the counting. Again, we can imagine that all this is so in the situation referred to in (M). Counting correctly will now consist in pointing to members of the class being counted, and with each pointing-gesture pronouncing a numeral word, whereby one is to point to all such objects once and only once, and to pronounce the numeral words in their correct order starting from "One". This procedure, and any mistakes in it, consist of essentially perceivable events, just as the entry, or the sudden materialisation, of an extra child is an essentially perceivable event. A child which appears in any of the groups must appear in it somewhere, and a suitably placed observer must be able to see this happen: likewise a suitably placed observer must be able to hear if the counter misses out "Eleven" in the third count. Now we are to imagine a troupe of observers following the experiment as closely as they can, each (or even several) of them with the task of concerning himself with some single feature of the situation or procedure. Thus one is to watch a particular child to make sure that he is pointed to once and once only, another is detailed to watch a certain small area for the possible appearance of extra children there, and so on. Then we are to imagine further, that the three counts give the results 5, 7, and 13 respectively, but that to each individual observer it seems just as if his part of the experiment had proceeded perfectly, and that it would still have seemed to him to have proceeded perfectly, however extensive the checks he had been allowed to make. This is to imagine that there was the best possible perceptual evidence for a counter-arithmetical conclusion, and our central question is, whether it really can be imagined or not.

## V

Is (M) logically possible? At first sight it looks as if it is, and one might give various reasons for thinking so. For example: three distinct countings are needed to reach the anti-arithmetical result, and they take place, we have supposed, successively. If we consider each counting by itself there is no difficulty. A count of the boys can certainly have the result 5, while seeming to all observers to have been flawlessly executed. And in just the same way a count of the girls can certainly yield 7, and a count of the children can yield 13. But the counts do not overlap temporally, and it is widely held that any non-overlapping sequence of consistent events is itself consistent—this is the principle that underpins Hume's arguments about induction. Or we might reach the same conclusion by a quite different route: we have a number of observers, each of them watching his own allotted part of the operation, and we are to suppose that to each of them it seems just as if his part had been performed correctly. Now even if two of them were following the *same* part, and disagreed about it, that would surely be perfectly consistent—for few philosophers seem keen to assert that the fact that one person has had certain perceptual experiences could ever entail that another person has had similar ones. So that in the case which we are actually considering the consistency is even more obvious, since no two observers have the same task assigned to them. If our descriptions of each individual observer are consistent in themselves, the total description must therefore be consistent as well. Conformably to Conventionalism, (M) appears to be contingent.

I believe that this impression is deceptive, and that the deception is masked by the choice of a comparatively complex example as the starting point. We will be much less ready to accept it after we have looked at the simplest case, that of a single observer surveying the counting of a very small number of objects, and have then added the complications gradually.

Suppose we begin by considering what is likely to prove the most awkward counter-arithmetical proposition, $0+0 = 1$. We find ourselves facing difficulties which are, to say the least, formidable. What we have to imagine is an observer to whom it (i) seems just as if no boys were present, and (ii) seems just as if no girls were present, and then (iii) seems just as if one child were present, whilst (iv) seeming to him just as if no child appeared in the region in question during the relevant period. The trouble, of course, is this: in describing an observer of whom (i), (ii), and (iii) were true, we have exactly described an observer of whom (iv) was false. Now the reader will notice that one possible reason for saying that (i), (ii), and (iii) are conjointly incompatible with (iv) is this: that any observer of whom (i), (ii), and (iii) are true will at once conclude, on the grounds of his faith in the arithmetical truth that $0+0 < 1$, that a child must have appeared, hence (iv) will not be true of him. But I hope that the reader will also anticipate that this reason is not my reason—I have explained in the previous section why it is that any demonstration of the impossibility of (M) which was allowed to proceed on the assumption that all observers accept elementary arithmetic would be of no use or interest to us. Rather, what I have in mind is this: if one were to describe such a series of perceptual experiences as would make (i), (ii), and (iii) true, one would have described a perceptual experience such that to anyone who had it, it would seem as if a child had appeared, quite irrespective of any arithmetical beliefs he might hold. That is to say, he would have perceptions as of an area containing no children, followed by perceptions as of the same area containing one child, and these taken together are precisely perceptions as of seeing a child appear. But if he has had a perceptual experience as of a child appearing, it is impossible that it should seem to him *just as if* no child had appeared, or that he should have the best possible perceptual evidence for that conclusion. For he will have had at least one experience which is evidence against it, and from the definition of "best possible perceptual evidence" it follows that he cannot have the best possible perceptual evidence for it.

If anyone is inclined to think that he really can imagine the experiences one must have for (i), (ii), and (iii) to be true, without *ipso facto* imagining the experience of its "seeming as if a child appeared", I have no supporting argument. I can do no more than offer the proposition for inspection, in the belief that it will then be accepted. But one thing that might cause disagreement would be that the dissenter had in mind a situation slightly different from that which is to be envisaged. He might be thinking of an experiment in which our observer surveys not the whole of the relevant area for the whole of the relevant time, but scans parts of it successively, or for brief periods does not observe it at all. Then perhaps it is possible for it to seem to him that there is no boy, no girl, and then one child, without having the experience as of a child suddenly appearing—rather, it would be describable as "the experience of finding a child there". To attach any weight to this point, however, would be to forget about the requirement that it has to seem to the observer *just as if* the various things were the case. He is to be able to have the best possible perceptual evidence for the conclusion, and this cannot be if there was a place which he was not observing at a time when something could have happened there which would have made a difference to the result. To put the point slightly differently: it may be true that to the observer who scans the area rather than surveying it all continuously, it does not seem just as if a child appeared; but it is not true that it seems to him just as if no child appeared. It is the second of these which would have to be true for (iv) to hold.

It might be thought that in taking "o+o = 1" as an example we have selected a special case. The idea could be that the presence of two zeros on the left-hand side somehow makes it hardly an arithmetical proposition at all, but just a matter of whether there was or was not something of a certain kind in the observer's field of view. I am not sure that any such distinction can be sustained, but even if it can it would not be important. For I think that anyone who asks himself the corresponding questions about, e.g., "$1+1 = 3$", will come to just the same conclusions. He will be unable to see how it could seem to an observer just as if one boy were present, just as if one girl were present, and then just as if three children were present, without at some stage seeming to him as if a child appeared. And the same would be true of any instance where the number of objects involved was small enough for the observer to take them in "at one go", that is, without having to scan them successively, leaving others temporarily unattended to.

We now turn to the consideration of the case in which there are two observers. Each of them has to survey the whole of an area and count the number of some easily perceivable and stable kind of object contained in it. Observer A counts one, and another one, and no more, and reports accordingly. Observer B, on the other hand, reports having counted three. Now even if we suppose that each was being sincere and attentive, and that it really did seem to him just as he reported, it is clear that this does not put either of them on the way to having the best possible perceptual evidence that one and one have made three, since, as we have described the events, neither has good evidence, let alone the best possible, that the other has done his part correctly. Again it is to be understood that this is not said for the reason that Observer A (for instance) has perceptual evidence that there is one and one other and *hence* (since $1+1 \neq 3$) that anyone who counted three must have miscounted; it is said for the reason that neither has had any opportunity to perceive the counting process by which the other has arrived at his result. This we can immediately rectify by supposing one of them to count aloud, pointing clearly to the counted objects as he does so; but we shall find that this does not get either observer any nearer to having the best possible perceptual evidence for the anti-arithmetical result.

Let it be Observer B who counts aloud. Our question is, what is Observer A supposed to perceive? We have to remember that it seems to him *just as if* there was one object there, and another, and no more, and that is how it must go on seeming to him throughout the whole exercise. Now he sees his partner point and say "One", and it must seem to A that B pointed to one or other of the objects which he, A, perceives, otherwise he will have some evidence of miscounting. Then he sees B point and say "Two", and this time he must seem to point to the other object that A perceives. Our problem is to decide what seems to Observer A to happen next. Nothing can be imagined except what will either provide him with some evidence of miscounting by B, or with some evidence that he himself was wrong in thinking there to be just the one object, and the other, and no more. In the light of what we have already seen there is nothing surprising about this, for what we have done, in effect, is to reduce this case to the single-observer case which has already been considered. Observer A may have excellent grounds for thinking B to be sincere and competent, but if he has not himself followed the counting process that no more provides him with the best possible perceptual evidence that it was carried out correctly than the fact that we know, for example, that horses do not materialise out of the air means that I now have the best possible perceptual evidence that one has not just sprung into being in the next room. And as soon as we try so to alter our imaginary experiment as to put A in a position to have the best possible perceptual evidence we see that we are going to draw a blank. Completeness would require us to repeat this argument for the further case in which we have many observers, all of whom observe different parts of the operation. But this I omit, as an unnecessary burden on the reader, since exactly the same principles apply.

What is quite certain is that there is no single person in any of our examples who can himself come into possession of the best possible perceptual evidence for an anti-arithmetical conclusion, and the examples give us good reason to think that we cannot imagine any such person. For a case involving only the very small numbers we cannot, as we have just seen, and this must at least suggest that we cannot do it for larger numbers either. The suggestion can be backed up. In order to make it possible that our observer should have the best possible perceptual evidence we will have to imagine a peculiarly favourable situation (for instance, one in which all the objects to be counted remain stationary and fairly close together, perhaps one in which they also have numbers clearly written on them) and if necessary an observer whose perceptual powers exceed ours in that he is capable of attending simultaneously to all the relevant elements. That he should find the situation "completely surveyable" in this sense is obligatory if we are to be able to credit him with the best possible perceptual evidence that nothing has moved or changed. Whether that means attributing to him powers beyond those of a normal human being will of course depend on the number and positions of the objects concerned.

Suppose that now, in accordance with these *desiderata*, we arrange the boys and girls of our previous experiment in a row in front of the observer, boys on the left, girls on the right. Let the boys carry cards with numbers on them from 1 to 5; and let the girls have similar cards showing on the upper half the numbers from 1 to 7, on the lower half the numbers from 6 to 12. So the observer finds himself facing a pattern like this:

$$1 \quad 2 \quad 3 \quad 4 \quad 5 \quad 1 \quad 2 \quad 3 \quad 4 \quad 5 \quad 6 \quad 7$$
$$6 \quad 7 \quad 8 \quad 9 \quad 10 \quad 11 \quad 12$$

What we have to imagine is that while it seems to our observer just as if the top line goes from 1 to 5 and then from 1 to 7, with no numerals missed out, it also seems to him just as if the line consisting of the boys' cards and the lower line of the girls' cards runs from 1 to 13, likewise with no omissions, and without any card having two numbers on its lower line. No such series of experiences can be imagined.

That is all I shall say about the question whether a single observer can himself have the best possible perceptual evidence for a counter-arithmetical conclusion. But even if all I have said is held to be beyond doubt, one may wonder whether it is really to the point. We began by asking whether there could ever be the best possible perceptual evidence for a certain sort of conclusion, and it is not immediately obvious that the answer to this must be the same as the answer to the question whether any single person could by himself possess such evidence. Have we not agreed that, provided we divide the observation of the counting experiment between a number of people, each one can easily be imagined to have the best possible perceptual evidence for events which, taken together, amount to something that goes against arithmetic? And if this is agreed, is the fact that the evidence has to be spread among different observers of any importance?

## VI

In this section I shall give my reasons for thinking that the fact just mentioned, namely that in order to make it look as if there may be the best possible perceptual evidence for an anti-arithmetical statement we are compelled to *distribute* the evidence among

several observers, is indeed of decisive importance for our view of
the proposition (M), and hence for our view of Conventionalism
as a theory of Arithmetic. But before embarking on the exposition of these reasons I should like to turn aside for a moment in
order to combine an acknowledgement with a small historical
point.

The argument I shall use is a modification of one introduced by
J. F. Bennett in his discussion of Locke's distinction between Primary
and Secondary Qualities (Bennett [1965] and [1971] §20). Bennett
had the idea of comparing a person who is insensitive to differences
in Secondary Qualities (he considered the case of a colour-blind
subject) with that of an imagined person who is insensitive to differences in Primary Qualities (where the examples he worked out in
detail were those of size and shape). What he found was a failure of
parallelism; whereas colour-blindness is a comparatively minor
defect, a person who was "size-blind", who could not perceive by
any method the differences of size between objects, would be
effectively out of contact with us altogether. For it turns out that
there have to be so many events and states of affairs which we perceive and this subject does not (if his mistakes about size are to be
more than momentary errors which we can get him to correct by
presenting the objects to him in slightly different situation), that
"it is no longer clear that we share with him a sensory awareness of a
single objective world" (Bennett [1971] p. 98). I propose to offer a
similar argument about the status of Number. Now the historical
point is this: in his list of the "Primary Qualities of Bodies", Locke
included the item "Number" (Locke [1690] II.8.9). The tendency
amongst modern commentators, who have learnt the lesson that
Number is not so much a property of objects as a relation between
objects and concepts, has been to think of this as one of those aberra-
tions which, since they have no further harmful consequences, it is
kindest to forget. And being kind men, they have generally acted
accordingly. But perhaps we have the opportunity to do Locke an
even greater kindness. For if we accept Bennett's way of establishing
the reality of the Primary/Secondary distinction, we shall have to
agree that it places Number firmly where Locke originally placed
it—on the Primary side. Seen from the vantage point provided by
this argument, the affinities between Number and the other Primary
Qualities are more striking than their admitted differences. We
might say that Locke was right when he said that Number was

Primary, even if he was careless to imply that it is straightforwardly a Quality.

Back now to the argument itself. One difference between the single- and multiple-observer situations is that the latter allow of the possibility that the observers are not perceiving the same area, nor even parts of the same spatio-temporal system of objects. Returning to our two observers A and B, let us imagine that it seems to A just as if the area he is perceiving contains one object of some easily identifiable kind, whereas to B it seems just as if the area *he* is perceiving contains no such object. What is to be said about this situation depends crucially on the way in which we are using the expression "seems just as if". If it meant no more than: seems just as if *at a certain time from a certain position,* and perhaps to sight or touch only, then it would of course be perfectly possible that one of the observers is just making a perceptual mistake, is subject to some sort of illusion, and that on closer inspection this will become obvious to everybody, himself included. When understood in this sense, "it seems to him just as if" is clearly at a great remove from "he has the best possible perceptual evidence", and it would be much too weak to be of any interest here. When we ask whether perceptual criteria for statements about the numbers of objects could clash with the arithmetical criteria for the same statements, we are not asking whether mistakes can occasionally be made which cause temporary numerical disagreements. We are asking whether there could be a clash which turned out only to be confirmed by further investigation. So that if it is to mean anything serious, "seems just as if" must imply "seems and continues to seem just as if", and that is how I am using it.

To require that, in this strong sense, it should seem to A and B respectively just as if there were and were not a single object of the given sort present, is to impose a very strict condition, as becomes apparent when one tries to imagine in detail how the discrepancy between the two observers is to work out. It is to seem to A just as if there were, let us say, exactly one glass on the table, and to B exactly as if there were no glass there. To begin with, suppose each has the appropriate tactual and visual data. What is to happen next? We have to consider the results of different sorts of test which it would be open to A to carry out.

Firstly, a glass is a solid object, and as such can have effects on people's bodies, sometimes painful or even fatal effects. Suppose that A, enraged by B's failure to acknowledge what is (to A) so obviously the case, takes the glass and throws it at him.[3] It has to go on seeming to A just as if there were a glass there, so he must find himself able to get hold of it, and it must have more or less normal glass-like effects. To B, on the other hand, it must continue to seem just as if no glass were there. One possibility is that at first it seemed to him that there was nothing on the table at all, but that he now sees someone making motions as of throwing and feels something hit him. In this case he now has some perceptual evidence that there was something on the table after all. (Not yet, of course, that there was a *glass* on the table—that will have to await the result of further tests, such as I shall describe later.) An alternative would be that B feels no effects of A's throw. But when we remember that we can think of these effects as being quite drastic (as it seems to A), this begins to look like saying that B is not associated with, nor does he even perceive, the body at which A threw the glass, and which is facing the area which A is observing. If among B's sensory data there is nothing to correspond to many things which A perceives, such as injuries to the body supposed to be B's, then we who have placed ourselves in the god-like position of being able to look in on both sets of sensory data will, or ought to, lose confidence that it is really the same physical place that A and B are perceiving. That, however, was to be an essential feature of the story. Once we have significant evidence against that, no report of the perceptual intake of A and B can possibly provide the best possible perceptual evidence for any counter-arithmetical statement.

The basic source of the trouble is plain to see. Given the original difference between the two observers, plus the condition that neither is to have any grounds for thinking that he has made a mistake, no matter how he tries to test his judgement, we can amplify the divergence between their perceptual states until there is no reason to say that they are observing the same spatio-temporal region at all. So far we have followed up only one of the many tests with which A might seek to reassure himself, and two of the possible reactions of B. Other avenues lead to much the same place. We may try, as another example, the hypothesis that B does perceive something on the table, but that it is not a glass. The point to be made is in principle identi-

---

[3] I shall sometimes use this form of words instead of the cumbersome "suppose A has perceptions just as if he took the glass . . . etc." Nothing will turn on this— there is no assumption involved that A is somehow right and B wrong.

cal. Just as the effects which can be produced if there is nothing on the table differ from those which can be produced if there is a glass on the table, so the situations in which there is a glass on the table and that in which there is something other than a glass there differ in the range of their possible effects. If A is to have the best possible perceptual evidence that there is a glass there, it will have to seem to him that all the right things happen; if B is to have similar evidence that there is no glass but something else it will have to seem to *him* that all the right things happen, and they may be very different. Perhaps A takes a bottle of beer and pours it into the glass. What does B then see? If he does not see the beer at all there is immediately another large difference between his perceptions and A's, which could be even further magnified by having A spill the beer over him, and so on. If, on the other hand, he does see the beer, where does it appear to him to go when A pours it out? If all over the table, we have another large difference between him and A. Possibly he sees a column of beer mysteriously supporting itself on the table. But if we take this alternative, we are again beginning to lose an essential feature, namely that it should seem to B just as if there were no glass there—we are approaching the situation where it seems to him somewhat as if there were a glass there, but one that is invisible to him.

Here it can be said that B does not yet have any evidence that what is on the table is a glass. It could be any other kind of container of the same sort of shape. This we may admit, but we must not forget that plenty of other possible tests bear on this issue. Suppose that A now takes a hammer and gives his glass a sharp tap. What does B find? If he cannot perceive that there is beer all over the room, and that he cuts his fingers if he fumbles around the table, we are back to the situation of the preceding paragraph, where extensive differences are already showing between his perceptions and those of A. But if he does perceive these things, he really is beginning to have some evidence that there was a glass there, and so it ceases to be possible for him to have the best possible perceptual evidence that there was none. Since glasses behave differently from things which are not glasses, what A and B perceive, if neither of them is to be brought to realise or at least to suspect his mistake, has to drift further and further apart. And it can very soon be driven past the point where we, surveying the sensory data of each of them from our grandstand seat, can find grounds for holding that they are both perceiving the same spatio-temporal region. That calls for a fairly high degree of correlation between their experiences, and there is good reason to think that it cannot be maintained.

As in the discussion of the case involving only a single observer, I have selected as the starting point an example where the numbers are 1 and 0; this has simplified the details of the argument, but again nothing of importance hangs on it. Other cases can be treated by first reducing them to the "1–0" situation. To get some idea of how this would work, let us imagine that it seems to A just as if two glasses were on the table, and to B just as if there were three. Suppose now that B chooses two of the three glasses he sees, and takes up one in his left hand and the other in his right. It must then seem to him that he has one in each hand and that one remains on the table. How do things now seem to A? There are various possibilities. It might seem to him that there is no glass in B's left hand, or that there is no glass in his right hand, or that there is no glass left on the table. But since it has to seem to B that there is exactly one glass in each of these places, any of the alternatives brings us straight back to a "1–0" situation, from which we can proceed to magnify the divergence between A and B as before. Something else that has to be taken into account is that it should seem to A that B has only put out one hand. As our hypothesis was that it should seem to B that he has put out two, this gives us a "2–1" position; and we only have to imagine that B now moves his hands some distance apart to get a clear "1–0" position, since it seems to B that there is a hand on, say, the left-hand edge of the table, and one on the right-hand edge of the table, whereas if it is to go on seeming to A that there is only the one hand there it must seem to him that there is no hand in at least one, if not both, of these places. So again we find ourselves back at the case we have already thought about. Anyone with a taste for the macabre will be able to invent other possibilities, but I do not anticipate that he will succeed in inventing one which cannot be dissolved by similar treatment.

One might still think that with more than two observers this type of argument would break down, on the grounds that we could then have a situation in which no two of them were in conflict with each other. Suppose that an observer A surveys the whole of the table, and that it seems to him just as if there were three glasses on it. Observers B and C each survey one half of the table, and it seems to each just as if there were one and only one glass on his half. At first glance one might think that there was no conflict between any two of them. That there are three glasses on the table is compatible with there being only one in B's half of it, since there might be two in the other half. So there is no conflict between A and B, and for just the same reason there is no conflict between A and C either. And it is quite obvious that the reports of B and C, that their respective halves of the table contain just one glass, are not in conflict. But the trouble is this: as we saw right at the beginning of the argument, or rather as an obvious variant of what we then saw, it cannot seem to A just as if there were three glasses in all if it seems to him just as if there is one and only one in each half of the table. It must seem to him that there are at least two in one half or the other, and that means that his perceptions must in fact be in conflict either with those of B or with those of C. We are, after all, still in the same position as that discussed in the preceding paragraph.

The argument I have now given is an argument of a kind that can of its nature never be stated fully. Its conclusion is that a certain situation cannot coherently be imagined, and the method has been to inspect some of the most immediately plausible attempts to imagine it. Necessarily one cannot in this way cover with certainty all the attempts that might be made, and it remains possible that some important approach has been overlooked. But while I cannot be said to have proved that the situation described in our original proposition (M) cannot be imagined, nonetheless what I have written so far strongly inclines me to think that it cannot, and I believe that the techniques used in the last few pages will prove adequate to deal with any putative counter-example that may be proposed.

## VII

The conclusion to be drawn is that for the sentences of elementary arithmetic, their acceptance as wholes is not independent of the conventions linking their constituents to types of perceptual situation, and that Conventionalism, which requires them to be independent, is therefore false. But it is quite possible that someone who has been satisfied by the foregoing disproof of independence may still feel able to hold a form of Conventionalism. My argument has drawn on the fact that certain situations, such as that described by the conjunction of (i)–(iv) (p. 17) cannot be imagined, but it has not said *why* they cannot be imagined. And it may be suggested that perhaps the reasons for this are conventionalist reasons. That is to say, perhaps there are linguistic conventions to the effect that such sentences as that represented by "(i) & (ii) & (iii) & (iv)" are always to be regarded as false, so that the Conventionalism operates, so to speak, at the level of the "purely perceptual" propositions and not at that of the ordinary arithmetical ones.

Now I can do nothing more to persuade the reader to accept the main part of my argument, but I can at least point out that *if* he has accepted it then he has already, in effect, rejected this further suggestion. If Conventionalism is to be an adequate account of these purely perceptual propositions, it must make the claim that the conventions in question are ones which apply directly to the *whole sentences* expressing them. (The reasons for this are exactly the same as those given earlier in section II.) But in fact there are no such conventions, or if there are, they are redundant, and this follows from something that has already been decided, namely that given the present conventions about the perceptual conditions which have to obtain if each of (i)–(iv), considered separately, is to be true, we will then, without the need for any further conventions, find ourselves quite unable to envisage any perceptual circumstances in which all four are true together. Once we accept the rules for the individual sentences we find ourselves with no choice but to regard their conjunction as false. So Conventionalism really does fail as a doctrine of arithmetic, and we must look instead to an account which calls not only on meaning-stipulations but on the phenomenology of perception as well.

The untutored reaction to the suggestion that our arithmetic might be changed is often to say, "I just can't imagine it any other way." The contention of this paper is that this answer is not only true but also fundamentally the right thing to say. The consideration of the experiences of perceiving groups of objects is crucial to any explanation of the status of arithmetic in our thinking. Conventionalism tries to get by without it, and that, ultimately, is why it fails.

## VIII

I mentioned earlier that my argument had consequences for our view of the nature of necessary truth which are wider in scope than the method of exposition would at first indicate. Quine is not a

conventionalist in the sense I have been discussing. He denies that
there are necessary truths, if that is to mean statements which are
absolutely mandatory, which means that he can deny my original
proposition (B) (p. 4) and is not therefore forced into the position
which it has been the principle object of this paper to refute.
Nevertheless, when he writes "any statement can be held true come
what may, if we make drastic enough adjustments elsewhere in the
system", we are surely entitled to ask what the adjustments would
in fact have to be if we were to adopt a different set of arithmetical
statements as our favoured set. For the more drastic they would
have to be, the less the force of the claim that our present system is
not absolutely obligatory on us.

Now the argument I have stated does give us some purchase here.
It indicates that, if arithmetic is to be a theory applicable to an
objective interpersonal world, we could adopt an arithmetic that
conflicted with our present one only on one of two conditions. One
would be that we severed the present links between individual
numeral words and types of perceptual situation (though since that
would be to change their meanings it would not by itself amount to
more than a change in notation). The other would be that we were
prepared to accept that objects were constantly doing things which
it was impossible for us even to imagine ourselves perceiving.

That, however, is only an approximate formulation of the second
alternative, and one which may make it sound objectionable only
to those of positivistic leanings. We must get a clearer idea of what it
amounts to. After all, it will be said, at least one theory, namely
Quantum Mechanics, has won acceptance as a theory of the objective world in spite of the fact that it posits physical processes that
are not visualisable. I shall assume without question that that is
true; nevertheless, it is a very different situation from that which
constitutes our second alternative. For in the Quantum-mechanical
case it is not supposed that we can visualise the events or objects in
question at all, so that the application of any definite numeral
terms to them would involve, by the criterion I have been using, a
change of meaning and not a genuinely conflicting arithmetic. The
situation we have to consider is one in which we know very well
what it is like to perceive one thing, two things, etc., and where
indeed these are just the same types of perceptual experience as they
are now, *but* in which our theory tells us that, e.g., one thing and one
thing gives us three things altogether. And while we can understand

the individual parts of this assertion we cannot imagine how one could ever perceive it to be true, and find ourselves, still worse, unable to imagine, let alone perform, the feat of perceiving one and one as anything other than two, which is what our theory tells us is false. And if we now look away from pure logic and think in terms of what is a practical possibility, I would have thought that this fact alone was enough to guarantee that a theoretical scheme containing a deviant arithmetic would never be adopted. Such a scheme might conceivably have some predictive powers, for all this paper has shown to the contrary, but to adopt it would be entirely to abandon the attempt to clarify the world to ourselves in any intellectually satisfying way. It may be that we could adopt a deviant arithmetic if we were ready for "drastic changes elsewhere in the system". But the point I am making now is that we would not only require drastic changes *within* the system; we would also have renounced one of the main points of having such a system at all. It is significant that this feature of theoretical systems is played down by modern writers in the pragmatist tradition—they concentrate attention on the predictive powers of theories.

The view advanced in this paper also suggests Kantian parallels, parallels which will strike the reader as more or less close according to where he would himself place the main emphasis in his exposition of Kant's thought. Kant held that there are different sorts of necessary truth, and that the necessity of one sort cannot be understood without reference to the nature of the quasi-perceptual "pure intuition". This paper has not shown that there are any necessary truths whose explanation does not involve such reference, but it has shown that some do, and it confirms Kant's opinion that arithmetical statements are amongst them.

The necessity of analytic statements has often been felt to be unproblematic, so much so that many discussions of the topic easily give the impression that all difficulty will be at an end if only the claims of a few remaining candidates for synthetic necessity can be beaten down. In introducing the analytic/synthetic distinction, philosophers rarely fail to point out that the notion of conceptual "containment" needs literalising and supplementing, since there is much necessity that is not of subject-predicate form, and since it is not a wholly clear concept even for that special case. But it is not so common to find it explained just what analyticity must be if it is to provide an account of necessity without serious residual problems.

I have tried to argue that, if it is to do so, analytic statements must be understood as statements whose truth is the object of a convention, and of a convention which applies directly to the whole sentence rather than to its individual constituents. And I hope to have shown further, that anyone who had this in mind when speaking of analyticity would be quite right to class arithmetic as synthetic; and he would also be right if he went on to make the Kantian claim that in order to see why it is necessarily true one must ask oneself certain questions about what it is like to *perceive* groups of objects.

Of course, none of this justifies any transcendental explanation of our perceptual abilities and inabilities, or, for that matter, any other type of explanation—in my argument there is nothing which allows us to make any advance on just noting them as brute facts. The insight of Kant was the attempt to base arithmetic on perception, and indeed on "pure" perception—not what we actually perceive, but what our perceptual imagination will and will not stretch to. One may conjecture that we could find this sort of foundation for other classes of necessity as well, such as the theorems of propositional and predicate logic.

# 2

# "Alternative" in "alternative logic"

## SUSAN HAACK

There are many systems of logic—many-valued systems and modal systems for instance—which are non-standard; that is, which differ in one way or another from classical logic. Because of this plurality of logics, the question whether, or in what way, non-standard systems are "alternatives" to classical logic, naturally arises. I shall try, in this paper, to throw some light on this question. The procedure adopted will be as follows. We begin by distinguishing (section I) a weaker and a stronger sense in which non-standard systems may be "alternatives" to classical logic. We then investigate (section II) whether there is any formal criterion by which to judge in which category a system falls. We find that any formal test needs to be supplemented by considerations of meaning, and that there are arguments which, if sound, would show that there can be *no* system which is an alternative to classical logic in our stronger sense. In section III these arguments are shown to be inadequate. And so, in section IV, we proceed to investigate some of the possible varieties of change of logic.

### I

*Rival versus supplementary logics*

Sometimes non-standard systems have been devised and investigated out of purely formal interest. Often, however, the construction of non-standard systems is motivated by the belief that classical logic is in some way mistaken or inadequate. And when we investigate the motivation for non-standard systems more closely, we notice a difference between the kind of change of logic which a proponent of, e.g. Intuitionist or many-valued logic takes himself to be advocating, and the kind of change which, e.g. the modal logician advocates. To speak roughly at first: an important difference between the claims

32

made by an Intuitionist or a many-valued logician, on the one hand, and the modal logician, on the other, seems to be that the former takes his system to be an alternative to classical logic in the strong sense that we should employ his system *instead* of the classical, whereas the latter takes his system to be an alternative to classical logic only in the weaker sense that we should employ it *as well as* the classical. A symptom of this difference—which is noticed by Ackermann in [1967] p. 15—is that the former tends to regard classical logic as *mistaken*, as including assertions which are not true, whereas the latter tends to regard classical logic as *inadequate*, as not including assertions which are true. Let us say that the Intuitionist or many-valued logician takes himself to be proposing a rival, whereas the modal logician takes himself to be proposing a supplement, to classical logic. A rival system is, then, one the use of which is incompatible, and a supplementary system one the use of which is compatible, with the use of the standard system.

We can now readily enough distinguish the systems which are proposed as rivals from those proposed as supplements:

| *Systems proposed as rivals* | *Systems proposed as supplements* |
|---|---|
| Intuitionist logic. | Modal logics (e.g. T, the Lewis systems; not Łukasiewicz's 4-valued 'modal' logic). |
| Minimal logic. | Epistemic logics. |
| Łukasiewicz's, Bochvar's many-valued logics. | Deontic logics. |
| Van Fraassen's presuppositional languages. | Tense logics. |
| Reichenbach's, Destouches-Février's, Birkhoff and von Neumann's logics for quantum mechanics. | |

The question, whether a system is proposed as a rival or as a supplement to classical logic, should not be confused with either of two other kinds of question which also arise in the philosophy of non-standard logics: questions concerning the kind of ground which might be given for the choice of logic, and questions concerning the view which should be taken of the scope of application of an alternative system.

Some of those who propose systems which they take to be rivals to classical logic think that logic may be in some absolute sense verified or falsified; we shall call these realists. Others think that our choice of logic is to be made on grounds of convenience, simplicity, economy; we shall call these pragmatists. Brouwer, for example, is in our sense a realist—he thinks that classical logic can be shown to be mistaken. (See Brouwer [1952].) Putnam, on the other hand, is in our sense a pragmatist—he thinks that a relatively simple physics and Birkhoff and von Neumann's logic should be preferred, on grounds of simplicity and economy, to a more complex physics and the standard logic. (See Putnam [1969].) The distinction between proponents of rival, and proponents of supplementary, systems should not be confused with the distinction between realists and pragmatists. (Rescher in [1969] chap. 3 is in some danger of making this confusion.) Among proponents of allegedly rival systems there are both realists and pragmatists.

Again, some of those who propose systems which they take to be rivals to classical logic think that their system should replace classical logic in *all* applications; we shall call these global reformers. Others think that their system should replace classical logic only in *some* applications; we shall call these local reformers. Dummett, for instance, is a global reformer—he wants to replace classical by Intuitionist logic in all applications (see Dummett [1959a]); whereas the traditional Intuitionists are local reformers—they take classical logic to fail only in mathematical reasoning. The distinction between proponents of rival, and proponents of supplementary, systems should not be confused with the distinction between global and local reformers. (Farber [1942] is in some danger of making this confusion.) Among proponents of allegedly rival systems there are both global and local reformers. It is, indeed, arguable that a proponent of a rival system ought to be a global reformer; but this is a separate issue.

It is tempting to take the claims made by proponents of nonstandard logics at their face value; to assume, that is, that Intuitionist or many-valued logics really are, as their proponents say they are, rivals to classical logic, whereas modal logics really are, as their proponents say they are, supplements to classical logic; and there to leave the question, in what sense non-standard logicals are alternatives to classical logic. But this would obviously be unsatisfactory. We need, at least, to raise the question, whether Intuitionist or many-valued logics really are, as is claimed, alternatives to classical logic in the strong sense that they are in conflict with it. A natural way to tackle this question is to ask whether there is any *formal* feature of these systems by which we can recognise their rivalry to classical logic.

## II

*Deviant versus extended logics*

Systems may differ from each other *syntactically* (i.e. with respect to the set of theorems) or *semantically* (i.e. with respect to interpretation) or, of course, both. We begin by investigating the possible syntactic differences between systems.

Differences between the theorem sets of two systems $L_1$ and $L_2$ may or may not be associated with differences in vocabulary. We distinguish three relevant possibilities:

(1) the class of wffs of $L_1$ properly includes the class of wffs of $L_2$ and the class of theorems/valid inferences of $L_1$ properly includes the class of theorems/valid inferences of $L_2$, the additional theorems/valid inferences of $L_1$ all containing essentially occurrences of $L_1$'s additional vocabulary.

In this case we call $L_1$ an extension of $L_2$. For the case where $L_2$ is classical logic, we call $L_1$ an *extended logic*.

*Examples*: classical propositional calculus is an extension of the implicational fragment; modal logics such as T, the Lewis systems, are extensions of classical propositional calculus.

(2) the class of wffs of $L_1$ and the class of wffs of $L_2$ coincide, but the class of theorems/valid inferences of $L_1$ differs from the class of theorems/valid inferences of $L_2$.

In this case we call $L_1$ and $L_2$ *deviations* of each other. For the case where $L_2$ is classical logic, we call $L_1$ a *deviant logic*.

*Examples*: Łukasiewicz's 3-valued logic (without the addition of the Słupecki 't' operator) is a deviation of classical 2-valued logic, its theorems being a proper subset of the theorems of classical logic.

(3) the class of wffs of $L_1$ properly includes the class of wffs of $L_2$ and the class of theorems/valid inferences of $L_1$ differs from the class of theorems/valid inferences of $L_2$ not only in that $L_1$ includes additional theorems involving essentially the additional[1] vocabulary, but also in that the sets of theorems involving only the common vocabulary differ.

In this case we call $L_1$ and $L_2$ *quasi-deviations* of each other. For the case where $L_2$ is classical logic, we call $L_1$ a *quasi-deviant logic*.

*Example*: Reichenbach's 3-valued logic is a quasi-deviation of classical 2-valued logic.

If $L_1$ is a quasi-deviation from $L_2$, there is a subsystem of $L_1$, obtained by excising from $L_1$ all additional vocabulary over and above that of $L_2$, which is a deviation from $L_2$. So in what follows we shall refer to both deviant and quasi-deviant systems as Deviant logics.

Now the systems proposed as supplements to classical logic typically differ from it in the first way, and the systems proposed as rivals typically differ from it in the second or third ways. It is therefore tempting to conclude that extended logics are supplements to, and deviant and quasi-deviant logics rivals of, classical logic. This conclusion seems plausible, especially in view of the following consideration: the proponent of a deviant or quasi-deviant logic would take his system to be a rival to classical logic precisely because it lacks certain theorems which classical logic has, or, more rarely, but, e.g. in the case of Post's many-valued systems, vice versa. There are, that is to say, principles to which the classical logician assents but to which the Deviant logician does not (or rarely, vice versa), and this is why a Deviant system rivals the classical. (It may be worth observing that the rule of thumb used by Hackstaff in [1966] p. 207, to discriminate "non-standard" systems is that if a system lacks certain "characteristic" theorems of classical logic, it is to count as non-standard.)

We should, perhaps, distinguish two possibilities; that a Deviant system should have as a theorem the contradictory of a wff which classical logic has as a theorem; and that a Deviant system should

---

[1] The question, which vocabulary is 'additional', is easy to answer for, e.g. modal systems, but may be tricky for, e.g. many-valued logics with, say, more than one 'implication'.

merely lack as a theorem a wff which classical logic has as a theorem. It is the second possibility which is realised in the case of the systems we are considering. However, in accepting, say, "$p$ or not $p$" as a theorem the classical logician is asserting something implicitly general (that, whatever $p$ may be, "$p$ or not $p$" is true), and when, e.g. the Intuitionist refuses to accept "$p$ or not $p$" as a theorem he does so because he thinks that in certain instances "$p$ or not $p$" is not true. So although the conflict is not as sharp as it would be in the case of a logic with "not ($p$ or not $p$)" as a theorem, still, there is, apparently, conflict—something, that is, which the classical logician asserts and the Deviant logician denies.

Similarly, it seems plausible to expect extended systems to be supplements to classical logic—one would expect the proponent of an extended logic to take his system to be a supplement, precisely because it takes nothing away, but adds new vocabulary, in terms of which new theorems are expressible.

Nevertheless, it would be a mistake too hastily to take Deviance as the test of rivalry. The difficulties come from two directions. First, there is a question whether Deviance is a necessary condition for rivalry, for there are some logics in our list of "systems proposed as rivals" which may fail to satisfy the criteria of Deviance.

Van Fraassen's "presuppositional languages" are in this category; see van Fraassen [1966], [1968], and especially [1969]. Such languages have exactly the theorems of classical logic; but they are interpreted in such a way as to allow truth-value gaps. For a "supervaluation" assigns to a molecular wff components of which lack truth-value that value which any classical valuation would assign it, if there is a unique such value, and otherwise no value. Thus a supervaluation would assign "true" to "$p$ v $\sim p$", since both the classical valuation in which "$p$" is assigned "true" and the classical valuation in which "$p$" is assigned "false", give it "true"; but it would assign no value to "$p$ v $q$" since some classical valuations (e.g. $|p| = |q| =$ t) give it "true" and others (e.g. $|p| = |q| =$ f) give it "false". In consequence we shall have as designated wffs all and only the classical tautologies. This suggests that we should regard such languages as semantically non-standard although syntactically conventional. Van Fraassen claims, however, that the change he proposes has consequences for deducibility, though not for theoremhood. (See [1969] pp. 79–86.) So it is possible that his presuppositional languages *are* within the scope of our definition of deviance.

There is also some difficulty with Bochvar's 3-valued logic. For the truth-tables for the "internal" connectives are such that whenever there is intermediate ("paradoxical") input, there is also intermediate output, so that there are no uniformly t-taking wffs containing only internal connectives. And the "external" connectives are defined in terms of the internal connectives and an "assertion" operator, which takes "true" if its argument takes "true", but otherwise "false", so that their truth-tables are such that whatever the input, the output is always classical. This suggests that it would be natural to think of the external connectives as corresponding to their classical counterparts, and the internal connectives as the new vocabulary. On this interpretation Bochvar's appears as an extended rather than a Deviant logic. (Cf. Rescher [1969] pp. 30–2.) But, of course, this might lead us to the conclusion that Bochvar's logic is a supplement rather than a rival, instead of the conclusion that Deviance is not after all a necessary condition of rivalry.

The second, and more serious difficulty, is that it is not certain whether syntactic Deviance is *sufficient* for rivalry. For suppose we were to ask how "classical logic" is to be demarcated. This is to be done, we have supposed, by reference to its set of theorems and valid inferences. Any system with the same theorems/inferences as, say, *Principia Mathematica*, counts as a formulation, a version, of "classical logic". In particular, a system which differs from that of PM only in employing a distinct, but intertranslatable, notation—say "&" in place of "." for conjunction—is only a *notational variant* of classical logic. But now we are faced with the following problem: a system, $L_1$, which has as theorems a typographically distinct set of wffs from the set of wffs of PM is, we should say, only a notational variant of that system, if uniformly replacing certain symbols of $L_1$ by symbols of PM renders the set of theorems identical. Someone who thought that $L_1$ was a rival to PM just because such wffs as "$p.q \supset p$" were lacking from its set of theorems would, we should say, have mistaken a purely typographical difference for a substantial disagreement.

And now the question arises, whether the apparent disagreement between Deviant and classical logicians may not similarly be mere appearance. We supposed Łukasiewicz's 3-valued logic, for instance, to be a rival to classical logic, because classical logic has as theorems certain wffs, such as "$p \vee \sim p$", which are not theorems of Łukasiewicz's logic. But the mere absence from the set of theorems of $Ł_3$ of wffs of a certain typographical form is not sufficient, as we can now see, to show that there is real conflict between $Ł_3$ and classical logic. There remains the question, whether those wffs, so to speak, mean the same in both systems. If, for example, we came to believe that Łukasiewicz was employing "v" as a (perverse) notation for the operation usually written "&", we should certainly not suppose that the absence from the set of theorems of $Ł_3$ of the wff "$p$ v $\sim p$" showed $Ł_3$ to be a rival to classical logic.

So we are faced with another problem. We have found formal features—deviance and quasi-deviance—which it seemed plausible to take as sufficient conditions of rivalry. And so it looked as though there were systems, the deviant and the quasi-deviant logics, which we could properly describe as *rivals* of classical logic, *alternatives* to it in a strong sense of 'alternative'. But now we realise that it could be argued that this appearance of rivalry is misleading. We must investigate this line of argument.

### III

*The argument against genuine rivalry*
While there is no doubt that deviant and quasi-deviant systems have been proposed as rivals to classical logic, some writers have argued that the systems so proposed turn out not really to be rivals at all, because their apparent incompatability with classical logic is explicable as resulting from change of meaning of the logical constants. Quine, for example, writes:

departure from the law of excluded middle would count as evidence of revised usage of 'or' or 'not' . . . For the deviating logician the words 'or' and 'not' are unfamiliar or defamiliarised . . .

(Quine [1960a] p. 396)

and

Alternative logics are inseparable practically from *mere change in usage of logical words.*

(Quine [1960a] p. 389, my italics)

The train of thought which leads to this position seems to be somewhat as follows:

(a)  if there is change of meaning of the logical constants, there is no real conflict between Deviant and classical logic,

(b) if there is Deviance, there is change of meaning of the logical
   constants,

so

(c) there is no real conflict between Deviant and classical logic.

Putnam, whose attitude to Deviant logic is more sympathetic than
Quine's, writes:

> the logical words 'or' and 'not' have a certain core meaning which is . . .
> *independent* of the principle of the excluded middle. Thus in a certain sense
> the meaning does not change if we go over to a three-valued logic or to
> Intuitionist logic. Of course, if by saying that a change in the accepted
> logical principles is tantamount to a change in the meaning of the logical
> connectives, what one has in mind is the fact that changing the accepted
> logical principles will affect the global use of the logical connectives, then
> the thesis is tautological and hardly arguable. But if the claim is that a
> change in the accepted logical principles would amount *merely* to redefining
> the logical connectives, then, in the case of Intuitionist logic, this is demon-
> strably false.
>
> (Putnam [1962] p. 377)

As this passage suggests, discussion of this kind of attempt to trivialise
Deviance in logic has concentrated on premiss (b); (a) has been conceded or ignored.

However, it is not hard to see that premiss (a) is, as it stands,
false. It says that if it can be shown that the Deviant logician means
by his logical constants something different from what is meant by
the classical logical constants, it follows that there is no real conflict
between the Deviant and the classical systems. Now suppose the
Deviant logician means by a certain connective, $c$, something
different from what is meant by the typographically identical connective of classical logic. Then, if the Deviant logic lacks as a theorem
a wff, $w$, which is a theorem of classical logic and contains $c$ as
sole connective, then, in an important sense, what the Deviant
logician denies is not what the classical logician asserts. However, it
does not follow from the fact that what the Deviant logician denies,
when he denies that $w$ is logically true, is not what the classical
logician asserts, when he asserts that $w$ is logically true, that *nothing*
the Deviant logician says is inconsistent with *anything* the classical
logician says; there may none the less be conflict.

For consider the following case: a Deviant logician $D$ denies that
the wff "$(p \lor q) \supset (\sim p \supset q)$" is logically true. The classical

logician, $C$, takes this wff to be a theorem. However, it is discovered that $D$ means by "v" what $C$ means by "&". It follows that when $D$ denies that "$(p \text{ v } q) \supset (\sim p \supset q]$" is logically true, what he denies is not what $C$ asserts when $C$ asserts that "$(p \text{ v } q) \supset (\sim p \supset q)$" is logically true. But it does not follow that there is no real disagreement between $C$ and $D$. For $C$ also thinks that "$(p \text{ \& } q) \supset (\sim p \supset q)$" is logically true, so when $D$ denies that "$(p \text{ v } q) \supset (\sim p \supset q)$" is logically true, what he denies *is* after all something which $C$ accepts. This shows that difference of meaning of the connectives between classical and Deviant systems is not sufficient to establish lack of rivalry between them.

Another consideration supports the same conclusion. For there are some cases at least of difference between logics which, *prima facie*, resist explanation of apparent conflict in terms of difference of meaning of connectives. If $L_D$ (the Deviant system) lacks certain principles which $L_C$ (the classical system) accepts, and these principles contain *no* occurrences of any connectives, then the apparent difference between $L_D$ and $L_C$ can hardly be explained away as due to an idiosyncracy in the meanings of the connectives of $L_D$. Since (in a consistent system) atomic formulae are not provable, the possibility of explanation in terms of changed meaning of connectives is always available when the difference between $L_D$ and $L_C$ lies in the set of theorems. But now consider Gentzen's formulation of minimal logic ($L_j$): it differs from classical logic, not in respect of the introduction and elimination rules for the connectives, but in respect of the structural rules for deducibility; namely, it results from restricting the rules for classical logic ($L_k$) by disallowing multiple consequents. Since this restriction involves no essential reference to any connectives, it is hard to see how it could be explicable as arising from divergence of meaning of connectives. The same argument applies to the Heyting calculus, which results, in Gentzen's formulation, from adding to $L_j$ the rule "from $A$ and $\daleth A$ to infer $B$", while retaining the restriction on multiple consequents. The argument is not wholly conclusive, since it could be suggested that the reason for the restriction on deducibility lies in a desire to avoid certain theorems, e.g. "$p \text{ v } \daleth p$", that and the desire to avoid these theorems may spring from idiosyncracy of connectives. But the argument is at least suggestive. And it cannot be dismissed by suggesting that the difference between classical and minimal logic be attributed to idiosyncracy in the meaning of

"⊢". The advocate of minimal or Intuitionist logic is not comparable to those philosophers who have been sufficiently impressed by the "paradoxes" of strict implication to deny that strict implication can be identified with entailment or logical consequence. Such writers might (as suggested in Smiley [1959]) propose alternative principles for "⊢", and if they did so it would be precisely because of their special interpretation of "⊢". The Intuitionist, by contrast, means the same by "⊢" as the classical logician, but nevertheless believes that a principle for "⊢", which the classical logician accepts, does not hold.

So change of meaning is not sufficient for absence of conflict. As our example (pp. 40–1) shows, whether difference of meaning is sufficient to account for apparent conflict depends upon the exact nature of the meaning change. However, there are arguments which, if sound, would show that adoption of a Deviant system must involve a wholesale change in the meanings of the logical connectives which would be sufficient to account for the appearance of incompatability with classical logic So we now turn to these.

(i)  *The argument from the theory-dependence of the meanings of connectives*
The most obvious argument for a strong version of premiss (b) would appeal to the thesis that the meaning of the logical connectives is wholly given by the axioms and/or rules of inference of the system in which they occur. (See Carnap [1937], and cf. Fremlin [1938], Campbell [1958].) It presumably follows immediately from this thesis that adoption of a Deviant axiom set entails wholesale change in the meaning of the connectives. For consider the question, how we are to individuate sets of axioms of rules. A proponent of the thesis that the meanings of the connectives are given by the axioms or rules of the systems in which they occur would presumably wish to count two axiomatisations as, from this point of view, the same, if, although there were not the same wffs in each set, the sets were equivalent, i.e. yielded the same set of theorems; since otherwise he would be forced to say that the connectives differed in meaning in alternative axiomatisations of the classical propositional calculus. So he would count two axiom sets involving the same connectives as different only if they yielded different sets of theorems, i.e. were Deviations of each other.

There is an interesting analogy between the view we are considering and Feyerabend's thesis, that differences between two ostensibly rival scientific theories involve differences of meaning of terms occurring in the theories (analogue: differences between two ostensibly rival logics involve differences of meaning of logical constants); and between premiss (a) and the criticism made of Feyerabend, e.g. by Shapere, that his meaning-variance thesis would entail that scientific theories which are proposed as rivals to each other are not really incompatible after all (analogue: what the Deviant logician denies is not, appearances to the contrary, anything the classical logician asserts). (Cf. Feyerabend [1962], [1963], Shapere [1966].)

Indeed, *prima facie*, at least, the meaning-variance thesis sounds more plausible when applied to logics than when applied to scientific theories, for in the latter case there seem to be certain restraints upon the meanings of the theoretical terms, to the extent that they have some connection with observables, whereas in the former case there are no such apparent restraints upon the meanings of the connectives.

The possibility of this kind of argument is recognised both by Quine, in "Carnap and Logical Truth" [1960a], and by Putnam in "Is Logic Empirical?" [1969]. However, neither Quine nor Putnam thinks that the concept of meaning is sufficiently clear for the thesis that the meaning of the constants of a system is given by the axioms/rules of the system to amount to anything upon which such weight could be placed. Putnam, indeed, offers against this argument the following considerations, which are especially interesting in view of the analogy noted above between meaning-variances theses for scientific theories and for logics. He suggests that for logical as for scientific terms there are operational constraints, which provide a degree of community of meaning between theories sufficient to allow genuine incompatibility. He argues, further, that just as, with relativity theory, the cluster of laws, geometrical and physical, involved in the Euclidean concept of a straight line "fall apart", so, with quantum mechanics, the cluster of laws, logical and physical, involved in the classical concepts of conjunction and disjunction have "fallen apart". The solution he proposes is:

to *deny* that there are *any* precise and meaningful operations or propositions which have the properties classically attributed to 'and' and 'or'.

(Putnam [1969] p. 232)

So, he argues, we must replace the old logic by a new one, and the old concepts of conjunction and disjunction by new ones, but ones

which share a "core" of meaning with the old. (Cf. Putnam [1957]
for the notion of "core" meaning, and [1962] for the notion of
"law cluster concept".)

However, it may not be necessary, in order to avoid the meaning
change argument, to agree with Putnam that there are operational
constraints upon even logical terms. For the premiss upon which the
argument rests—that the meanings of the logical connectives are
given by the axioms and/or rules of inference of the system in which
they occur—has been challenged.

Prior tries in [1960] and [1964] to show that the meanings of the
connectives *cannot* be given by the axioms/rules of a system, by
inviting us to consider a system which includes the connective
"tonk", governed by the rules:

From $A$ to infer $A$ tonk $B$

and

From $A$ tonk $B$ to infer $B$

However, the conclusion which Prior apparently favours, that the
connectives must have independently specified meaning before we
can discover what logical principles hold for them, rather than
specification of those principles *constituting* giving their meaning,
hardly follows. For it is clear that there are independent arguments
against the "tonk" rules, which are neither syntactically adequate,
since they would allow $A \vdash B$, nor semantically adequate, since no
unique truth-table could be given for "tonk" consistent with them.
(Cf. Belnap [1961] and Stevenson [1961], respectively, on these
points.) Since the "tonk" rules are unacceptable, it is not surprising
if they cannot give the meaning of "tonk". It does not follow that
*no* rules could give the meanings of the connectives occurring in
them.

Even so, however, it is doubtful whether the thesis that meaning is
given by axioms and/or rules of inference can be made to support a
strong version of the meaning variance thesis for Deviant logics.
For the typical situation with Deviant systems is that their axioms/
rules of inference are very similar to but not quite the same as those
of classical logic. For instance, as Putnam points out in [1969], in
Birkhoff and von Neumann's as in classical logic all the following
rules for "&" and "v" are valid:

$A, B \vdash A \& B$
$A \& B \vdash A$
$A \& B \vdash B$
$A \vdash A \lor B$
if $A \vdash C$ and $B \vdash C$, then $A \lor B \vdash C$

but nevertheless this system deviates from the classical, notably in lacking the distributive laws for "&" and "v". Because there is such a degree of overlap, even if we were convinced of the thesis that the meanings of the connectives are given by the axioms/rules of the system, the conclusion, that Deviant logics must involve a degree of meaning variance sufficient to dispose of all apparent rivalry with classical logic, would hardly be unambiguously forthcoming. For the thesis that the meaning is given by the axioms/rules yields, in the case of axioms/rules partly but not wholly differing from the classical, only the conclusion that the meanings of the connectives in such systems are partly but not wholly different from their meanings in the classical; and this gives us no clear answer to the question, whether there is real rivalry.

Some similar difficulties would arise if it were suggested, as by Stevenson, that the meaning of the connectives is given, at least in part, by their truth-tables. (Cf. Lewis [1932].) Suppose it were asked whether, on this view, the connectives of, say, $Ł_3$, differ in meaning from their typographical analogues in classical logic. One might say that they do, since the truth-tables of $Ł_3$ are different, being 3-valued, from those of $L_C$. On the other hand, one might say that they do not, since the truth-tables of $Ł_3$ are normal, i.e. they have classical, true or false, output wherever they have classical input. (Cf. here the "conditional" account of the meaning of the connectives in Strawson [1952] p. 19.) And there are further difficulties. What are we to say of the meanings of the connectives in systems such as Intuitionist logic which have no finite characteristic matrix? And of the meanings of the connectives in a system like van Fraassen's which is conventional so far as its theorems are concerned, but semantically deviant?

Prior seems to think that since, as he supposes, he has shown that the thesis that meaning is given by the axioms/rules of a system is untenable, the meanings of the connectives can only be fully specified with reference to their ordinary language readings. If this view were adopted, we should presumably think that the meanings of the connectives do *not* change in the move to Deviant logics, since Deviant logicians employ the usual ordinary language readings for their connectives. (Except, that is, for the Intuitionists, who sometimes employ idiosyncratic readings.) However, since so many writers have found difficulty with the usual ordinary language readings of the connectives (consider, e.g. the literature which exists on the question, how proper a reading of " ⊃ " is "if... then...""?) Prior's thesis, that the meaning is finally and fully given by the ordinary language reading, is not obviously any more acceptable than the alternatives already considered.

So no conclusive argument has yet been given, from an acceptable premiss concerning the meanings of the connectives, to the conclusion that in Deviant logics meaning variance accounts for apparent rivalry.

Quine has, however, a different argument for the same conclusion.

### (ii) *The argument from translation*

Quine's argument purports to show that *apparent conflict in logic should always be accounted the result of mistranslation.*

In "Carnap and Logical Truth" [1960a] the argument appears in a form which appeals directly to standards of translation between one language and another:

Oversimplifying, no doubt, let us suppose it claimed that ... natives accept as true certain sentences of the form '*p* and not *p*'. Or—not to oversimplify too much—that they accept as true a certain heathen sentence of the form '*q* ka bu *q*', the English translation of which has the form '*p* and not *p*'. But now just how good a translation is this, and what may the lexicographer's method have been? If any evidence can count against a lexicographer's adoption of 'and' and 'not' as translations of 'ka' and 'bu', certainly the natives' acceptance of '*q* ka bu *q*' counts overwhelmingly ... prelogicality is a myth invented by bad translators.

(Quine [1960a] p. 387)

In *Word and Object* [1960b] also, this argument is deployed against the possibility of prelogical peoples. In *Philosophy of Logic* [1970c], however, the argument is applied to "translation" of the deviant logician's "dialect" into our own:

We impute our orthodox logic to [the deviant logician], or impose it upon him, by translating his deviant dialect.

([1970c] p. 81)

It is worth observing that this argument of Quine's—which, if it were sound, would show that there can be no genuine rivals to classical logic—is incompatible with another thesis, propounded in, e.g. the last section of "Two Dogmas of Empiricism" (Quine [1951]), to the effect that none of our beliefs, beliefs about the laws of logic included, is immune from revision in the light of experience. According to this view it is at least theoretically possible that we should revise our logic. In practice, as Quine observes in "Two Dogmas", he is inclined to be conservative about his logic, for the ramifying adjustments necessitated by a change of logic are liable to be excessively widespread. But, in principle at least, the possibility of revising logic is left open. However, the *Philosophy of Logic* thesis is that there can be no such thing as a real, but only an apparent change of logic.

The *Philosophy of Logic* thesis derives from Quine's theory of translation (see Quine [1953a], [1959], [1968b], and, especially, [1960b], Ch. 2). In *Word and Object* [1960b], Ch. 2, Quine is arguing for the thesis of the *indeterminacy of translation*, which may be summarised thus:

QIT Alternative, and mutually incompatible, translations may conform to all data concerning speakers' dispositions to verbal behaviour.

The primary interest here is in the reasons for an exception which Quine makes to QIT: translation of the truth-functional connectives is, he claims, immune from indeterminacy.[2]

In order to understand the reasons for excepting the truth-functions, and the relevance of this exception to Deviant logics, we shall have, however, to look more closely at QIT. We find in Quine's work on translation three theses:

(1) There is *inductive uncertainty* in the translation even of *observation sentences*.

(2) There is *radical indeterminacy* in the translation of *words and phrases*.

(3) There is *radical indeterminacy* in the translation of *theoretical sentences*.

---

[2] So the present concern will be, not the adequacy of Quine's arguments for QIT, but the adequacy of his arguments for his exception to QIT. On the former question cf. Blackburn, "The Identity of Propositions", section II, Chapter 6 in this volume.

Theses (2) and (3) together constitute QIT: although Quine accepts thesis (1) he takes pains to emphasise that it is distinct from, and less important than, his indeterminacy theses.

Quine begins from the premiss that the evidence for a linguistic theory consists of information concerning the verbal behaviour and dispositions to verbal behaviour of the speakers of the language being translated. He takes assent and dissent as basic behavioural co-ordinates, and defines the affirmative/negative stimulus meaning of a sentence for a speaker as the class of all stimulations which would prompt his assent/dissent, and the stimulus meaning of the sentence for the speaker as the ordered pair of its affirmative and negative stimulus meanings. He then points out that there are certain difficulties even in discovering the stimulus meaning of observation sentences, since natives' assent to or dissent from a sentence may depend upon collateral information. These difficulties arise, then, from the underdetermination of a linguistic theory by its data, from the availability of alternative ways of accounting for given evidence. This is thesis (1). But Quine takes this merely inductive uncertainty relatively lightly. (See [1960b] p. 68.)

Radical indeterminacy is a much more serious matter; where it arises, the problem is not that there is difficulty in finding a translation, but rather, that there is no uniquely correct translation to be found. Radical indeterminacy arises at the level of analytical hypotheses—hypotheses, that is, concerning the segmentation of heard utterances into meaningful units, and the parsing and translation of these units. For alternative analytical hypotheses, incompatible with each other but yielding the same net output at the observation sentence level, will always be available, since compensating adjustments, either in the choice of meaningful unit, e.g. construing some segment as pleonastic, or in the form of the hypothesis that the meaning of certain segment(s) is context dependent, are always possible. (See [1968b].) This is thesis (2).

Radical indeterminacy also arises at the level of translation of certain sentences, those, namely, which are theoretical rather than observational. For consider how we are to translate theoretical sentences, given only evidence concerning speakers' dispositions to verbal behaviour. Assent to or dissent from a theoretical sentence does not depend in any direct way upon stimulation; indeed, in [1970a] this is treated as a defining characteristic of non-observationality of sentences. Now suppose that we have translated all the

observation sentences which constitute the data for a native theory
$T$, the sentences of which we wish to translate. By the "Duhem
theses", the theses, that is, that no hypothesis can be conclusively
verified or falsified by any amount of data, these observation sentences are compatible with rival theories, say $T$ and $T'$. And so $T$
and $T'$, though *ex hypothesi* incompatible, are indistinguishable in
point of stimulus meaning. To put the argument in another way; if
meaning is given by assent/dissent conditions (the "Dewey principle") and if the assent/dissent conditions of theoretical sentences are
indeterminate (the "Duhem theses") then the meanings of theoretical
sentences are indeterminate. (See [1970b].) This is thesis (3).

Now on this interpretation we have some explanation of why
Quine should make the exception to QIT which interests us—
the alleged determinacy of translation of the truth-functional
connectives. In sections 12–13 of *Word and Object* Quine argues that,
whereas the quantifiers are vulnerable to the radical indeterminacy,
the truth-functions are not. The discrimination here between quantifiers and truth-functions is comprehensible, now, if we remember
that the truth-functions *link* whole sentences, whereas the quantifiers
occur *within* whole sentences. More precisely, the truth-functional
operators are sentence-forming operators on sentences, while the
quantifiers are sentence-forming operators on open, i.e. incomplete,
sentences. Therefore the quantifiers, but not the truth-functions, are
vulnerable to that form of radical indeterminacy which strikes
below the sentence level; for we can give semantic criteria, in terms
of assent and dissent, for the truth-functions, but not for the quantifiers.

It has been shown why Quine should except the truth-functions
from QIT, why he should take them to be determinately translatable. We have yet to show how their translatability is supposed to
yield a meaning variance thesis for deviant logics. The argument
seems to run as follows: we can give semantic criteria, in terms of
assent and dissent, for the truth-functional connectives; when an
expression fulfils these criteria, this is sufficient reason to translate
it by the appropriate truth-function. And this rules out the possibility
of a correct translation in accordance with which the natives dissent
from (classical) tautologies or assent to (classical) contradictions.
Thus, Quine is maintaining both:

(1) It is possible to tell that a certain expression of (the language

being translated), $L$, should be translated by a certain connective,
e.g. "and"

and

(2) It is not possible that a correct translation of expressions of $L$
by sentential connectives should be such that sentences translated
by (classical) contradictions are assented to by speakers of $L$,
nor that sentences translated by (classical) tautologies are dis-
sented from by speakers of $L$.

We shall argue that even if (1) is true, (2) follows only given some
further assumptions which are themselves doubtful, so that Quine's
argument against rivalry between logics fails.

The assumptions which support Quine's claim that correct translation to a native's or a Deviant logician's utterances must be such
as to make them conform with classical propositional calculus are:

(a) the principle of maximising agreement (hereafter $M$)
(b) the adoption of classical criteria for the truth-functions
and, supporting (b),
(c) the adoption of assent and dissent as behavioural co-ordinates.

Quine recognises that he is taking for granted the principle that we
should so translate another's utterances as to maximise agreement
between us. He writes:

the maxim of translation underlying all this is that assertions startlingly
false on the face of them are likely to turn on hidden differences of language.
(Quine [1960b] p. 59)

and

It behooves us, in construing a strange language, to make the obvious
sentences go over into English sentences which are true and, preferably,
also obvious.
(Quine [1970c] p. 82)

To put the matter another way: faced with a choice of attributing to
the native, or to the Deviant logician, a disagreement in belief or a
divergence in meaning, we should choose the latter rather than the
former. Now $(M)$ yields (2) in conjunction with the assumption that
the person doing the translating accepts classical logic. And just this
assumption is embodied in (b)—Quine's adoption of criteria for
the truth-functional connectives which (with "assent" replacing

"true" and "dissent" replacing "false") simply follow the 2-valued matrices.

This choice of criteria is, in turn, made plausible by Quine's adoption of assent and dissent as co-ordinates. For suppose we took three co-ordinates, assent, dissent, and puzzlement, as basic. Then we could state alternative criteria, e.g. as follows:

> The *disjunction* of two sentences is that sentence to which one would assent if one assents to either component, from one which one would dissent if one dissents from both components, and to which one would react with puzzlement if one reacts with puzzlement to both components, or reacts with puzzlement to one component and dissents from the other.

> The *negation* of a sentence is that sentence to which one would assent if one dissents from the sentence, from which one would dissent if one assents to the sentence, and to which one would react with puzzlement if one reacts with puzzlement to the sentence.

On *these* criteria the possibility that natives might fail to assent to some sentence translatable as "*p* or not *p*" is not at all absurd— and might be evidence that they employ a 3-valued logic. And if we used these criteria Quine's (1) could be true but (2) false.

That in order to yield the conservative conclusion that everybody really accepts classical logic, (*M*) must be supplemented by the further assumption that classical logic is correct, can be seen clearly, if it is not already sufficiently apparent, by the following consideration. Suppose that our linguist were an Intuitionist. If he accepts (*M*), he will so translate the natives' (or our) utterances as to attribute to them (us) an Intuitionist logic. To an Intuitionist linguist it would be absurd to suppose that a sentence which commands invariable assent could correctly be translated "*p* or not *p*". Quine might object that although an Intuitionist would indeed so translate native sentences that natives do not invariably assent to the sentence he translates as "*p* or not *p*", the Intuitionist does not mean by that sentence what the classical logician means. But this form of argument simply is not legitimately available to Quine at this stage—for he has yet to establish that an Intuitionist cannot mean the same as a classical logician by "*p* or not *p*".

The principle of maximising agreement entails that correct translation invariably preserves classical logic in a privileged position, only if we assume that classical logic is the right one. When

Quine asks 'Not to be dogmatic about it, what criteria for the connectives might one prefer?', his rhetorical question only thinly masks the *petitio principii*. His maxim, 'Save the obvious', preserves classical logic only granted that classical logic *is* obvious.

A further difficulty with Quine's argument is that it seems most doubtful whether, even supposing (b) granted for the sake of argument, $(M)$ would take the weight Quine places on it. $(M)$ may, quite properly, be thought of as a pragmatic principle applying to our choice of linguistic theory: the principle that, if it is reasonably obvious to the translator that $p$, and the translator has no special reason to suppose that this is not obvious to his respondent, then a translation which preserves the translator's and the respondent's agreement that $p$ is preferable to one that does not. This pragmatic principle may be given a certain amount of support by the consideration that without assumption of *some* agreement in beliefs between translator and respondent, translation could hardly begin.

Still, if $(M)$ is a sensible pragmatic principle, still it is only a pragmatic principle; it may be overridden. Sometimes translations violating it might be simpler than translations in conformity to it. $(M)$ surely has greatest weight in cases like that of the fictional logician of *Philosophy of Logic* [1970c], who takes all classical laws governing conjunction to govern disjunction, and vice versa, where the beliefs that would have to be attributed to the respondent in order to preserve homophonic translation are very extraordinary. It has less weight in cases, like that, say, of Birkhoff and von Neumann's logic, where we should have a large though incomplete measure of agreement in belief even under homophonic translation. Worse, its verdict is quite ambiguous where the Deviant logician holds, besides his (apparently) idiosyncratic logical beliefs, the further belief that he disagrees with the classical logician.

We may also observe that, if $(M)$ were as unreservedly acceptable as Quine supposes, it would yield not only the conclusion that Deviance in propositional calculus is attributable to idiosyncracy of meaning of the truth-functional connectives, but also the conclusion that Deviance in predicate calculus is attributable to idiosyncracy of meaning of the quantifiers. This is, indeed, a view to which Quine seems sympathetic in *Philosophy of Logic*, e.g. when he discusses what the Intuitionist means by "$(\exists x)\ldots x$". But once we have noticed this, we cannot avoid the conclusion that Quine must have overestimated the importance of the exceptions to the indeterminacy of translation in the case of the truth-functions. That is, if the predicate calculus analogue of (2) follows from $(M)$, even without the predicate calculus analogue of (1), the connection between (1) and (2) themselves must be less close than, in *Word and Object*, Quine seems to suppose.

So, we conclude, Quine's argument from translation is no more successful than the argument from the theory dependence of the meanings of logical terms in establishing that there can be no real rivals to classical logic.

We have found no general argument adequate to show that Deviance must involve wholesale meaning change, or, therefore, adequate to show that genuinely rival logics are impossible. It does not, however, follow from this failure—and neither do we assert—that Deviant logics never involve any meaning change, or that all Deviant logics necessarily stand in real conflict with classical logic. We shall suggest, in what follows, that the extent to which a Deviant system involves change of meaning may depend upon the particular system in question.

IV

*Varieties of Deviance*

It is unsurprising, in view of their contrasting attitudes to Deviant logics, to find Quine concentrating on the fictional logician of *Philosophy of Logic*, when the plausibility of the thesis that the change is *only* one of notation is maximal, and Putnam concentrating on the kind of Deviance typified by the Intuitionist or by Birkhoff and von Neumann, when the plausibility of the thesis that the change is only one of notation is minimal.

Short of the possibility of straightforward rivalry, when there is Deviance unaccompanied by any meaning variance, we might distinguish three kinds of possible case. Quine more or less explicitly acknowledges their possibility, but concentrates almost wholly on the first, which is the most favourable to a conservative position.

(A) One possibility is that all theorems of the Deviant logic, $L_D$, can be translated into theorems of classical logic, $L_C$, and vice versa. This is the situation with Quine's fictional example; if we translate each wff $A$ of $L_C$ by the wff $A'$ of $L_D$ which results from replacing all occurrences of "&" in $A$ by "v" and all occurrences of "v" in $A$ by "&", then $\vdash_{L_C} A$ iff $\vdash_{L_D} A'$. Quine concludes, very plausibly, that $L_D$ should be regarded as only a notational variant of $L_C$.

But there is a second possibility, viz:

(B) that we should be unable to translate everything which the Deviant logician asserts into something to which the classical logician would assent and everything from which the Deviant logician dissents into something from which the classical logician would also dissent. Suppose, e.g. that for every wff $A$ of $L_C$ we can find a translation $A'$ of $L_D$ such that if $\vdash_{LC} A$ then $\vdash_{LD} A'$, but there are some theorems of $L_D$ which have no translations in $L_C$. Then $L_D$ is, if not a rival, at least a supplement (and not merely an uninteresting notational variant) of $L_C$.

A quasi-deviant system which might not implausibly be thought of as falling into this category is that of "Sense without Denotation" (Smiley [1960]), which is formally similar to Bochvar's. Here there is some reason to say that the secondary connectives do not differ in meaning from the classical connectives, since exactly the same logical principles hold for these as for those. The primary connectives now appear as new connectives, bearing some, but only an imperfect, analogy to the old, and the system appears as an extenson of the classical.

Another possibility is

(C) that a system should employ a set of connectives differing in meaning from those of classical logic, while lacking the means to express classical connectives. Such a system would be neither straightforwardly a rival, nor straightforwardly a supplement, of classical logic.

An example might be the 3-valued system considered in Lewis [1932]. Let $1$ = certainly true, $2$ = certainly false, $3$ = doubtful. In terms of these categories, Lewis argues, the meaning of the classical "or" is simply inexpressible. For consider what value we are to give to "$p$ or $q$" when $|p| = |q| = 3$. If "$p$" and "$q$" are doubtful, is "$p$ or $q$" also doubtful? Well, generally yes; but not if "$p$" and "$q$" are so related (as when "$p$" = "$\sim q$") that when "$p$" is true, "$q$" must be false, and vice versa. The moral to be drawn is, presumably, that the question, whether at least one of "$p$", "$q$" is true, cannot be answered given only information, concerning "$p$" and "$q$", whether they are certainly true, certainly false, or not certainly either.

Quine comes close to explicit recognition of the possibility of cases of types (B) and (C) when he writes:

> There may of course still be an important failure of intertranslatability, in that the behaviour of certain of our logical particles is incapable of being duplicated by paraphrases in the native's or deviant logician's system or vice-versa. If translation in this sense is possible . . . then we are pretty sure to protest that he was wantonly using the familiar particles 'and' and 'all' (say) when he might unmisleadingly have used such and such other familiar phrasing.
>
> (Quine [1960b] p. 386)

The important conclusion which, returning to his conservative mood, Quine leaves undrawn, is this: that if straightforward and wholesale intertranslation is *not* possible, we shall have to take the Deviant logician seriously after all.

We have up to now been considering the question, whether Deviant logics really are, as their proponents claim, rivals of classical logic, or whether considerations of meaning inevitably show that the rivalry is only apparent, and we have concluded that genuine rivalry *is* possible. But there is another point, so far neglected, that deserves mention. It is this: even if the edge of the disagreement between the classical and a Deviant system is blunted by some degree of meaning change, this meaning change may be neither unmotivated nor unimportant. Quine is half aware of this:

> in repudiating '$p$ v $\sim p$' the deviant logician is . . . giving up classical negation, or perhaps alternation, or both; and *he may have his reasons.*
>
> (Quine [1970c] p. 87, my italics)

Putnam is acutely aware of it, when he stresses [1969] that a change of logic, even if less than a genuine repudiation of the classical system, may constitute an important "conceptual revision".

And so I make, against those who would trivialise "alternative logics", two claims: that it is not true that there can be no such thing as a genuine rival to classical logic; and that it is not true, either, that adoption even of a Deviant system which involves some degree of meaning variance may not constitute a real and interesting change of logic. Of course, the question, whether there could be *good reasons* for adopting an alternative logic, remains.[3]

---

[3] Craig ("An Approach to the Problem of Necessary Truth", Chapter 1 in this volume) argues for a negative answer to this question. I should argue for an affirmative answer. (See Haack [1974], Chapter 2)

# 3

# Quantification, modality, and indirect speech[1]

## THOMAS BALDWIN

### I

A familiar group of problems in philosophical logic and the philosophy of language concern the use of quantification in modal and
indirect speech constructions. The problems raised are important
for two reasons. At the level of the specific concepts employed, one
wants to know what, if anything, is meant by such sentences as:

There is someone whom the police suspect to be a spy.
The structure of British society might not be what it is.

which would naturally be understood in a theory based on predicate
logic to involve the use of a variable within a subordinate clause
that is bound by a quantifier outside the subordinate clause. At a
more general level, the adequacy of any theory of language and
logic is tested by its ability to handle sentences such as those above.
The problems to which these sentences give rise have proved so
persistent for the paradigm theory which derives from Frege and
Tarski that one may regard them as a serious anomaly to that paradigm, one which signals the present fluid and critical state of linguistic theory.

In this essay I shall concentrate on this second aspect of these
problems, on their general significance for theories of language and
logic. It may seem that another essay on this subject is otiose; that,
after the consumption of so many hundreds of trees in the produc-

[1] I should like to express my gratitude to Simon Blackburn both for his patience
as editor and for his helpful comments on an earlier draft of this paper. I should
also like to record the stimulation I have received in thinking about these matters
from lectures by and conversations with Timothy Smiley.

tion of publications on this subject, one should leave further trees untouched. But the fact remains that today, thirty years since Quine raised these problems (cf. Quine [1943]), there is still no consensus of opinion on their solution. Despite undeniable advances in logical and linguistic theory in this period, there is still no philosophical treatment of the problems of quantification into modal and indirect speech contexts which commands general assent. In this essay I shall argue that several current treatments of the problems are definitely mistaken and I shall make tentative proposals of my own. But the reason for continuing discussion of these problems is not just that they have as yet no agreed solution: it is primarily that their solution has a fundamental significance for theories of logic and language. For the concepts which inevitably arise in any discussion of the problems are among the basic concepts of any logical and linguistic theory.

A clear way to approach the problems of quantification into modal and indirect speech contexts lies through examination of four claims, each of which is plausible by itself, but whose conjunction is inconsistent:

(A) There are acceptable sentences of natural languages in which pronouns inside a subordinate clause in a modal or an indirect speech construction have their antecedent outside that clause.

(B) The logical form of sentences embodying pronominal constructions such as those mentioned in (A) is displayed by equivalent sentences in which quantifiers outside a subordinate clause bind variables within it.

(C) Contexts for singular terms inside a subordinate clause in a modal or an indirect speech construction are referentially opaque.

(D) One cannot interpret quantification into opaque contexts.

An example will help: a sentence of the kind described in (A) is

(1) There is someone of whom Ralph believes that he is a spy.[2]

If (B) is accepted, then the logical form of (1) will be displayed by

(2) $(\exists x)$ (Ralph believes that $x$ is a spy)

(where S displays the logical form of S', I shall often say that S' should be *construed* as S). But, as (C) claims, it is plausible to regard

---

[2] Where sentences are numbered, as here, the numbering begins afresh in each section of the essay.

the context for singular terms "Ralph believes that...is a spy" as opaque. So, if (D) is accepted and applied to this context, one cannot interpret a sentence such as (2) since the variable here occurs in an opaque context.

Each of the claims (A)–(D) is initially plausible and any three of them are consistent. It is just the conjunction of all four which is inconsistent. Actually, it is really the conflict between (C) and (D) which is fundamental; the first two claims, (A) and (B), just serve to set up a class of sentences whose interpretation is contingent on one's attitude to (C) and (D). One way to view the conflict between (C) and (D) is to consider the generalised principle of the substitutivity of identity:

(3) $(x)(y)(x = y \to (Fx \to Fy))$.

This principle is equivalent to

(4) $(x)((\exists y)(x = y \ \& \ Fx) \to Fy)$

and it is the apparent logical truth of this latter principle which stands behind (D), the claim that quantification into opaque contexts cannot be interpreted. However, (C), the claim that contexts for singular terms in modal and indirect speech constructions are opaque, involves the denial of just this same generalised principle of the substitutivity of identity, (3). So the fundamental question to be resolved is whether the substitutivity of identity holds for modal and indirect speech contexts. Nevertheless, it is worth considering carefully what is involved in the assertion of (A) and (B), and I shall begin by discussing views which conflict with them. But before I do so, I shall introduce some concepts which will have a crucial role in this essay.

First, there is the concept of a quantifier. Loosely speaking, quantifiers are phrases such as "some..." which form noun phrases out of general terms. More accurately, quantifiers are phrases such as "it is true of some...that—", which form complete sentences when the first space is filled by a general term and the second by a sentence which contains an appropriate pronoun. In most books, the only use of quantifiers that is discussed is that which involves single-sorted quantification, where quantifiers are taken to be always attached to the single general term "thing". Occurrences in a sentence of the phrase "it is true of some thing that—" are abbreviated as "$(\exists x)(—)$", "$(\exists y)(—)$", etc., and the letters "$x$", "$y$", etc., are used as bound variables to replace pronouns which have a relevant occurrence of "some thing" as their antecedent. Clearly, this is a very limited approach to the use of quantifiers, and one wants to allow also for many-sorted quantification, where quantifiers are attached to other general terms. Initially, many-sorted quantification, as in a sentence which begins "it is true of some men that—", can be represented by use of the general term to which the quantifier is attached, as in "$(\exists \text{ man}, x)(—)$", where "$x$" occurs merely as an index to show that later occurrences of "$x$" as a bound variable have the phrase "some men" as antecedent. But in a systematic construal of such sentences, one needs to replace a simple general term such as "man" by another which uses a restrictive clause to include the predicate that corresponds to the original general term, such as "thing such that it is a man". Thus, in place of "$(\exists \text{ man}, x)(—)$" one needs, for systematic purposes, "$(\exists x : x \text{ is a man})(—)$", where "$x$" no longer occurs as an index. It it also useful sometimes to abbreviate a general term that crops up frequently by using a single letter as a sorted variable; for example, instead of "$(\exists x : x \text{ is a sequence})(—)$", I shall write simply "$(\exists s)(—)$".

In my discussion I shall use the same language (English) as both object-language and metalanguage, and I shall use "L" within the metalanguage to refer to the object-language. I shall, however, make one distinction between the object-language and the metalanguage for expository purposes. I shall use letters from the Roman alphabet as variables and schematic letters in the object-language and letters from the Greek alphabet as variables and schematic letters in the metalanguage (thus object-language "$Fx$" and "$Gy$" become metalanguage "$\Phi\mu$" and "$\Psi\nu$"). There will be one exception to this general distinction, however: I shall use Cyrillic letters "а" and "б" as sorted variables of the metalanguage to take as their domain singular terms of the object-language (thus "$(\exists \text{а})(—)$" abbreviates "$(\exists \mu : \mu \text{ is a singular term of L})(—)$").

It will be necessary to discuss carefully in this essay the proper interpretation of sentences with quantifiers. It is generally only sentences with single-sorted quantification that are thought to be amenable to direct interpretation. Two opposed interpretations of such sentences can be introduced at once. In the standard interpretation, which derives from Tarski (cf. Tarski [1936]), one introduces talk of sequences in the metalanguage, and says

"$(\exists x)(x$ is a spy)" is true in L iff
$(\sigma)(\exists \sigma')(\sigma'$ differs in at most the first place from $\sigma$ &
$\sigma'$ satisfies in L "$x_1$ is a spy")

The reasons for the complexity of this will be discussed later. In the alternative substitutional interpretation, which derives in recent times from Mates (cf. Mates [1950]), "$(\exists x)(x$ is a spy)" is said to be true if and only if there is a singular term of the object-language whose substitution for "$x$" in "$x$ is a spy" yields a true sentence. This can be straightforwardly expressed as:

"$(\exists x)(x$ is a spy)" is true in L iff
$(\exists a)(\ulcorner a$ is a spy$\urcorner$ is true in L)

(I use here the square brackets "$\ulcorner \urcorner$" in the manner introduced by Quine, so that "$\ulcorner a$ is a spy$\urcorner$" is short for "the result of replacing "$x$" by a in "$x$ is a spy"").

Next, a distinction between the use of intensional idioms and that of linguistic idioms can be introduced. Someone who favours the use of intensional idioms will regard truth as primarily a property of propositions, and will formulate his general theory of truth in similar idioms. Someone who favours the use of linguistic idioms will regard truth as primarily a property of sentences, perhaps with some added specification of a context of their utterance. I shall be largely concerned here with linguistic idioms, but it will be useful initially to have intensional idioms at hand. The two interpretations of quantifiers given just above were both set in linguistic idioms. In intensional idioms it is the proposition that $(\exists x)(x$ is a spy) which should be susceptible of two interpretations. The standard interpretation is easy:

that $(\exists x)(x$ is a spy) is true iff
$(s)(\exists s')(s'$ differs in at most the first place from $s$ & $s'$
satisfies that $x_1 : x_1$ is a spy)

(where "that $x_1 : x_1$ is a spy" names a property). It should be noted here that the distinction between the object-language and the metalanguage does not apply and that the concepts of truth and satisfaction need not be relativised to a language. Propositions are abstract objects and not parts of any language. The correct substitutional interpretation in intensional idioms is less easy, for talk of substitution only appears sensible when one is dealing with bits of language. This talk of substitutions, however, can be replaced by talk of linguistic functions (one can regard sentences of the form "F*a*" as values of functions from singular terms). Now it is easy to find something analogous within intensional idioms: one may regard propositions as the values of functions from objects. This suggests that, analogous to the ordinary substitutional interpretation in linguistic idioms, one should have within intensional idioms:

that $(\exists x)(x$ is a spy) is true iff
$(\exists x)($that $x$ is a spy is true)

(where "that $x$ is a spy" expresses a function onto propositions).

In my use of linguistic idioms I shall make a slightly improper use of quotation marks. First, I shall use them to form structural-descriptive names of sentences; i.e. I shall use " " $(\exists x)(x$ is a spy)" " " not just as a name of "$(\exists x)(x$ is a spy)" (which it clearly is), but also as a name of that sentence for which one may prove, in an adequate semantic theory, equivalences such as

"$(\exists x)(x$ is a spy)" is true in L iff $(\exists \mu)(\mu$ is a spy).

Secondly, I shall allow myself to quote schematic letters in order to express generalisations about the truth-conditions of sentences of a given form. For example, I shall be happy to say

"$p$ & $q$" is true in L iff "$p$" is true in L & "$q$" is true in L.

I am well aware that both these uses of quotation marks are improper, but nothing of substance in what I say is thereby vitiated. My reason for adopting these uses is that they are simpler and clearer than more respectable alternatives.

There is, finally, the concept of a singular term, which the substitutional interpretation of quantifiers has already used. This connection with the use of quantifiers is, indeed, one of the key features of singular terms. Another key feature of singular terms is that they are phrases which are used to name, or refer to, just one item in a given piece of discourse. Thus in a semantic theory, singular terms are typically assigned referents, and their reference is at least their primary contribution to the interpretation of sentences in which they occur. The sorts of phrase which are therefore candidates for the status of singular term are proper names, definite descriptions, and functional expressions; whether all such phrases really are singular terms will be an issue of importance in the ensuing discussion. It is important to realise in advance that this issue is not a simple grammatical one; rather, it is a question of how the use of, say, definite descriptions connects with the use of quantifiers, and how far their semantic role is fruitfully approached by assigning referents to them in a semantic theory.

## II

I return now to my original problem and the formulation of it in the previous section as arising out of the inconsistency of the four claims (A)-(D). One may start by trying to query (A): is it just a mistake to suppose that there are acceptable sentences in which pronouns inside subordinate clauses in modal and indirect speech constructions have their antecedent outside these clauses?

In the case of indirect speech it is hard to accept that this is a mistake. For sentences of this kind are needed to express important claims about our understanding of the world and ourselves. Sentences such as "Moore knew what was in the room" would be ruled out; yet without such sentences it would be impossible to express the force of the claim that empirical knowledge is knowledge of a common external world. Again, the expression of self-consciousness, as in "Wittgenstein knew that he was in pain" would be ruled out, although there are special problems about the interpretation of sentences of this kind.

In the case of modal constructions, the matter is equally clear. Quite ordinary sentences such as "My character might not be as unpleasant as it is" would be ruled out. But it seems an essential feature of any serious moral and political consciousness that one should have beliefs about which aspects of one's moral and political situation can be changed and which cannot. Similarly, sentences such as "The colour of grass could not be other than it is" would be ruled out. But it seems equally an essential feature of our understanding of nature that we should have beliefs about those aspects of nature which are accidental and those which are not.

Sentences with pronouns in subordinate clauses in modal constructions sometimes express claims about the essential properties of an object (a property of an object is essential to it if it is a property which the object must possess if it is to be what it is). Claims of this kind often provoke a negative reaction from contemporary philosophers; but sometimes their attacks are ill-judged. A typical (although perhaps rather unfair) example is provided by Bennett (cf. Bennett [1966], p. 211):

Could there be a necessarily private hat, i.e. one which could not be worn by more than one person? The question is absurd: it is a piece of pre-Lockean essentialism, an ellipsis which we are not told how to expand. Any expression of the form 'an X which is necessarily G' requires expansion into something of the form 'an X which is F (where F is a non-modal property)— and necessarily any X which is F is G'.

Unfortunately for Bennett, if 'expansion' involves the production of an equivalent sentence, his suggestion has the consequence that all properties are essential. For

There is an *x* which is F

is equivalent to

There is an *x* which is F and necessarily any *x* which is F is F

and this, by Bennett's suggestion, would be equivalent to

There is an *x* which is necessarily F.

# III

It is Quine, more than any other recent philosopher, who has called attention to the problems raised by the inconsistency of (A)–(D). For modal contexts, Quine simply denies (A) (cf. Quine [1953b]). His reason for doing so appears to be just the inconsistency of (A)–(D) and the acceptability of each of (B)–(D). Quine's treatment of indirect speech, however, is more interesting (cf. Quine [1956]). Here it is not (A), but (B), which Quine denies. That is, Quine does not deny that a sentence such as

(1) There is someone of whom Ralph believes that he is a spy

is an acceptable sentence. Instead, he denies that the logical form of (1) is correctly displayed by

(2) $(\exists x)$(Ralph believes that $x$ is a spy).

In place of (2), Quine argues that we should recognise in (1) a transparent sense of "believe", in which it takes a complex construction which includes a transparent context outside any subordinate clause. Thus for Quine the logical form of (1) is displayed, not by (2), but by

(3) $(\exists x)$(Ralph believes of $x$ that $y{:}y$ is a spy).

This requires not just two senses of "believe" (an opaque and a transparent one), but an indefinite number of them. For the verb must now have a different sense in each sentence of the form

(4) There are at least n people whom Ralph believes to spy on each other.

In general, a separate sense of "believe" is needed for each number of transparent contexts which Quine's account of a belief-sentence requires.

Yet these senses cannot be independent of each other; there must be some systematic connection between them. Although various suggestions as to this connection have been made (cf. Kaplan [1969]), the simplest approach is to take as primitive a relation which holds between a property and a sequence of objects just when the property is believed to be true of the members of the sequence. Then one can introduce each of Quine's senses of "believe" according to the polyadicity of the property in question, and take the opaque sense as the limiting case in which the property is a complete "zero-adic" proposition. The idea is basically to use the idioms of the standard interpretation of quantifiers, with "satisfies" replaced by "is believed to satisfy". However, what is proposed is not a new interpretation of belief-sentences, but a new construal of them which uses within the object-language idioms of the standard interpretation that are usually confined to the metalanguage. Thus, if one takes this approach one will say that the logical form of (1) is properly displayed, not by (3), but by

(5) $(\exists s)$($s$ is believed by Ralph to satisfy that $y{:}y$ is a spy),

where the fact that the property that $y{:}y$ is a spy is monadic shows that (5) introduces Quine's first transparent sense of "believe" in which it takes just one transparent context.

Although Quine's treatment of these matters is widely accepted, it is unsatisfactory. It is surprising that it has escaped notice that this is so, since Quine's theory differs in few respects from Russell's multiple-relation theory (cf. Russell [1910]), and the latter is well-known to be unsatisfactory. The only important difference between

Russell and Quine is that Russell does not allow properly for Quine's opaque sense of "believe". The similarity between the two theories is brought out by the fact that in the multiple-relation theory "believe" is also ambiguous according as to what is believed. The inadequacy of the multiple-relation theory is best demonstrated by the fact that it cannot account properly for the difference in sense between sentences such as:

Othello believes that Desdemona loves Cassio

and

Othello believes that Cassio loves Desdemona.

For the difference between

Believes (Othello, Desdemona, loving, Cassio)

and

Believes (Othello, Cassio, loving, Desdemona)

shows only a difference in the order in which Desdemona and Cassio are related by "Believes (...)", and not the required difference in the order in which they are believed to be related by "...loves...". This is, indeed, the basis of part of Russell's own critique of the multiple-relation theory (cf. Russell [1919], p. 61):

There are really two main things that one wants to notice is this matter that I am treating of just now. The *first* is ..., and the *other* is the impossibility of putting the subordinate verb on a level with its terms as an object term in the belief. That is a point in which I think that the theory of judgment which I set forth once in print some years ago was a little unduly simple, because I did then treat the object verb as if one could put 'loves' on a level with Desdemona and Cassio as a term for the relation 'believe'.

A similar inadequancy afflicts Quine's theory. Suppose Quine is to construe

(6) Othello believes of Desdemona and Cassio that the former loves the latter.

The obvious application of Quine's initial suggestion, that which gives (3) as a construal of (1), yields

(7) Othello believes of Desdemona and Cassio that $xy:x$ loves $y$.

But (7) does not distinguish between (6) and

(8) Othello believes of Desdemona and Cassio that the latter loves
the former.

The natural way to modify (7) in such a way that the distinction
becomes clear is to remove the property name "that $xy:x$ loves $y$",
and replace it by the functional expression "that $x$ loves $y$", where
"$x$" and "$y$" are to be bound by quantifiers elsewhere in the sentence, as in

(9) $(\exists x)(\exists y)(x =$ Desdemona & $y =$ Cassio & Othello believes of
$x$ and $y$ that $x$ loves $y$)

which seems a suitable construal of (6), as opposed to (8), which
can be construed as

(10) $(\exists x)(\exists y)(x =$ Desdemona & $y =$ Cassio & Othello believes
of $x$ and $y$ that $y$ loves $x$).

But the trouble for Quine with (9) and (10) is that they involve
the use of variables within a subordinate clause in indirect speech
which are bound by quantifiers outside the clause. For the whole
point of Quine's new senses of indirect speech verbs was to keep
such bindable contexts out of subordinate clauses in indirect speech,
since contexts there for singular terms were assumed to be opaque.
So it looks as if Quine's new senses of indirect speech verbs either
will not express obvious distinctions, such as that between (6) and
(8), or will involve precisely the sort of quantification they were
designed to avoid.

   The point becomes more complex and more interesting if Quine's
theory is modified along the lines of the standard interpretation of
quantifiers, as suggested above (i.e. the theory is modified so that
(1) is construed as (5), and not as (3)). There have, somehow, to be
modifications to

   $\langle$Desdemona, Cassio$\rangle$ is believed by Othello to satisfy that
   $xy:x$ loves $y$

to mark the difference between (6) and (8). In the standard interpretation of quantifiers a similar trick is done by indexing variables
systematically, and using the indices to determine which members
of a sequence satisfy which properties. The same could be done here,
so that (6) would be construed as

(11) ⟨Desdemona, Cassio⟩ is believed by Othello to satisfy that $x_1x_2:x_1$ loves $x_2$

and (8) would be construed as

(12) ⟨Desdemona, Cassio⟩ is believed by Othello to satisfy that $x_1x_2:x_2$ loves $x_1$.

There is no doubt that (11) and (12) are equivalent to (6) and (8), if the role of the indexed variables is understood in the usual way. So doesn't this solve Quine's problem?

In a sense it does. But if one reflects on the use of the indexed variables in (11) and (12), one will see, I think, that the problem has only been avoided in this case by an ingenious technical device. It is clear that (11) and (12) will be equivalent to (6) and (8) only if the indexed variables are understood to satisfy principles of the form:

(13) $s$ is believed by Othello to satisfy that $x_ix_j:x_iRx_j$ iff Othello believes of the $i$th member of $s$ and the $j$th member of $s$ that the former R the latter.

(13) indicates, therefore, that if the indexed variables of (11) and (12) are to perform the role which one expects of them, they must be understood in such a way that, in general, "$x_i$" abbreviates "the $i$th member of $s$", where "$s$" takes sequences as values. Thus (11) is more clearly expressed as

(14) ⟨Desdemona, Cassio⟩ is believed by Othello to satisfy that $s$: the first member of $s$ loves the second member of $s$.

What is important about (14) is that in (14) the property which is believed to be satisfied is a monadic property of sequences. Thus (14) only employs Quine's first transparent sense of "believe" in which it takes one transparent context for a singular term. My initial presentation of the modified version of Quine's theory was, therefore, misleading; the point of the introduction of sequences is not that it enables one to represent all the different transparent senses of "believe". Rather it enables one to reduce them all to the single case in which "believe" takes one transparent context. Thus (14) can be re-expressed as

(15) Othello believes of ⟨Desdemona, Cassio⟩ that $s$: the first member of $s$ loves the second member of $s$

which has exactly the same form as (3). The effect of this reduction is that it enables one to avoid all the difficulties about ordering which face any sense of "believe" which takes more than one transparent context.

So far as I know, this kind of reduction can always be carried out, although the details of it become increasingly complex as one considers cases of multiple quantification. It does provide, therefore, one apparent way of vindicating Quine's kind of approach to quantification into indirect speech. Nevertheless, I want to say, the use of sequences to avoid the problem of ordering in this way is only an ingenious technical device and does not really yield a satisfactory account of the matter. The requirement that the logical form of (1),

(1) There is someone of whom Ralph believes that he is a spy

be given, not by (2),

(2) $(\exists x)$(Ralph believes that $x$ is a spy)

nor even by (3) or (5), but by

(16) $(\exists s)$(Ralph believes of $s$ that $s'$: the first member of $s'$ is a spy)

is not really acceptable. For the very content of Ralph's belief has been changed in the change from (1) to (16): (1) is a belief about people, (16) is a belief about sequences of them. So, although there is a close connection between (1) and (16), one may well deny that they are equivalent (perhaps Ralph has no idea what sequences are). At any rate, I want to say, (16) differs too much from (1) in both structure and content for it to be acceptable to suppose that (16) gives the logical form of (1). Quine's original proposal for the logical form of (1), (3)—

(3) $(\exists x)$(Ralph believes of $x$ that $y$:$y$ is a spy)

—was at least an appropriate candidate for the logical form of (1); but it could not be systematically generalised without the introduction of sequences. Once sequences are introduced, however, one has moved from a description of the original belief to a description of a different belief that is only equivalent, in some sense, to the original one. So the logical form of the first description has not been properly given.

It seems to me, therefore, that Quine's kind of approach to belief cannot be elaborated in such a way as to do justice both to the structure and to the content of our beliefs. Perhaps in some Quinean possible world people only have beliefs about sequences of things; but such a possible world (if it really is possible) is not our world, and thus any proper account of our beliefs must allow for the fact that we can have relatively complex beliefs about things other than sequences. What I have argued here is that there is no way of properly expressing the logical form of descriptions of such beliefs unless one allows for quantification into indirect speech. The question that remains to be settled is how such quantification is possible.

## IV

In the previous section I suggested that one interesting way of viewing Quine's account of indirect speech was to view it as modelled on the standard interpretation of quantifiers. I argued, however, that even this way of viewing it would not save Quine's account. In the course of that argument a proper understanding of what is involved in the standard interpretation of quantifiers was a crucial issue, and it is to this matter that I now turn.

The fundamental idea behind the standard interpretation of quantifiers within intensional idioms is that one can give the truth-conditions of propositions in terms of the conditions under which properties are satisfied. This is clear right from the very first stage at which one says

(1) that $p$ is true iff $(s)(s$ satisfies that $p)$

in which one treats even propositions as zero-adic properties. In stating the conditions under which properties are satisfied, one has no problems with monadic properties, for one can see at once the truth of

(2) $a$ satisfies that $x: Fx$ iff $Fa$.

But where properties are dyadic, the trouble begins: is one to say

$a$ and $b$ satisfy that $xy: xRy$ iff $aRb$

or

$a$ and $b$ satisfy that $xy: xRy$ iff $bRa$?

The natural response to this problem lies through the use of quantifiers and bound variables, as in

(3) $(\exists x)(\exists y)(x = a \ \& \ y = b \ \&$ that $xRy$ is true) iff $aRb$

but to take this response is to destroy the idea that it is the conditions under which properties are satisfied which are the fundamental element of a semantic theory. For the phrase "that $xRy$" does not name a property; rather, it expresses a function onto propositions. Within the standard interpretation, therefore, an alternative response is used. Sequences are introduced, and with them one is able to replace n-adic properties by monadic properties. Thus in place of (3) one has

(4) $\langle a,b \rangle$ satisfies that $s$: the first member of $s$ R the second member of $s$ iff $aRb$

which is usually abbreviated, in misleading form, as

$\langle a,b \rangle$ satisfies that $x_1 x_2 : x_1 R x_2$ iff $aRb$.

It is essential to the standard interpretation that one should be able to carry out this replacement of n-adic by monadic properties, and it is only to achieve this end that sequences are introduced. The complexity of the standard interpretation of quantifiers:

(5) that $(\exists x)(Fx)$ is true iff
$(s)(\exists s')(s'$ differs in at most the first place from $s$ & $s'$ satisfies that $x_1 : Fx_1$)

is wholly to be explained by reference to this end, by the need to replace n-adic properties of things by monadic properties of sequences of things. So far as I know, this kind of replacement can always be carried out, even where many-sorted quantification occurs. But it is a tedious device, and the problem for which sequences are introduced is much better solved by doing away with reference to properties altogether and using instead functions onto propositions, as in (3). Once this step is taken, however, one is committed to regarding atomic propositions as the values of functions, and to giving their truth-conditions by equivalences of the form:

(6) $(x)$(that $Fx$ is true iff $Fx$).

An interpretation of quantifiers which fits in with this approach is easy:

(7) that $(\exists x)(Fx)$ is true iff $(\exists x)$(that $Fx$ is true).

(6) and (7) enable one to infer, as one would hope,

(8) that $(\exists x)(Fx)$ is true iff $(\exists x)(Fx)$.

(7), however, should be familiar. It is exactly my suggestion in the first section of this essay for an intensional version of the substitutional interpretation of quantifiers.

Both the standard and the substitutional interpretation yield technically adequate accounts of the truth-conditions of propositions which involve quantification. But of the two, the substitutional interpretation seems to me clearly preferable here. Not only is it far simpler than the standard interpretation; it also has the great merit of yielding directly what was wanted on the right-hand side. There is none of the lengthy excursus through sequences that is characteristic of the standard interpretation. One would like to be able to show further that the substitutional interpretation is, in some sense, the fundamental interpretation of quantifiers within intensional idioms. However, to show this one would have to be able to show independently that the conditions under which properties are satisfied are, in some fundamental sense, to be understood as the conditions under which corresponding propositions are true, that "true of" is derived from "true". It is very natural to think that this is so, but, given the adequacy of the standard interpretation, I can see no way of proving that it is so.

Once one shifts from intensional to linguistic idioms, the matter becomes more complex, but is not essentially different. The fundamental idea of the standard interpretation in this case is that the truth-conditions of sentences be given by giving the conditions for the satisfaction of predicates. Thus the basic principles which give the interpretation of primitive predicates must have the form:

(9) $\alpha$ satisfies in L "F'x" iff $\Phi\alpha$

(the dash in "F'..." is to indicate that the predicate is a primitive predicate of the object-language). Dyadic predicates, therefore, present the same old problem; how is one to choose between

$\alpha$ and $\beta$ satisfy in L "xR'y" iff $\alpha P \beta$

and

$\alpha$ and $\beta$ satisfy in L "xR'y" iff $\beta P \alpha$?

The same old solution is used: one is to turn all n-adic predicates into monadic predicates by introducing talk of sequences. Thus one has

(10) $\langle \alpha, \beta \rangle$ satisfies in L "the first member of $s$ R' the second member of $s$" iff $\alpha P \beta$

which has basically the same form as (9). (10) is, of course, usually abbreviated as

$\langle \alpha, \beta \rangle$ satisfies in L "$x_1 R' x_2$" iff $\alpha P \beta$

I do not dispute that this approach yields a technically adequate account of the truth-conditions of sentences with quantifiers. As the preceding discussion of intensional idioms will have indicated, however, I favour substitutional interpretations for a more natural style of interpretation. One can best approach this kind of interpretation through the problem of saying when a dyadic predicate is satisfied by a pair of things. The problem is this: how is one to modify

$\alpha$ and $\beta$ satisfy in L "$xR'y$"

in order to secure an unambiguous result? The solution to the corresponding problem within intensional idioms was easy: one was to use quantifiers and bound variables, as in

(3) $(\exists x)(\exists y)(x = a \,\&\, y = b \,\&\, \text{that } xRy \text{ is true})$ iff $aRb$.

The natural application of this idea to linguistic idioms would seem to be

(11) $(\exists \mu)(\exists \nu)(\mu = \alpha \,\&\, \nu = \beta \,\&\, \text{"}\mu R' \nu\text{" is true in L})$ iff $\alpha P \beta$.

But this is clearly wrong. For in ""$\mu R' \nu$"" in (11) metalanguage variables occur in an incongruous way within what was supposed to be an object-language predicate. Instead of (11), I think, one is bound to use substitutional quantification, as in

(12) $(\exists a)(\exists \sigma)(\text{ref}(a,L) = \alpha \,\&\, \text{ref}(\sigma,L) = \beta \,\&\, \ulcorner aR'\sigma \urcorner \text{ is true in L})$ iff $\alpha P \beta$

(where "ref(a, $\sigma$)" abbreviates "the reference of a in L"). For although "a" and "$\sigma$" are metalanguage variables, "$\ulcorner aR'\sigma \urcorner$" avoids the incongruity that afflicts ""$\mu R' \nu$"" of (11) because "a" and "$\sigma$" do not occur within the object-language in "$\ulcorner aR'\sigma \urcorner$".

Once principles of the form of (12) are introduced in place of (10), one must abandon the fundamental idea of the standard interpretation that the truth-conditions of sentences be given by giving the conditions for the satisfaction of predicates. Instead, one is committed to the view that simple subject–predicate sentences are the values of functions from singular terms, and to regarding "⌜Fa⌝" as a functional expression in exactly the way in which "that F*x*" is similarly regarded within intensional idioms. Just as within intensional idioms the basic principles for giving the truth-conditions of atomic propositions should have the form.

(6) $(x)$(that F*x* is true iff F*x*)

within linguistic idioms, the basic principles for giving the truth-conditions of simple subject–predicate sentences should have the form

(13) $(a)$(⌜F′a⌝ is true in L iff $\Phi(\mathrm{ref}(a,L))$).

Substitutional quantification is, naturally, central to the substitutional interpretation of quantifiers:

(14) "$(\exists x)(Fx)$" is true in L iff $(\exists a)$(⌜Fa⌝ is true in L).

If one puts together (13) and (14) one can infer at once

(15) "$(\exists x)(F′x)$" is true in L iff $(\exists a)(\Phi(\mathrm{ref}(a,L)))$.

(15), however, is not what one really wants; it is rather

(16) "$(\exists x)(F′x)$" is true in L iff $(\exists\mu)(\Phi\mu)$

that one wants, and one must ask what extra assumptions are needed to enable one to infer (16) from (15). It is clear that two extra assumptions are needed:

(17) $(a)(\exists\mu)(\mathrm{ref}(a,L) = \mu)$

(18) $(\mu)(\exists a)(\mathrm{ref}(a,L) = \mu)$.

Both these assumptions raise interesting questions: (17) rules out singular terms which lack a reference, and (18) makes the interpretation of quantification over non-denumerable domains at least more difficult to understand than one would have expected, since it requires that the number of singular terms be at least as great as the number of any kind of thing which forms a domain for quantification. One can, however, easily dispense with the need for the first assumption (17) by modifying the interpretation of quantification in such a way as to require that the singular terms used to interpret quantifiers be non-empty, i.e. by having in place of (14)—

(19)  "$(\exists x)(Fx)$" is true in L iff
      $(\exists \mu)(\exists a)(\text{ref}(a,L) = \mu$ & $\ulcorner Fa \urcorner$ is true in L).

Since there are phrases in natural languages which appear to lack a reference while remaining singular terms, this modification of the substitutional interpretation seems desirable.

No such simple modification will remove the need for the other assumption, (18), but I think that with a little further complexity even this difficulty can be overcome. I have so far presented and discussed interpretations of quantifiers that make no reference to the role of context of utterance in determining the truth-conditions of a sentence. In order to present an account of the truth-conditions of sentences with demonstratives, however, one must introduce the idea of context, for the truth or falsity of a sentence such as "he is a spy" obviously depends in part on who is referred to on each occasion of its utterance, that is, upon the context of utterance (I take the context of utterance of a sentence to be sufficient to specify what is referred to by all the demonstratives that occur in the sentence). In order to accommodate this point the basic principles that give the truth-conditions of simple subject-predicate sentences must include reference to a context of utterance, $\xi$, and thus have the form:

(20)  $(\xi)(a)(\ulcorner F'a \urcorner$ is true in L in $\xi$ iff $\Phi(\text{ref}(a,L,\xi)))$.

In spelling out the truth-conditions of complex sentences in terms of those of simpler sentences, the relativity of truth to context of utterance generally features only as an idle parameter. But, I suggest, when one comes to give the truth-conditions of sentences with quantifiers, reference to context assumes a more active role. Instead of just modifying the substitutional interpretation in the obvious way, one should introduce a new context on the right-hand side, to get—

(21)  $(\xi)($"$(\exists x)(Fx)$" is true in L in $\xi$ iff
      $(\exists \mu)(\exists a)(\exists \xi')(\mu = \text{ref}(\exists,L,\xi')$ & $\xi'$ differs at most in assignment to a from $\xi$ & $\ulcorner Fa \urcorner$ is true in L in $\xi'))$.

The clause "$\xi'$ differs at most in assignment to a from $\xi$", so reminiscent of the standard interpretation, is required for cases of multiple quantification. The idea behind (21) is that the sentence "it is true of some men that they are spies" is true in any context if and only if the sentence "they are spies" is true in some context in which one refers to some men. This equivalence requires one to include possible as well as actual contexts of utterance, but this does not seem objectionable since one would have wanted it anyway. Behind this idea lies the thought that a substitutional interpretation should make use of the fact that in English and other languages much the same phrases occur, now as pronouns with antecedents, now as demonstratives. For this suggests that the interpretation of sentences with quantifiers should proceed not by substituting for a bound variable any non-empty singular term, but, rather, only a specifically context-dependent one, whose context of utterance is to be considered as given by the phrase which was the antecedent of the bound variable.

If one does take (21) as the preferred substitutional interpretation, one may ask again what assumptions are needed to pass from (21) and principles of the form of (20) to what one wants here—

(22) $(\xi)(\text{``}(\exists x)(\text{F}'x)\text{''}$ is true in L in $\xi$ iff $(\exists \mu)(\Phi\mu))$.

It is clear that one now needs only the assumption

(23) $(\xi)(\mu)(\exists a)(\exists \xi')(\mu = \text{ref}(a,L,\xi')$ & $\xi'$ differs at most in assignment to a from $\xi$)

and this assumption differs crucially from the earlier assumption (18) which the simple substitutional interpretation required. For whereas with (18) it was difficult to see how quantification over non-denumerable domains was to be understood, (23) requires only that the cardinality of the set of pairs of singular terms and contexts be at least as great as the cardinality of any set that forms a domain of quantification. With this requirement, non-denumerable domains are no problem, since they only give rise to a non-denumerable number of possible contexts of utterance, and are quite consistent with there being only a finite number of singular terms.

Despite its undesirable complexity, therefore, (21) seems to me the preferable formulation of a substitutional interpretation of quantifiers within linguistic idioms. The technical details of the resulting interpretation resemble those of the standard interpretation. Nevertheless, the two interpretations remain, at a fundamental level, quite distinct: where the substitutional interpretation uses substitutional quantification to connect language and the world, the standard interpretation employs only a bare confrontation between the two. I know of no conclusive arguments in favour of one style of interpretation, but in respect of its naturalness of idiom the substitutional interpretation seems to me preferable, and I shall use it in what follows. Since the full details of the complete interpretation (21) are tedious to work with in practice, I shall revert to the simpler interpretation (19)—

(19) "$(\exists x)(Fx)$" is true in L iff
$(\exists \mu)(\exists a)(\mu = \text{ref}(a,L)$ & $\ulcorner Fa \urcorner$ is true in L)

although I shall have to discuss further modifications even of this. The application of this interpretation requires, of course, the old assumption (18) and my discussion can be regarded as initially limited to domains for which this assumption is reasonable.

## V

In my initial statement in section one of the problem of quantification into modal and indirect speech contexts, I suggested that the fundamental difficulty arose from the conflict between the claim (C) that contexts for singular terms within modal and indirect speech constructions are referentially opaque, and the claim (D) that one cannot interpret quantification into opaque contexts. In this section I shall argue that, at least in its application to modal constructions, (C) is false; that is, I shall argue that contexts for singular terms within modal constructions are referentially transparent.

A problem with which any account of quantification into modal contexts must come to terms is that raised by the use of existential generalisation. There must be some way of blocking an inference such as

Nec(the number of planets = the number of planets)

so:

$(\exists x)\text{Nec}(x = \text{the number of planets})$,

for the premiss is indisputable, but the conclusion is unacceptable. What I shall argue here is that the most natural way of solving this and similar problems commits one to the view that modal contexts are referentially transparent.

One natural response to this problem is to try to introduce a modal restriction on existential generalisation, such that instead of

(1) $((\exists x)(x = a) \ \& \ Fa) \rightarrow (\exists x)(Fx)$

one has only the principle

(2) $((\exists x)Nec(x = a) \ \& \ Fa) \rightarrow (\exists x)(Fx).$

If one favours this response, one must find a modified interpretation of the existential quantifier. For the ordinary (substitutional) interpretation

(3) "$(\exists x)(Fx)$" is true in L iff
  $(\exists \mu)(\exists a)(ref(a,L) = \mu \ \& \ \ulcorner Fa \urcorner$ is true in L$)$

validates (1) at once. The obvious way to modify (3) is to introduce a modal restriction into the metalanguage (cf. Hintikka [1963] pp. 71–3), as in

(4) "$(\exists x)(Fx)$" is true in L iff
  $(\exists \mu)(\exists a)(Nec(ref(a,L) = \mu) \ \& \ \ulcorner Fa \urcorner$ is true in L$).$

(4) certainly no longer validates (1), and it looks as though it will validate (2), given suitable assumptions about the interpretation of modal operators. However, in order to prove from (4) and principles of the form

(5) $(a)(\ulcorner F'a \urcorner$ is true in L iff $\Phi \ (ref(a,L)))$

the kind of simple equivalence one wants—

(6) "$(\exists x)(F'x)$" is true in L iff $(\exists \mu)(\Phi \mu)$

—one needs to assume, not, as before,

(7) $(\mu)(\exists a)(ref(a,L) = \mu)$

but rather

(8) $(\mu)(\exists a)(Nec(ref(a,L) = \mu)),$

which embodies an extremely strong claim about the availability of suitable singular terms. In the previous section I tried to ease the discomfort caused by the need to assume (7) through the introduction of a 'contextual' interpretation of quantifiers, which required one to assume, not (7), but (in effect)

(9) $(\mu)(\exists a)(\exists \xi)(ref(a,L,\xi) = \mu).$

The application of the same argument in this case allows one to replace (8) by

(10)  $(\mu)(\exists a)(\exists \xi)(\mathrm{Nec}(\mathrm{ref}(a,L,\xi) = \mu))$

and this perhaps does something to ease the discomfort (8) produces. I shall discuss further the kind of problem which (8) raises in the next section.

So far as I can see, this approach yields a formally adequate solution to the problem raised by the use of existential generalisation in modal contexts. I shall have more to say about it later. But for the moment I want to note that it requires an explicit modal restriction in the interpretation of quite ordinary non-modal quantification. This seems at least unnatural, and it would perhaps be preferable to find a solution to the problem raised here which does not have this feature.

Suppose one thinks of the condition "$(\exists x)\mathrm{Nec}(x = a)$" not as a restriction on existential generalisation in modal contexts, but rather as a condition on a phrase's being a singular term at all. If this is adopted, (1) and (2) above will be equivalent, and the ordinary interpretation of the existential quantifier, as in (3), can be retained for all contexts. Since the phrase "the number of planets" fails to satisfy this condition, it is not to be regarded as a singular term and the initial problematic inference can be set aside as not being a proper case of existential generalisation at all. Here, then, is an easy solution to the problem. It is a consequence of this solution that the nature of the interpretation of sentences in which the phrase "the number of planets" occurs will have to be different from that which would have been the case had this phrase been a singular term; but it is not difficult to formulate different accounts, and I shall explore some of them in a later section.

The purpose of introducing this modal condition "$(\exists x)\mathrm{Nec}(x = a)$" on singular terms is to deny singular term status to phrases such as "the number of planets" which make trouble for existential generalisation in modal contexts. The question that may now be raised, therefore, is whether the phrases that make trouble in this way are exactly the phrases whose behaviour makes one want to say that modal contexts are referentially opaque. For if this is so, then the adoption of this solution would commit one to the view that modal contexts are referentially transparent.

One can show that modal contexts will not be opaque if and only if all singular terms satisfy the condition "$(x)(x = a \rightarrow \text{Nec}$ $(x = a))$". It is clear that necessary identities warrant substitutivity within modal modal contexts, and to establish the converse implication, one need only recall the familiar argument:

suppose that the substitutivity of identity holds for modal contexts, and thus that:

$(x)(x = a \rightarrow (\text{Nec } Gx \rightarrow \text{Nec } Ga))$

then, in particular,

$(x)(x = a \rightarrow (\text{Nec}(x = x) \rightarrow \text{Nec}(x = a)))$

hence:

$(x)(\text{Nec}(x = x) \rightarrow (x = a \rightarrow \text{Nec}(x = a)))$

but identity is necessarily reflexive, i.e.

$(x)(\text{Nec}(x = x))$

so one can conclude:

$(x)(x = a \rightarrow \text{Nec}(x = a)).$

The answer to the question raised above, therefore, turns on the relation between the conditions "$(\exists x)\text{Nec}(x = a)$" and "$(\exists x)$ $(x = a \,\&\, (y)(y = a \rightarrow \text{Nec}(y = a)))$". It is easy to see that the latter implies the former; so, if modal contexts are transparent, there will be no problems about existential generalisation in modal contexts. However it is the converse implication that really matters:

(11)  $(\exists x)\text{Nec}(x = a) \rightarrow (\exists x)(x = a \,\&\, (y)(y = a \rightarrow \text{Nec}(y = a)))$

and here the situation is less clear. There is no direct way of showing that (11) is correct, for without assuming the very substitutivity of identity in modal contexts that is at issue, one cannot get a contradiction out of

(12)  $(\exists x)\text{Nec}(x = a) \,\&\, (\exists y)\text{Nec}(y = b) \,\&\, a = b \,\&\, {\sim}\text{Nec}(a = b).$

But, at an informal level, it seems to me that (11) is correct, for there are no natural instances of (12). The reason for this is complex and relates to the natural assumption that there is a general equivalence between the conditions "$(\exists x)(x = a \,\&\, Fx)$" and "$(x)(x = a \rightarrow Fx)$".

It is by assuming the equivalence of these conditions that it is possible to dispense in logic with what one might call "individual quantifiers"—expressions of the form "it is true of $a$ that—", which may be abbreviated as "$(a,x)(—)$". For the role of these individual quantifiers is exhausted by the equivalence "$Fa \leftrightarrow (a,x)(Fx)$", and if one uses in place of "$(a,x)(Fx)$" the conditions "$(\exists x)(x = a$ & $Fx)$" and "$(x)(x = a \rightarrow Fx)$", it is easy to see that existential generalisation and universal instantiation, respectively, will yield this equivalence. It follows, therefore, that if the equivalence of these conditions (barring difficulties with empty singular terms) is at risk in modal contexts, as the denial of (11) would imply, it is not possible to dispense with individual quantifiers in modal contexts. This is not by itself objectionable, but, I think, if one does introduce individual quantifiers, one can see more clearly the reason for thinking that modal contexts are referentially transparent, and thus that (11) is correct after all.

One would normally expect the inference "$Fa \rightarrow (a,x)(Fx)$" (which I shall call "individual generalisation") to hold without restriction. It is certainly validated by the natural interpretation of individual quantifiers:

(a) ($\ulcorner(a,x)(Fx)\urcorner$ is true in L iff
(ref(a,L),$\mu$) ($\exists \sigma$) (ref($\sigma$,L) = $\mu$ & $\ulcorner F\sigma\urcorner$ is true in L)).

However, once modal contexts are introduced, unrestricted individual generalisation seems to run into trouble, as in

Nec(the number of planets = the number of planets)

so:

(the number of planets,$x$)Nec($x$ = the number of planets).

Clearly, this difficulty is exactly similar to that which I have been discussing with respect to existential generalisation. It would be possible to remove this difficulty by introducing a modal restriction into the interpretation of individual quantifiers when they bind variables within modal contexts, as was discussed earlier for the existential quantifiers, but in the context of the present argument the relevant solution is to require that singular terms satisfy the condition "$(a,x)\text{Nec}(a = x)$". One may now ask whether the application of this condition rules out the possibility of referential opacity in modal contexts, i.e. whether

(13) $(a,x)\text{Nec}(x = a) \rightarrow (x)(x = a \rightarrow \text{Nec}(x = a))$.

Again, there is no independent way of showing that (13) is correct; but in this case it seems to me clear that the formula analogous to (12):

(14) $(a,x)\mathrm{Nec}(x = a)$ & $(b,y)\mathrm{Nec}(b = y)$ & $a = b$ & $\sim\mathrm{Nec}(a = b)$

does embody a contradiction. For the condition "$(a,x)\mathrm{Nec}(x = a)$" embodies the thought that $a$ must be what it is, and, if $a$ and $b$ are one and the same, and $a$ must be what it is and $b$ must be what it is, then it does not seem possible that $a$ and $b$ should have been different.

I do not claim to have given here any formally conclusive argument in favour of (13) or (11). Indeed I do not think that any formally conclusive argument could be given. It is possible to construct semantic theories in which (13) is a logical truth; it is also possible to construct theories in which it is not. In this respect (13) is similar to Lewis's S4 principle "Nec $p \to$ Nec Nec $p$", and I think that both principles have much the same status: they are both substantive truths about the nature of necessity. One can usefully contrast (13) and (14) with similar epistemic formulae:

(15) $(a,x)$Ralph knows that$(x = a) \to (x)(x = a \to$ Ralph knows that$(x = a))$

(16) $(a,x)$Ralph knows that$(x = a)$ & $(b,y)$(Ralph knows that $(b = y))$ & $a = b$ & $\sim$Ralph knows that$(a = b)$.

I want to say that unlike (13), (15) is false, as one can see from the fact that (16) does not embody any contradiction. The condition "$(a,x)$Ralph knows that$(x = a)$" embodies the thought that Ralph knows what $a$ is, and, even where Ralph knows what $a$ is and what $b$ is, it does not follow that where $a$ and $b$ are the same he knows that they are. Indeed the difference between necessity and knowledge in this respect seems to me to indicate a deep difference between these concepts. One can persuade oneself with a bit of strain that epistemic sentential logic should mirror modal sentential logic (where epistemic logic is regarded as the logic of a rational reconstruction of knowledge). One cannot persuade oneself that epistemic predicate logic should mirror modal predicate logic, for the simple reason that (13) is true and (15) is false.

Once (13) is accepted, and it is also accepted that, in order to avoid difficulties with regard to individual generalisation in modal contexts, singular terms should satisfy the condition "$(a,x)\text{Nec}(x = a)$", one is bound to conclude that modal contexts are referentially transparent. In this situation, one might as well simply require that all singular terms satisfy the condition "$(x)(x = a \to \text{Nec}(x = a))$". For one thereby guarantees that there will be no problems with regard to existential and individual generalisation, and that one does not need to countenance quantification into opaque contexts when dealing with modal constructions.

At the start of this section I described an alternative solution to the difficulty raised by unrestricted application of existential generalisation. It may seem that this solution, for all its complexity, does show one way in which one may deny that modal contexts are referentially transparent, even if one admits the truth of (11) and (13). This is, indeed, the case; but once (11) and (13) are accepted, the denial that modal contexts are transparent loses most of its force. For if (11) is accepted, then the corresponding metalinguistic principle should also be accepted:

(17) $(\exists\mu)\text{Nec}(\mu = \alpha) \to (\exists\mu)(\mu = \alpha \,\&\, (\nu)(\nu = \alpha \to \text{Nec}(\nu = \alpha)))$.

Once (17) is accepted, then even on this interpretation of quantification:

(4) "$(\exists x)(Fx)$" is true in L iff
$(\exists\mu)(\exists a)(\text{Nec}(\text{ref}(a,L) = \mu) \,\&\, \ulcorner Fa \urcorner$ is true in L)

the generalised principle of substitutivity of identity within modal contexts,

(18) $(x)(y)(x = y \to (\text{Nec } Gx \to \text{Nec } Gy))$

will be validated. What are not validated, of course, are all the particular principles of the form

(19) $a = b \to (\text{Nec } Ga \to \text{Nec } Gb)$.

The reason for this asymmetry is the modal restriction on the interpretation of quantification in (4). This asymmetry indicates that the two aspects of singular terms which are usually combined—the semantic aspect of being assigned a referent in a semantic theory, and the syntactic aspect of instantiating generalisations—are here pulled apart. Singular terms are assigned referents, but do not always instantiate generalisations. The important point in the present context, however, is that (18) is validated on this interpretation.

As a result, even this interpretation does not allow for quantification into opaque contexts. So the sense in which it allows for the opacity of modal contexts does not amount to much.

It matters little, in the end, whether one chooses to adopt a view such as that exemplified by (4), in which one places a modal restriction on the interpretation of quantifiers, or a view such as that discussed in most of this section, in which one places a similar modal restriction on what is to count as a singular term. The way in which I have so far allowed for empty singular terms by placing an existential restriction on the singular terms used to interpret quantifiers suggests that I should, if only for the sake of consistency, adopt the former view. Somewhat inconsistently, I prefer the latter view, since it seems to me to yield a simpler theory. The virtue of this kind of approach is that one does not have to pull apart the concept of a singular term. Singular terms remain largely identifiable as those phrases which both instantiate generalisations and are assigned a reference in a semantic theory. Yet there is certainly nothing incoherent in pulling apart the concept of a singular term by taking the other view. But I think that if one does do this, it will nevertheless be natural to introduce some restricted class of singular terms to instantiate generalisations in modal contexts, which will coincide exactly with the class of singular terms under the kind of interpretation I favour.

## VI

If, as I have argued, the problems of quantifying into modal contexts are to be resolved by denying that such contexts are referentially opaque, the task of giving an interpretation to a sentence such as

(1) There is something which must be greater than 5

ought to be straightforward. (1) can be construed as

(2) $(\exists x)\mathrm{Nec}(x > 5)$

and it should be easy to provide a theory which will have as a theorem:

(3) "$(\exists x)\mathrm{Nec}(x > 5)$" is true in L iff $(\exists \mu)\mathrm{Nec}(\mu > 5)$.

Surely, it will be said, all one needs to add to ordinary axioms giving the interpretation of singular terms, predicates, connectives, and quantifiers, is an axiom which gives the interpretation of the modal operator "Nec", in the natural style of

(4) "Nec $p$" is true in L iff Nec("$p$" is true in L).

Unfortunately it is not so easy. (4) introduces a modal operator into the metalanguage, and thus raises the question of what is to warrant substitutions within such a modal operator in the metalanguage (cf. Wallace [1970] pp. 139–40). The natural answer to this question is to strengthen the axioms of one's semantic theory in such a way that one can prove, for any sentence "$p$" of the object-language, an equivalence of the form:

(5) Nec("$p$" is true in L iff $\pi$).

The trouble with this answer, however, is that one is naturally inclined to feel that the sentences of a language might not have meant what they do mean, and thus might not have had the truth-conditions which they do have. One may nevertheless persist with this answer, and argue further that although a sentence of one language might have had a different meaning in another language, languages are identified in such a way that the sentences of any language must mean in that language what they do mean in it. Of course, new sentences with new meanings can always be added to any given language; what is important is that the sentences already in the language cannot change their meaning without a change in the language. This argument requires a very stringent identification of languages; the English language is not to be identified as the language spoken by English people, since it is clear that English people might use the sentences of English with quite different meanings from those which those sentences do have. Instead, the language is to be identified as the language in which these sentences have these meanings etc.... When regarded in this way, natural languages are regarded very much as formalised languages, as extraordinarily complex systems of communication whose structure is wholly essential to their identity.

If one accepts this argument, one will be prepared to countenance a theory with theorems of the form of (5), in which it will be possible to prove (3). It is not difficult to describe such a theory. One must have axioms for the interpretation of primitive predicates, primitive singular terms, and functional expressions of the form:

(a)(Nec(⌜F′a⌝ is true in L iff Φ(ref(a,L)))))
Ref("a′",L) = α
(a)(ref(⌜f(a)⌝,L) = φ(ref(a,L))))

(as before, "F′..." is schematic for primitive predicates, and "a′" is similarly schematic for primitive singular terms, such as most proper names), together with axioms for the interpretation of connectives, quantifiers, and modal operators, such as

Nec("*p* & *q*" is true in L iff
    "*p*" is true in L & "*q*" is true in L)
Nec("(∃x)(Fx)" is true in L iff
    (∃μ)(∃a)(ref(a,L) = μ & ⌜Fa⌝ is true in L))
Nec("Nec *p*" is true in L iff
    Nec("*p* "is true in L)).

In addition, one needs an axiom to the effect that everything is referred to by a singular term, i.e.

(μ)(∃a)(ref(a,L) = μ).

I shall call a theory with these axioms TL; it will be clear that TL embodies very strong claims about the essential structure of the language L, i.e. of the English language. The fact that the axioms giving the interpretation of singular terms have only the form "Ref("*a*",L) = α" should not mislead. In TL one must assume that "Ref("*a*",L)" is a singular term of the metalanguage; thus, given that in TL all identities are necessary, one will have as a theorem of TL:

Ref("*a*",L) = α → Nec(ref("*a*",L) = α).

If one recoils with horror from TL, one must reject the style of the interpretation of the modal operator "Nec" which first led one to introduce a modal operator into the metalanguage. In short, one must reject (4). One suggested alternative to (4) uses possible worlds (cf. Wallace [1970] pp. 140–1); in place of (4), one is to have:

(6) "Nec *p*" is true in L in Ω iff (ω)("*p*" is true in L in ω)

(where "Ω" refers to the actual world and I use a simple S5-type interpretation of necessary truth as truth in all possible worlds, with no restriction on what possible worlds are to be considered). However, if one adopts (6) one has not only to countenance the metaphysical implications of possible worlds, but also to provide a theory which enables one to prove theorems of the form:

(7) $(\omega)($ "*p*" is true in L in $\omega$ iff $\Phi(\omega))$.

Yet this requirement is certainly no less intuitively problematic than the requirement that one's theory have theorems of the form of (5). The change of idiom in the metalanguage to talk of possible worlds is useless as a response to this difficulty.

There is, however, yet another alternative to (4) which seems to provide a distinctly different approach. The idea here is to interpret necessity as a property of propositions, so that, instead of (4) one has:

(8) "Nec *p*" is true in L iff NEC(ref("that *p*",L))

(where "NEC..." is a predicate true of propositions). In order to carry through this approach systematically, it is only necessary to provide a theory which will enable one to prove theorems of the form

(9) Ref("that *p*",L) = that $\pi$.

Appearances are, however, misleading. Just as was the case with TL, in a theory of this kind it will be the case that all identities are necessary, and thus that one will have as a theorem:

Ref("that *p*",L) = that $\pi \to$ NEC(that ref("that *p*",L) = that $\pi$).

So all the essentialist claims about language are as much a feature of a theory of this kind as they are of TL.

The claim that all identities are necessary is not just thrown into the last theory for the reasons given in the previous section. It is built into the metalanguage through the use there of reference to propositions. As I argued in section IV, any recursive specification of propositions will have to use the idea that propositions are the values of functions, and will thus have the principle:

$\alpha = \beta \to$ (that $\Phi\alpha =$ that $\Phi\beta$)

hence, in particular,

$\alpha = \beta \to$ (that NEC(that$\Psi\alpha$) = that NEC(that$\Psi\beta$))

from which one can easily infer

$\alpha = \beta \to$ NEC(that$\alpha = \beta$).

Talk of propositions, therefore, is sheer nonsense unless it is taken for granted that, for the things of which propositions are functions, all identities are necessary.

It seems, then, that there is no real alternative to the essentialist claims about language which are explicit in TL, if one is to provide any systematic interpretation of modal constructions. Incidentally, it will be clear that this matter is quite unaffected by the choice, discussed in the previous section, between introducing a modal restriction on singular terms and introducing a modal restriction on the interpretation of quantifiers. TL is designed to fit in with the former alternative, but one could easily modify it to fit in with the latter. The only way I can envisage at present of avoiding this conclusion lies through the radical idea that necessity amounts to no more than provability in an appropriate theory. For although "Nec" cannot be sensibly interpreted as a simple predicate true of sentences, "it is provable in T that..." can certainly be interpreted in this way. This suggests, therefore, that a new approach to the problem may be possible by exploiting this idea. In order to follow it through properly, however, one would have to develop in detail an account of the interpretation of sentences of the form "it is provable in T that $p$", and I shall not undertake this here.

I have pursued this matter at considerable length because it seems to me to constitute the most important general philosophical problem raised by the use of modal concepts. Curiously, it has received little discussion and, so far as I know, the problem was first explicitly stated by John Wallace (in Wallace [1970]). I am inclined, however, to credit Quine with a subliminal perception of these difficulties, despite the fact that this matter is never mentioned in Quine's numerous critiques of modal concepts.

## VII

I showed in section v that in order to guarantee the referential transparency of modal contexts, it is both necessary and sufficient to require that singular terms satisfy the condition "$(x)(x = a \rightarrow \text{Nec}(x = a))$". One can ask, therefore, what kinds of phrase in a natural language such as English this will allow one to count as singular terms. Of course, one may want to deny that modal contexts are referentially transparent. But, as I indicated at the end of section v, even if one does choose a view of this kind, one will still want to know which singular terms can be safely used to instantiate generalisations in modal contexts (such singular terms might be called "rigid designators"), and one determines this by determining what singular terms satisfy the condition "$(x)(x = a \to \mathrm{Nec}$ $(x = a))$". So much the same question arises whatever view one takes, and in my discussion I shall take it that the question is formulated in the first of these ways, as a question about what one is to count as a singular term at all.

It is easy to show, by contraposing an argument from Quine (cf. Quine [1960b] pp. 197–8) and Føllesdal (cf. Føllesdal [1965]) what one cannot count as a singular term. Whatever one's final judgement on the logical form of sentences with definite descriptions, one cannot dispute the equivalence:

$p \leftrightarrow$ (the number n such that n $=$ o & $p$
$\qquad =$ the number n such that n $=$ o).

Hence, if definite descriptions are singular terms, and therefore satisfy the condition "$(x)(x = a \to \mathrm{Nec}(x = a))$", one can infer:

$p \to \mathrm{Nec}$(the number n such that n $=$ o & $p$
$\qquad =$ the number n such that n $=$ o).

But the original equivalence is itself a necessary truth, so one can conclude:

$p \to \mathrm{Nec}\ p$

and thus collapse modal distinctions. The only way to block this argument is to deny that definite descriptions are singular terms at all. A similar argument will show that class abstracts are not singular terms; one need only employ the equivalence:

$p \leftrightarrow \{x : x = x\ \&\ p\} = \{x : x = x\}$

and then repeat the argument. Indeed, one can see now how to carry over this pattern of argument to more specific abstract phrases (except, of course, to intensional abstract phrases). A particular case with a colour abstract is as clear as any. One need only recognise the equivalence:

The sky is blue $\leftrightarrow$ The colour of the sky $=$ blue.

Hence, if colour abstracts are singular terms, one can infer:

The sky is blue → Nec(the colour of the sky = blue)

and, given that the original equivalence is itself necessary, conclude:

The sky is blue → Nec(the sky is blue).

On pain of collapsing modal distinctions, then, one cannot admit within this approach that definite descriptions and extensional abstract phrases are singular terms.

By contrast, it is clear that this approach allows one to count as singular terms names of abstract objects ("Blue", "9", "{9}", etc....). Furthermore, it also allows one to count as singular terms functional expressions drawn from arithmetic and other sciences ("$3^2$", "$H_2O$", etc....). The interesting case is that of proper names of concrete spatio-temporal objects, such as Edward Heath. Mere reflection on the truth or falsity of

$$(x)(x = \text{Edward Heath} \rightarrow \text{Nec}(x = \text{Edward Heath}))$$

is not very helpful. Instead, and here I largely follow Kripke (cf. Kripke [1972a], [1972b]), one needs to reflect on the truth or falsity of

Edward Heath must be who he is
No one else could have been Edward Heath.

There is, I think, some difficulty is grasping what is meant here. For there is a strong urge to regard sentences which begin "No one else could have been..." as completable only by a description, and thus to read some description into any proper name that is used. Thus the sentence "No one else could have been Mrs Wilson" is naturally understood as "No one else could have been the wife of Mr Wilson." Nevertheless, there remains a sense in which a sentence such as "No one else could have been Edward Heath" is true, just because there is no appropriate description with which to replace "Edward Heath". Clearly, someone could lead a life more or less similar to Edward Heath's life; but that person would not be Edward Heath. Again, Edward Heath might never have been born and his parents might have had another male son whom they called "Edward"; but such a person would still not have been Edward Heath (although he would have been called "Edward Heath"). In a thoroughly unexciting way, it seems that "No one else could have been Edward Heath" is true, and thus that one can count as singular terms "Edward Heath" and similar proper names.

It is an obvious consequence of the condition on singular terms "$(x)(x = a \rightarrow \mathrm{Nec}(x = a))$" that identity statements formed from two singular terms are necessary, if true. This has been thought to be unacceptable (cf. Dummett [1973] p. 270), and something needs to be said about it. It is less easy to find interesting examples of true identity statements which use two singular terms than one might expects, once one has set aside obvious examples from abstract sciences. For example, two different abbreviations of the same proper name scarcely count as two proper names, so the fact that M. Tullius Cicero is referred to as "Tully" and "Cicero" is not very impressive. Still, it's clear that when "Cicero" and "Tully" are used in this way "Cicero is Tully" is a necessary truth. A more satisfying case arises where someone adopts a special name for use when he performs a special role, such as that of popular entertainer. For, particularly if the man is successful in this role, the adopted name may become analytically separable from occasions on which the role is performed and come to function simply as an ordinary proper name whose use is just historically linked with certain public occasions. Such a man will then have two names at the same time. A case of this kind is that of Cliff Richard, whose ordinary name is "Harry Webb". In a case such as this, one can form the identity statement

(1) Cliff Richard = Harry Webb

and now properly raise the question as to whether or not it is to be regarded as a necessary truth. It seems clear to me that it should be regarded as such, once one accepts that "Cliff Richard" is a proper name and not just an abbreviation of "the successful singer of "The Young Ones", etc....". For how could Harry Webb not have been Cliff Richard? Of course, Harry Webb might not have adopted the name "Cliff Richard", might not have made the song "The Young Ones", etc....But these objections miss their mark. Harry Webb could only not have been Cliff Richard if he could have been a different person from that which he is. And that is not possible. Each person must be the person he is and not another person.

The impression that (1) is contingent is largely produced by the correct observation that it is neither an *a priori* truth (as Kripke has argued, cf. Kripke [1972a]), nor an analytic truth. It is not something whose truth a man could grasp independent of all experience;

for mere reflection on who Cliff Richard is and who Harry Webb is will not lead to the thought that they are the same. It is not something whose truth follows merely from the meaning of the words used; for whatever meaning they have, it is not sufficient to yield the consequence that a man who denies (1) thereby shows that he has not properly understood it. Nevertheless, (1) could not be false; it is necessary, but synthetic *a posteriori*, truth. To accept that (1) is a necessary truth is not to commit oneself to the view that anyone who denies it has thereby 'said nothing' or has contradicted himself. There has simply been a mistaken identification; but, unlike most mistakes, such a mistake is one which could not have been correct, however reasonable it may have been to make it.

I turn now to the question of how sentences with definite descriptions and extensional abstract phrases are to be construed and interpreted. Much the simplest approach to this matter, which derives from Russell (cf. Russell [1905]), is to regard definite descriptions as basically similar to indefinite descriptions, and thus to construe the role of the definite article in a sentence as that of a quantifier. It is by no means essential to this approach that one should accept the Russellian equivalence between sentences with definite descriptions and sentences without them, for one can treat the definite article as semantically primitive. With "$(\imath x : \ldots)(—)$" for "it is true of the $x$ such that...that—", one will have

"$(\imath x : Fx)(Gx)$" is true in L iff
$(\imath\mu : (\exists a)(\text{ref}(a,L) = \mu \ \& \ \ulcorner Fa \urcorner \text{ is true in L}))$
$\quad (\exists \delta)(\text{ref}(\delta,L) = \mu \ \& \ \ulcorner G\delta \urcorner \text{ is true in L}).$

It is important to recognise that "$(\imath x : Fx)(—)$" is, in this approach, a restricted quantifier, and not, as in Russell and Whitehead's *Principia Mathematica* notation, a term. In the notation here, the formula "$G(\imath x : Fx)$" is simply ill-formed.

This Russellian approach certainly provides an adequate treatment of sentences with definite descriptions. It is obviously attractive for sentences with phrases such as "the man with a martini", which do seem to behave just like sentences with the corresponding indefinite description "a man with a martini". This approach certainly also provides an adequate and interesting account of sentences with extensional abstract phrases. Although, on this approach, it is a mistake to assign referents to such phrases, it in no way follows that this approach embodies any hostility to abstract objects. Sentences such as

> The colour of the sky is blue
> $\{x : x$ is a planet$\}$ has nine members

are to be construed, respectively, as

> $(\imath x : x$ colours the sky$)(x =$ blue$)$
> $(\imath x : (y)(y \in x \leftrightarrow y$ is a planet$)(x$ has nine members$))$

in which there is explicit quantification over abstract objects. Nevertheless, the Russellian approach to extensional abstract phrases is not entirely natural: for example, replacement of the definite article by an indefinite article may yield a sentence whose sense is not clear, e.g.

> A number of planets is nine.

A common feature of abstract phrases of this kind is that there can only be one thing at any one time which satisfies them: thus, at any time, there can only be one number which is the number of planets. For this reason, phrases of this kind are very naturally construed as functional expressions; "the number of planets" is naturally construed, before one takes account of the complexities of modal contexts and suchlike, as of the form "the number of $(\{x : x$ is a planet at t$\})$", i.e. as expressing a function from the set of planets at a time onto numbers. Indeed, I think it may be partly the feeling that phrases of this kind are functional expressions which explains why one wants to insist that, for example, nothing can be two colours at the same time; for unless this were so, one could not properly regard "the colour of the sky" as a functional expression, as of the form "the colour of (the sky,t)". This point does not only apply to abstract phrases; almost any phrase in English of the form "the... of...", e.g. "the Queen of England", "the top of the mountain", can be naturally regarded as a functional expression.

If these phrases are construed as functional expressions, then it seems that they should be regarded as singular terms, for they will be assigned referents in a semantic theory. Once the problem of opacity in modal contexts is recognised, it is easy enough to switch across to Russellian idioms. For any functional expression "$f(x)$" one can always introduce a relational expression "$yRx$" such that $yRx$ iff $y = f(x)$, and then construe a sentence of the superficial form "F(f(x))" as of the logical form "(ʏy:yRx)(Fy)" (e.g., consider in English the functional expression "the father of *x*" and the relational expression "*y* is a father of *x*"). But to change idioms in this way is to reject the intuition that, in some way, phrases such as "the colour of the sky" are functional expressions. And the question that may be asked is whether there is any way of hanging on to this intuition while avoiding problems of opacity.

The answer is that this is possible, at the cost of adding to the complexity of one's semantic theory. First, the concept of a singular term must be pulled apart. In the Russellian theory, singular terms are the only phrases which instantiate generalisations and the only phrases which are assigned referents in a semantic theory. If one is to accommodate a treatment of phrases such as "the colour of the sky" as functional expressions within an interpretation of modal contexts, one must allow that phrases which are not singular terms are nevertheless interpreted as having a reference. I shall say that any phrase which is interpreted as having a reference is a *referring term*. Thus, on the present approach, "the colour of the sky" is a referring term, but not a singular term. By contrast, on the Russellian approach, all singular terms are referring terms. The situation within this new approach is, in fact, basically the same as that described at the close of section v in which I discussed the possibility of following through with a modally-restricted interpretation of quantifiers. For in that situation too the concept of a singular term was pulled apart, although in precisely the opposite direction from that envisaged here: in that case, the fundamental feature of singular terms was to be that they were assigned a reference, and it was not always true that singular terms instantiated generalisations. This difference, however, is merely a difference of style. Where I here distinguish among referring terms between those which are singular terms and those which are not, on the other view one distinguishes among singular terms between those which are rigid designators and those which are not.

One could develop theories which exploited these ideas by modifying in different ways the simple theory TL of section v. TL, however, has a modal metalanguage, and if one is impressed by a functional construal of a phrase such as "the colour of the sky", it may appear desirable to regard it as expressing a function not just from a time (and, perhaps, a place), but also from a possible world. This would require that the idea of interpreting modal operators as quantifiers over possible worlds be taken seriously, and not just used as a convenient algebraic device for formulating completeness proofs. It would be tedious to set out in detail all these different semantic theories, particularly with the need to take account within them of the distinction between singular terms and referring terms. But the differing natures of the theories can perhaps be appreciated by comparing the different interpretations to be put upon a sentence such as "The colour of the sky might not be what it is". In a simple Russellian theory, this will be interpreted as true if and only if:

$$(\imath\mu:\mu \text{ colours the sky})\text{Poss}(\imath\nu:\nu \text{ colours the sky})(\mu \neq \nu).$$

In a theory with a modal metalanguage which allows for a distinction between singular terms and referring terms, the same sentence will be interpreted as true if and only if:

$$(\text{the colour of (the sky, now)},\mu)\text{Poss}$$
$$(\mu \neq (\text{the colour of(the sky, now)}))$$

(I use here an individual quantifier in the manner explained in section v). Finally, in a possible world theory, the same sentence will be interpreted as true if and only if:

$$(\exists\omega)(\text{the colour of (the sky, now, }\omega) \neq$$
$$(\text{the colour of (the sky, now, }\Omega)))$$

(where "$\Omega$" refers, as before, to the actual world). My own preference, largely for reasons of simplicity, is for a Russellian theory, and I certainly feel no inclination to introduce reference to possible worlds at this stage. Fortunately, however, for my present purposes it is not essential to make any final choice. The solution to the problems of quantification into modal contexts is to this extent independent of the interpretation of modal constructions.

## VIII

If it is plausible to hold that contexts for singular terms in modal constructions are transparent, then it seems that one should try a similar hypothesis for indirect speech. The hypothesis here must be that all contexts for singular terms within indirect speech are transparent, and that any appearances to the contrary are the result of taking certain phrases to be singular terms when they are not.

In this case, however, potential conclusions about identity, analogous to the conclusion that all identities are necessary, seem to me unacceptable. Typical of the conclusions one would have to accept is the principle:

$(x)(y)$(Ralph knows that $x = x \rightarrow$
$$(x = y \rightarrow (\text{Ralph knows that } x = y))),$$

and by no stretch of the philosophical imagination is it possible to admit such a conclusion. An easy way of pressing this point is provided by the discussion of identity statements in the previous section. I argued there that an identity statement such as "Cliff Richard = Harry Webb" could plausibly be regarded as a necessary truth, and that impressions to the contrary could be explained away by allowing the statement to be nevertheless synthetic and *a posteriori*. However, these admissions cannot be sustained if one holds that contexts for singular terms in sentences prefixed by "it is an *a priori* truth that..." or "it is an analytic truth that..." are transparent, as the present hypothesis would require. For just as it is a necessary truth that identity is reflexive, it is equally an *a priori* analytic truth that it is reflexive. And therefore the conclusions

$(x)(y)(x = y \rightarrow$ it is an *a priori* truth that $x = y)$
$(x)(y)(x = y \rightarrow$ it is an analytic truth that $x = y)$

would be inescapable.

In discussing modal contexts, I argued in section v that difficulties with regard to individual and existential generalisation in modal contexts were most naturally solved by adopting a view which has the consequence that modal contexts are transparent. Similar difficulties clearly arise with regard to existential and individual generalisation in indirect speech, and one may wonder how these difficulties can be set aside without taking indirect speech contexts to be referentially transparent. The sort of inference which one must not validate is

Ralph believes that the tallest spy is a spy

so:

$(\exists x)$(Ralph believes that $x$ is a spy)

(cf. Kaplan [1969] pp. 220–1). In fact there is already an excellent reason for rejecting this inference: the phrase "the tallest spy" fails to satisfy the modal condition on singular terms which I introduced in section v—that singular terms be such that sentences of the form "$(x)(x = a \rightarrow \text{Nec}(x = a))$" are true. So now the question arises of whether one can rely on this modal condition alone in the interpretation of indirect speech.

In one respect it is not, I think, a sufficient condition. In the case of names of abstract objects, such as numbers, it lets in as singular terms phrases such as "$\sqrt{(3^2+(9-2))}$" which one may plausibly want to rule out. In this kind of case, one must appeal to some conventional notation which gives names of numbers—in our case it is usually decimal notation. However, just what one should say about names of real numbers is not clear to me. Is "$\sqrt{2}$" a singular term? Or is its decimal expansion? It seems to me that the sense of "Ralph knows what $\sqrt{2}$ is" and similar sentences is just not clear enough without further specification to provide an answer here. This is, however, a somewhat esoteric problem, whose solution belongs to the philosophy of mathematics and need not be taken any further here.

A more serious difficulty arises from the thought that in indirect speech, it is not the modal condition "$a$ must be what it is", but the epistemic condition "$y$ knows what $a$ is" that is relevant (where "$y$" takes as values the persons whose beliefs, etc., are under discussion). In some sense, this thought lies behind Russell's famous "fundamental epistemological principle" that "every proposition which we can understand must be composed wholly of constituents with which we are acquainted" (Russell [1911] p. 117; this principle is roughly formulated at the end of Russell [1905] and obviously links up in Russell's mind with the theory of descriptions). In more recent times, this thought is explicit in the work of Hintikka and Kaplan. Hintikka proposes to use the condition "$y$ knows what $a$ is" in the metalanguage as a restriction on the interpretation of quantification into indirect speech contexts (cf. Hintikka [1962] (Ch. 6)), very much in the way in which he proposes to introduce a modal restriction on the interpretation of quantification into modal contexts (cf. section v). Kaplan (in Kaplan [1969] section 9) proposes something like the condition "$y$ knows what $a$ is" as a condition of "$a$"'s being a singular term for $y$. Clearly, Kaplan's proposal is in line with my general approach in this essay, so I shall concentrate upon it; nevertheless, my discussion will have obvious implications for Hintikka's proposal.

If Kaplan's proposal were correct, there would be a contradiction in the statement:

There is someone whom Ralph believes to be a spy, although he does not know who it is.

That this statement is contradictory, however, is not at all obvious, and in order to grasp better the intended role of the epistemic condition on singular terms it will be helpful to consider a couple of arguments. First, there are arguments in which the condition "$y$ knows what $a$ is" is to figure as a sufficient condition for "$a$"'s being a singular term in the context of the argument. This applies particularly to arguments such as

Ralph believes that the man from MI5 is a spy
Ralph knows who the man from MI5 is

so:

$(\exists x)$(Ralph believes that $x$ is a spy).

For such arguments will not be validated by the modal condition on singular terms.

I do not deny that arguments such as this have some plausibility. But I do not see how one could convince a sceptic that the conclusion of the argument really is a logical consequence of the premisses. For someone who accepts only the modal condition on singular terms can also accept that people are committed to believing the logical consequences of what they believe and know to be the case. And with this principle, the two premisses above will yield the conclusion

$(\exists x)$(Ralph is committed to the belief that $x$ is a spy).

It seems to me that whatever intuitions one may have had about the original argument are as well accounted for by the second one, which does not require any epistemic condition on a phrase's being a singular term.

Those who introduce epistemic conditions want to use them not only as sufficient, but also as necessary conditions for a phrase's being a singular term in the context of a relevant argument. Thus an argument such as

Ralph believes that Ortcutt is a spy

so:

$(\exists x)$(Ralph believes that $x$ is a spy)

will be rejected as it stands. Only with the extra premiss "Ralph knows who Ortcutt is" should the argument be accepted. However, it seems to me that there is no natural reason why the argument should not be accepted as it stands. The only natural sense to be attached to the extra premiss "Ralph knows who Ortcutt is" is that there is some description of Ortcutt, say "the F", such that "Ralph knows that Ortcutt is the F" is true. Why such an extra premiss should be regarded as relevant to existential generalisation as in the argument above remains mysterious.

As far as difficulties with existential generalisation in indirect speech go, then, one can manage perfectly well with just the modal condition on singular terms. Epistemic conditions for a phrase's being a singular term introduce an immense complexity into the logic of singular terms and thus into any semantic theory which handles indirect speech. The only thing which could justify such complexity would be the hypothesis that if one used such conditions one could hold that indirect speech contexts are transparent (given his multiple relation theory of judgement, it must be this thought which lies behind Russell's 'fundamental epistemological principle'). Indeed, if such an hypothesis were sustained some of the complexities would be removed. However, as I argued at the start of this section, one cannot seriously hold the view that indirect speech contexts are transparent. Furthermore, the hypothesis itself is clearly mistaken. For even if Ralph knows who Cliff Richard is and who Harry Webb is, he may still not know that they are one and the same. Herein lies, as I suggested in section v, a fundamental contrast between knowledge and necessity. As a result referential opacity strikes much deeper in the case of indirect speech than in the case of modal constructions. There is no way in which one can winnow out a restricted class of singular terms that will enable one to maintain that indirect speech contexts are transparent after all.

## IX

If contexts for singular terms within indirect speech are referentially opaque, then any account of quantification into indirect speech

must show how quantification into opaque contexts can be interpreted. This is no minor undertaking. One of the claims which I
initially used to set up the problem of quantification into modal and
indirect speech contexts in the first section of this essay was precisely
the claim (D) that one could not interpret quantification into
opaque contexts. It is this claim which is here to be denied. The
difficulty of supporting this denial is greatly compounded by the
general difficulty of formulating a theory which yields anything like
an adequate interpretation of indirect speech. It is to this difficulty
that I shall first address myself.

One can dismiss at once, I think, any attempt to interpret indirect
speech verbs as simple operators on sentences (for suggestions along
these lines, cf. Prior [1971] pp. 18–21, Quine [1970b] pp. 32–3).
For one can see at once that the kind of equivalence which this
proposal requires:

(1) "Ralph believes that Ortcutt is a spy" is true in L iff
    ref("Ralph",L) believes that ("Ortcutt is a spy" is true in L)

is simply false. Ralph may well believe that Ortcutt is a spy while
having no beliefs at all about the sentence "Ortcutt is a spy". An
approach which avoids this objection will be one in which indirect
speech verbs are interpreted as expressing relations between subjects (generally, people) and propositions. This approach requires,
in place of (1), an equivalence such as

(2) "Ralph believes that Ortcutt is a spy" is true in L iff
    ref("Ralph",L) BELIEVES (ref("that Ortcutt is a spy",L))

(where "BELIEVES" expressed a relation between subjects and
propositions). This approach to indirect speech is analogous to the
approach I mentioned in section VI in which I considered briefly
the idea that necessary truth be interpreted as a property of propositions (cf. (8) of section VI). Within a straightforward theory of
this kind, the interpretation of quantification into indirect speech
will be easy, and it will be possible to prove natural equivalences
such as

(3) "($\exists x$)(Ralph believes that $Fx$)" is true in L iff
    ($\exists \mu$)(Ralph BELIEVES (that $\Phi\mu$)).

The objection to this theory arises from the fact, mentioned in section VI, that once one agrees that propositions are the values of functions, one cannot dispute the principle of extensionality

(4) $(\mu)(\nu)(\mu = \nu \rightarrow$ (that $\Phi\mu =$ that $\Phi\nu$))

and thus in particular

$(\mu)$ $(\nu)(\mu = \nu \rightarrow$ (that Ralph BELIEVES (that $\Phi\mu$) $=$ that Ralph BELIEVES (that $\Phi\nu$))),

from which one infers at once

$(\mu)(\nu)(\mu = \nu \rightarrow$ (Ralph BELIEVES (that $\Phi\mu$) $\rightarrow$ Ralph BELIEVES (that $\Phi\nu$))).

But since one can prove in this theory

(5) "$(x)(y)(x = y \rightarrow$ (Ralph believes that $Fx \rightarrow$ Ralph believes that $Fy$))" is true in L iff

$(\mu)(\nu)(\mu = \nu \rightarrow$ (Ralph BELIEVES (that $\Phi\mu$) $\rightarrow$ Ralph BELIEVES (that $\Phi\nu$)))

one is bound to validate the substitutivity of identity within indirect speech. Yet this, as I argued in the previous section, is something which cannot be seriously countenanced. So one must reject this theory.

In his famous paper "On Sense and Reference" (Frege [1892]), Frege argued that because of the failure of the substitutivity of identity within indirect speech, referring terms do not have the same reference in indirect speech as they have in direct speech. Instead, according to Frege, referring terms refer in indirect speech to what is normally their sense. It has been held against Frege that the idea of indirect reference does not allow for quantification into indirect speech (e.g., cf. Linsky [1969] p. 692). This view is, however, a mistake; indeed, I shall show that not only does Frege's idea of indirect reference allow for quantification into indirect speech, it allows for it to be interpreted in such a way that it amounts to quantification into opaque contexts. Any complete presentation of Frege's semantic theory would be a complex and controversial undertaking which I shall not attempt here. It is, however, possible to represent the idea of indirect reference in a theory that does not purport to be a complete Fregean theory, but which is nevertheless not too unfair to Frege's ideas. In the theory to be developed, both singular terms and sentences will be regarded as referring terms, and the reference of a referring term will be relative not only to the language to which it belongs, but also to the kind of context in which it occurs. For the moment, only two kinds of context need be considered, direct and indirect speech. I shall write "ref(a,L,dir)" for "the reference of a in L in direct speech", and "ref(a,L,ind)" for "the reference of a in L in indirect speech". One major point of contrast between this theory and any true Fregean theory is that in this theory predicates are not construed as referring terms, although they will be assigned different interpretations according as to whether they occur in direct or indirect speech. Given Frege's notorious troubles with the concept *horse*, this may be no bad thing.

The theory begins with an axiom that introduces the reference of all true sentences:

"$p$" is true in L iff ref("$p$",L,dir) = T

(where T is some appropriate abstract object). There will be obvious axioms giving the interpretation in direct speech of primitive predicates, primitive singular terms, and functional expressions, of the form:

$(a)(ref(\ulcorner F'a \urcorner, L, dir) = T$ iff $\Phi(ref(a,L,dir)))$
    $Ref("a'",L,dir) = \alpha$
$(a)(ref(\ulcorner f(a) \urcorner, L, dir) = \phi(ref(a,L,dir)))$.

Axioms giving the interpretation in direct speech of connectives and quantifiers will be typified by

$Ref("p \& q",L,dir) = T$ iff $ref("p",L,dir) = T \&$
                                    $ref("q",L,dir) = T$
$Ref("(\exists x)(Fx)",L,dir) = T$ iff
$(\exists \mu)(\exists a)(ref(a,L,dir) = \mu \& ref(\ulcorner Fa \urcorner, L, dir) = T)$.

One also needs, as usual, an axiom to the effect that everything is referred to by a singular term, i.e.:

$(\mu)(\exists a)(ref(a,L,dir) = \mu)$.

With these axioms one can prove natural equivalences such as

"$(\exists x)(F'x)$" is true in L iff $(\exists \mu)(\Phi \mu)$.

So far, reference has always been reference in direct speech. But with the introduction of an indirect speech verb, indirect reference is needed:

(a)(ref($\ulcorner$a believes that $p\urcorner$,L,dir) = T iff
ref(a,L,dir) BELIEVES (ref("$p$",L,ind))).

This axiom introduces indirect reference, which must now be filled out in a similar way. Axioms giving the interpretation in indirect speech of primitive predicates, primitive singular terms, and functional expressions, will have the form:

(a)(ref($\ulcorner$F'a$\urcorner$,L,ind) = that $\Psi$(ref(a,L,ind)))
    Ref("$a'$",L,ind)  = $\beta$
(a)(ref($\ulcorner$f(a)$\urcorner$,L,ind) = $\phi$(ref(a,L,ind)))

(where $\beta$ is the sense of a singular term and "$\Psi$" is a predicate true of such senses; I shall say that the senses of singular terms are individual concepts). Axioms giving the interpretation in indirect speech of connectives and quantifiers will be typified by

Ref("$p$ & $q$",L,ind) =
    that ref("$p$",L,ind) is true & ref("$q$",L,ind) is true
Ref("($\exists x$)(F$x$)",L,ind) =
    that ($\exists \varkappa$: $\varkappa$ is an individual concept)
        ($\exists$a)(ref(a,L,ind) = $\varkappa$ & ref($\ulcorner$Fa$\urcorner$,L,ind) is true).

One will also need, as one would expect, an axiom to the effect that every individual concept is referred to in indirect speech by a singular term, i.e.:

($\varkappa$: $\varkappa$ is an individual concept)($\exists$a)(ref(a,L,ind) = $\varkappa$).

In addition to these axioms, three other axioms are needed to make it possible to interpret quantification into indirect speech. First, one must have it as an axiom that all singular terms have an indirect reference, i.e.:

(a)($\exists \varkappa$: $\varkappa$ is an individual concept)(ref(a,L,ind) = $\varkappa$)).

Secondly, one must have a couple of axioms which give the relation between the indirect and the direct reference of a referring term. I shall say that the indirect reference unambiguously determines the direct reference; thus, for singular terms, one has the axioms:

(a)(ref(a,L,ind) determines ref(a,L,dir))
(a)($\mu$)($\nu$)((ref(a,L,ind) determines $\mu$ & ref(a,L,ind) determines $\nu$)
        $\rightarrow$ ($\mu = \nu$)).

I shall call a theory with these axioms "TF". In TF one can easily prove equivalences such as

(6) "$(\exists x)$(Ralph believes that $Fx$)" is true in L iff
    $(\exists \mu)(\exists \varkappa: \varkappa$ is an individual concept)...
        ($\varkappa$ determines $\mu$ & Ralph BELIEVES (that $\Psi\varkappa$)).

So one is certainly able to provide an interpretation of quantification into indirect speech within TF. Furthermore, the point of the idea of indirect reference in TF is that one is not able to prove in TF

(7) "$(x)(y)(x = y \to$ (Ralph believes that $Fx \to$ Ralph believes that $Fy$))" is true in L iff
    $(\mu)(\nu)(\mu = \nu \to$ (Ralph BELIEVES (that $\Phi\mu$) $\to$ Ralph BELIEVES that$(\Phi\nu)$)).

Instead of (7), one is only able to prove

(8) "$(x)(y)(x = y \to$ (Ralph believes that $Fx \to$ Ralph believes that $Fy$))" is true in L iff
    $(\mu)(\nu)(\varkappa: \varkappa$ is an individual concept)$(\lambda: \lambda$ is an individual concept)
        ($\mu = \nu$ & $\varkappa$ determines $\mu$ & $\lambda$ determines $\nu$) $\to$
        (Ralph BELIEVES (that $\Psi\varkappa$) $\to$ Ralph BELIEVES (that $\Psi\lambda$)),

which shows that the substitutivity of identity within indirect speech is not validated in TF. Thus TF certainly provides an interpretation of quantification into indirect speech which allows for quantification into opaque contexts. To this extent, therefore, TF succeeds in capturing what I take to have been the point of Frege's idea of indirect reference.

One difficulty which faces TF, and, indeed, any theory which attempts to capture Frege's idea of indirect reference, concerns the interpretation of sentences in which indirect speech verbs are iterated, as in "Mary hopes that Ralph believes that she loves him". The natural development of the theory, which is, indeed, suggested by Frege, is to ascribe a doubly indirect reference to referring terms within the scope of two indirect speech verbs. But this seems to require an indefinite number of indirect referents, corresponding to the possibility of indefinite iteration of indirect speech verbs (as in Grice's theory of meaning), and this requirement does not look attractive (cf. Carnap [1947] section 30). A much simpler approach, first hinted at by Carnap (in Carnap [1947]), and explicitly formulated by Dummett (in Dummett [1973] pp. 267–9), is to suppose that there is just one level of indirect reference, which is unaffected by the addition of further indirect speech verbs. The trouble with this approach, however, is that 'paradox of analysis' arguments can be formulated which seem to indicate the need of a hierarchy of indirect referents after all (cf. Church [1946]). I do not know of any way of resolving this difficulty, but more can be said on this matter, and I will not pursue it further here.

Since TF makes explicit use of reference to propositions, the fact that propositions, in so far as they are the values of functions, satisfy the principle of extensionality, will have certain consequences for TF itself. One can infer at once from this principle that TF will have as theorems both

(9) $(x:x$ is an individual concept$)(\lambda:\lambda$ is an individual concept$)$
  $(x = \lambda \rightarrow$ ANALYTIC $($that $x = \lambda))$

(10) $(\mu:\mu$ is a proposition$)$ $(v:v$ is a proposition$)$
  $(\mu = v \rightarrow$ ANALYTIC $($that $\mu = v)),$

and the principles corresponding to (9) and (10) for the concept of an *a priori* truth. Thanks to the idea of indirect reference, it does not follow from (9) and (10) that one thereby validates the principles that all identities or that all truths are analytic (or *a priori*). What does follow, however, is that all the axioms of TF which deal with indirect reference must be regarded as *a priori* analytic truths. This is a much stronger form of the conclusion which I discussed in section v with regard to the interpretation of modal constructions. I argued there that it was difficult to see how one could construct a semantic theory which enabled one to provide a systematic interpretation of modal constructions unless one took it that the semantic theory made claims about the essential structure of a language. In this case, the semantic theory must be regarded as giving *a priori* analytic truths about part of the structure of a language. This is not an agreeable conclusion, but it is certainly part of the price one must pay for using a theory such as TF.

The fact that (9) and (10) are theorems of TF has further consequences for TF. Although the substitutivity of identity and material equivalence in belief is not validated by TF, (9) and (10) guarantee that stronger principles of substitutivity will be validated, namely

(11) $(x)(y)$(Ralph believes that $x = x \rightarrow$

      (it is analytic that $x = y \rightarrow$ Ralph believes that $x = y$))

(12) (Ralph believes that $p \leftrightarrow p$

      (it is analytic that $p \leftrightarrow q \rightarrow$ Ralph believes that $p \leftrightarrow q$)).

Principles corresponding to (11) and (12) for the concept of an *a priori* truth will also be validated. The fact that these principles are validated by TF reinforces the conclusion that any serious adoption of TF requires great confidence in the concepts of an analytic and an *a priori* truth.

As long as one has such confidence, the acceptability of (11) and (12) indicate that one could formulate another theory, more or less equivalent to TF, in which one dispensed with reference to intensional objects. I argued at the start of this section that one could not interpret "believes that" as a simple operator on sentences. If, however, one slightly reconstrues a sentence such as "$(\exists x)$ (Ralph believes that $Fx$)" as

(13) $(\exists x)(\exists y : y$ is a belief)...

      (Ralph has $y$ & it is analytic that $y$ is true iff $Fx$)

one can find here the phrase "it is analytic that..." which it is natural to interpret as an operator on sentences, as in

(14) "It is analytic that $p$" is true in L iff

      it is analytic that ("$p$" is true in L).

(14) raises the question of what is to support substitutions within the scope of the operator "it is analytic that...". Naturally, only analytic equivalences will support such substitutions, so, as was the case with TF, it must be assumed that a semantic theory gives not only necessary, but even analytic, truths about the truth-conditions of the sentences of a language.

A theory that uses (14) to provide the basis for a systematic interpretation of indirect speech would be similar to the theory TL of section VI, in which the modal operator "Nec" was interpreted in a manner analogous to (14). However, in TL it was assumed that modal contexts are referentially transparent, whereas no similar assumptions are desirable for indirect speech. So the question may be raised as to whether one can have a theory in which (14) is employed without the assumption that indirect speech contexts are transparent. The answer is that this is certainly possible. All one needs to do is to strengthen all the axioms of TL, and in particular those that give the interpretation of primitive singular terms and functional expressions, by making them analytic truths themselves. Thus one needs, for singular terms, axioms of the form:

It is analytic that $(\text{ref}(``a\text{'''},L) = \alpha)$
(a)(it is analytic that $(\text{ref}(\ulcorner f(a) \urcorner, L) = \phi(\text{ref}(,aL)))$).

In addition one needs an axiom to the effect that for any singular term there is something to which it refers as an analytic truth, i.e.

(15)  (a)$(\exists \mu)$(it is analytic that$(\text{ref}(a,L) = \mu)$),

and a further axiom to the effect that for everything, there is a singular term which refers to it as an analytic truth, i.e.

(16)  $(\mu)(\exists a)$(it is analytic that$(\text{ref}(a,L) = \mu)$).

These axioms are needed to make it possible to interpret quantification into indirect speech without assuming that indirect speech is transparent. For while it is easy to see how one could prove an equivalence of the form

(17)  "$(\exists x)$(it is analytic that F$x$)" is true in L iff
        $(\exists \mu)(\exists a)(\text{ref}(a,L) = \mu$ & it is analytic that $\Phi(\text{ref}(a,L)))$,

if one inferred at once from (17), as looks tempting,

(18)  "$(\exists x)$(it is analytic that F$x$)" is true in L iff
        $(\exists \mu)$(it is analytic that $\Phi\mu$),

one would be assuming that contexts for singular terms within the scope of "it is analytic that..." were transparent. But it is just this assumption which is to be rejected. If one adds (15) and (16) to (17), however, one can now infer (18) with no assumptions about referential transparency.

   The assumptions embodied in (15) and (16) are not very attractive as they stand. However, one can dispense with the need to make just these assumptions if one employs much the same tactics as were employed before in the discussion of substitutional interpretations of quantification. One can dispense with the need to assume (15) at all if one builds an appropriate restriction into the interpretation of the existential quantifier, and one can do something to ease the discomfort that (16) causes by introducing reference to contexts. I am bound to admit, however, that the situation that presents itself here is not a philosophically attractive one, and there is certainly much more to be said on this matter. What I have tried to develop here is one line of thought which at least shows how one can begin to provide an account of indirect speech that allows for quantification into opaque contexts.

This modified version of TL (henceforth "modified TL") will validate much the same principles as TF. There are two main differences between the theories: first, TF makes use of reference to intensional objects, whereas modified TL makes no use of such reference. Secondly, TF allows one to construe sentences of the form "Ralph believes that $p$" as such, whereas in modified TL the same sentence has to be construed as of the form:

$$(\exists y\!:\!y \text{ is a belief})(\text{Ralph has } y \ \& \ \text{it is analytic that } y \text{ is true iff } p).$$

The first difference is the most important. The availability of modified TL seems to me to show that the kind of reference to intensional objects which TL embodies is unnecessary, but also quite harmless. Merely ontological anxiety about TF which does not apply in any way to modified TL would seem to me irrational. Some light can also be shed on the much-disputed matter of whether or not proper names have sense as well as reference. The availability of modified TL shows that there is no need to assign to a proper name any abstract object as the sense of that name. What is necessary, however, is that a semantic theory should not just assign a referent to a proper name; for in modified TL it must be regarded as an analytic truth that any proper name has the reference in a given language that it does have. In this way, therefore, even modified TL preserves the view that proper names have sense as well as reference.

As I have been careful to indicate clearly, both TF and modified TL require great confidence in the concept of analyticity. It is a feature of much contemporary philosophy, however, that no such confidence is justifiable, and one would certainly like to be able to formulate a theory which did not have to provide analytic truths about the structure of a language. Unfortunately, those who propound critical views of analyticity have still to suggest a style of interpretation of indirect speech that is remotely adequate, and it is therefore difficult to say whether or not one can provide, without analyticity, a systematic interpretation of indirect speech that allows for quantification into opaque contexts. I am inclined to think, however, that this should be possible. For any adequate interpretation of indirect speech that does not use the concept of analyticity must, I think, start from something like a construal of sentences of the form "Ralph believes that $p$" as

$$(\exists y{:}y \text{ is a belief})(\text{Ralph has } y \ \& \ \theta(y \text{ is true iff } p))$$

where "$\theta$" expresses the preferred condition, distinct from analyticity, for the interpretation of indirect speech. Where this is so, one need only make corresponding changes throughout modified TL, replacing "it is analytic that..." by "$\theta$" throughout, in order to have a theory which gives a systematic interpretation of indirect speech that allows for quantification into opaque contexts.

# 4

## Proper names, reference, and rigid designation[1]

### CHRISTOPHER PEACOCKE

Dissatisfied as we may now be with "disguised description" treatments of ordinary proper names, theories thus based at least purported to give an account of each of the following:

(a) the contribution made by a name to the truth-conditions of the sentences in which it occurs
(b) the requirements for mastery of a name in a language
(c) the alleged puzzles over names in existential and identity statements
(d) what is constitutive of a name in a community being a name of a given object
(e) what is constitutive of a speaker's denoting an object on a particular occasion of use of a name.

Any alternative view of names must speak to these issues, and my immediate concern in this paper is with the first of them, (a), together with the relation between the contribution made to truth-conditions by names and that made by other singular terms.

My starting point is the concept of a *rigid designator* introduced by Kripke in "Naming and Necessity" (Kripke [1972a]); for my first claim is that we can restate Kripke's thesis that proper names are rigid designators in a way free of the apparatus in terms of which it was made, a way that provides a plausible answer to issue (a).

[1] I have benefited from discussions on these matters with Richard Grandy, John McDowell, Dana Scott, and David Wiggins; and I am especially indebted to Gareth Evans for incisive remarks made in reply to an ancestor of the present paper.

## I

Kripke says "Let's call something a *rigid designator* if in any possible world it designates the same object." (Kripke [1972a] p. 269) The "in" in the definition could with increase of perspicuity be replaced by "with respect to". To ask whether an expression $\alpha$ is a rigid designator is not to ask a question about $\alpha$ *as used in* another possible world. Rather, we specify counterfactually a certain possible situation and then ask what $\alpha$, used as an expression of *our* actual language, denotes with respect to that possible state of affairs. (On the mistaken interpretation, it would be absurd to suppose that *any* expression is a rigid designator.)

Kripke's definition quantifies over possible worlds and appeals to transworld identity; our task is to avoid this, or at least provide an alternative. To avoid unnecessary complexity at this stage, we will offer a criterion for

$t$ is a rigid designator in language L

only for the case in which $t$ $(s, u, \ldots)$ ranges over singular terms and L over languages free of both ambiguity and indexicals. We will drop the last restriction later. Then we may say

$t$ is a rigid designator in L iff
there is an object $x$ such that for any sentence $G(t)$ in which $t$ occurs, the truth (falsity) condition for $G(t)$ is that $\langle x \rangle$ satisfy (respectively, fail to satisfy) $G(\ )$.

If we omit "there is an object $x$ such that" from the right-hand side we obtain a definition for

$t$ is a rigid designator of $x$ in L.

We may say, metaphorically, that we are here basing rigid designation on the idea of a certain object entering the truth-conditions of all the sentences of the language in which $t$ occurs. What a rigid designator designates is just the object that so enters the truth-conditions.

Definite descriptions, in the use of them with which Kripke was concerned when he denied that they are rigid designators, are not rigid designators on this criterion either. There is no object such that the truth-condition for $G$(the F) is that *that object* (or its unit sequence) satisfy $G(\ )$. The truth-condition for $G$(the F) is certainly not that the object *y* that is in fact the F satisfy G( ); that is not sufficient, for the truth-condition requires *y* also to be the F. And it is not necessary, since G(the F) would be true if any object other than *y* were the F and also satisfied G( ). This point, granted the notion of a truth-condition, can be made without appeal to the possible worlds apparatus; and it can be seen as an explicit formulation of one of the ideas in Russell [1905].

This criterion of rigid designation can be seen too as merely a more explicit formulation of an idea variously expressed as that of a term's "serving...simply to refer to its object" (Quine [1953b]), "tagging" an individual (Marcus [1961]), or in general of an expression's being "used to enable...individuals to be made subjects of discourse" (Mill [1843]); and the view that proper names are rigid designators in our sense seems a natural elucidation of Miss Anscombe's remark that the proper name contributes "to the meaning of the sentence precisely by standing for its bearer" (Anscombe [1958]).

There is a consequence of the view that proper names are rigid designators in our sense. If it is true, we can predict a point remarked by Geach (Geach [1972] pp. 117, 140, 144), that genuine proper names "gives us no scope trouble"; guinine proper names are "essentially scopeless". The point is that there is no difference in respect of truth-conditions between (for example)

Concerning Heath: he might not have been prime minister

and

It might have been the case that: Heath is not prime minister; whereas there is actually a difference in truth-*value* between

Concerning the prime minister: he might not have been prime minister

and

It might have been the case that: the prime minister is not prime minister.[2]

If "Heath" is a rigid designator, then by our criterion, there is an object *x* such that the truth-condition for "concerning Heath: he

[2] In this example, the first occurrence of "the prime minister" is intended to have large scope with respect to "not".

might not have been prime minister" is that: concerning it $(x)$, it might not have been prime minister. Similarly, the truth-condition for "it might have been the case that: Heath is not prime minister" is that the same object $x$ satisfies the condition: it might have been that ( ) is not prime minister. But of course, these are one and the same condition; there is no difference between being such that concerning it, it might not have been prime minister, and being such that it might have been that *it* is not prime minister. In this argument, the existential-universal ($\exists\forall$) form of our criterion is crucial; without it, we could not conclude that it is the same object that the truth-conditions of the two sentences both concern. One might say that proper names always have maximum scope, but of course one might equally say they always have minimum scope on the basis of *these* facts; rather, as Geach says, they are scopeless.

Kripke's definition of a rigid designator, no doubt because of the problems to which he was concerned to apply the notion, used specifically modal concepts. Ours uses none, and in virtue of this we have a bonus: any expression that is a rigid designator on our criteria is, as it were, a rigid designator with respect to *every* operator, modal or non-modal. An argument strictly parallel to that of the previous paragraph will yield the conclusion that the truth-conditions of

Concerning Heath: in the past, he edited *The Church Times*

and

In the past: Heath edited *The Church Times*

do not differ, as indeed they do not. We could, if we wished, set up a syntactical device which marked a distinction of scope for proper names as well as for definite descriptions; but it would be a distinction without a semantic difference.

Dummett holds that, for the sorts of cases so far considered, distinctions of scope with respect to operators apply to proper names as much as to definite descriptions (Dummett [1973], especially pp. 113–17). There is, he holds, a "clear sense in which we may rightly say, 'St. Anne cannot but have been a parent'", and we should give the same account of this as we give of the truth-conditions of the true sentence "The mother of Mary cannot but have been a parent", rather than invoke the *a priori*/necessary distinction. But there is an argument independent of the present issue against Dummett's position. On his view, there ought to be a true reading of almost any sentence of the form

α might not have been α

where α is a proper name, viz. that reading on which the first occurrence of α has wider scope than the modal operator, and the second narrower scope. For in the typical case, the object that is in fact α might not have satisfied our criterion (being the F, say) for recognising an object as the referent of α. Yet there seems to be no such reading of the sentence for genuine proper names.[3] Worse; in many cases, something other than the thing that is in fact α might be the F, and so on Dummett's view it ought (on one reading of the sentence) to be true to say

Something other than the thing that is α might have been α.

In general, we must distinguish between the true metalinguistic statement (i) and statement (ii):

(i) necessarily, if our criterion for recognising an object as the referent of α is that it be the F, the referent of α cannot be anything but the F

This is compatible with the falsity of the non-metalinguistic statement (on any reading),

(ii) α is necessarily F.

Kripke puts the relevant distinction here in terms of "fixing the referent" as opposed to "giving the meaning" (Kripke [1972a] pp. 273–7). Our criterion suggests another way of expressing it. One who holds both that a proper name α should be assigned a sense that is not uniquely determined by its referent and further holds that this sense "gives the meaning" of α will deny that there is an object $x$ such that what is (strictly and literally) said in an utterance of $G(α)$ is that $x$ satisfies condition $G(\ )$; one who holds that the sense serves only to "fix the referent" will not deny it. Frege (with an exception noted below) did in effect deny it; in his theory, what is said could only be the "thought" expressed by the sentence, and it is the sense, not the referent, of a singular term occurring in the sentence that contributes to the determination of this.

---

[3] The "St." in "St. Anne" may make one suspicious of whether this expression is such a genuine proper name.

The existence of a distinction between fixing a referent and giving the meaning shows that it is consistent to hold both that proper names are rigid designators on our criterion, and that no full account of the role of a proper name in the language of a community can be given without assigning it a sense not determined by its referent. But the claim that proper names are rigid designators must, if anything, help the case of those who deny, for one reason or another, there is a need to assign proper names a sense not fixed by their referent; for, if true, it shows that, at least in point of getting the truth conditions right, no such assignment is needed.

Someone may object, "Since we are not obliged to accept the possible worlds semantics for necessity, why do we need your criterion? Suppose we follow the convention that "$\alpha\beta$" is to abbreviate "the concatenation of expression type $\alpha$ with expression type $\beta$" and that object language expressions are used as names of themselves when they occur in expressions thus underlined. Then can we not simply say: $t$ is a rigid designator in L iff it is true in L that nothing else might have been $t$, or, more carefully, iff $T(\underline{\exists x(x = t \,\&\, \sim\Diamond\exists y(y = t \,\&\, y \neq x))}$, L)?" But this criterion is not necessary, for it presumes that the object language is capable of defining a possibility operator, which is not, intuitively, required for a language to contain rigid designators. It is not sufficient either; for if $t$ is, intuitively, a rigid designator, then so, by this criterion, is $(\imath x)$ $(x = t \,\&\, p)$, for any true sentence replacing $p$. The most we can say is that this criterion is necessary in the case in which L does contain a possibility operator. But that that it is so follows from our adopted criterion. By that criterion, for any rigid designator $t$ of L, there is an object $z$ such that the truth condition for the sentence mentioned in the alternative criterion is that

$$\langle z \rangle \text{ satisfy } \underline{\exists x(x = \xi_1 \,\&\, \sim\Diamond\exists y(y = \xi_1 \,\&\, y \neq x))}$$

and it is sufficient for this that

$$\langle z,z \rangle \text{ satisfy } \underline{\xi_2 = \xi_1 \,\&\, \sim\Diamond\exists y(y = \xi_1 \,\&\, y \neq \xi_2)}$$

But this last condition *is* so satisfied; for $z = z$, and it is *not* possible that there is an object both identical with $z$ and not identical with $z$. (No particular semantics for "$\Diamond$" are assumed here, but only the results that any coherent semantics will deliver.)

Our criterion of rigid designation, and much of the talk of this section, reifies *conditions*; it is our next task to try to avoid such reification.

## II

A natural way to try to eliminate talk of conditions, in a way that prevents the notion of a truth-condition of a sentence from collapsing into that of a material equivalent of it, is to *mention* the Tarski–Davidson truth theory for the language L in question. We label this theory $T_L$. The idea is more easily stated than implemented, and not until after the discussion of demonstratives in the next section can we have a plausible basis for a criterion.

Let "T" be the truth predicate for any given language, and let "$\vdash_{T_L}$" abbreviate "it is a theorem of $T_L$ that". One's very first thought in writing out "$t$ is a rigid designator in L" in terms of $T_L$ is to produce this piece of nonsense:

$$\exists x(\text{for all sentences } G(t) \text{ of L}, \vdash_{T_L} (T(G(t)) \equiv \langle x \rangle \text{ sats } G(\xi_1))).$$

This is nonsense for the same reason that

$$\exists x(\text{John said "I am going to } x\text{"})$$

is nonsense; the context governed by "$\vdash_{T_L}$" is of course quoted and not used.

One's second thought may be to move the existential quantifier inside "$\vdash_{T_L}$":

$$\text{for all sentences } G(t) \text{ of L}, \vdash_{T_L} \exists x(T(G(t)) \equiv \langle x \rangle \text{ sats } G(\xi_1)).$$

The difficulty with this formulation is that the objector can protest that, for classical formulations of the truth theory, the only reason that (for the case of first order extensional languages) proper names meet it and definite descriptions do not is that proper names that denote can be proved to denote in the truth theory, but "denoting" definite descriptions cannot. If we made the same assumptions about descriptions as we make about names in classical theory, then for such languages, definite descriptions meet the criterion in the case of such simple languages. A simple example brings home the general point. Suppose all descriptions were expanded out in Russell's fashion, so that for sentences in which the description had maximal scope, we had theorems of the form

$$T(G(\imath x)Fx) \equiv \exists x(\forall z(Fz \equiv z = x) \,\&\, Gx)$$

Then it is easily checked that if $T_L$ contains classical first-order logic,

$$\exists x(\forall z(Fz \equiv z = x)) \vdash_{T_L} \exists x(\forall z(Fz \equiv z = x) \,\&\, T(\underline{G(\imath x)Fx}) \equiv Gx)$$

So, granted the premiss $\exists x \forall z(Fz \equiv z = x)$, the analogue of which for proper names is a theorem of classical truth theories, definite descriptions even when handled in Russell's way would meet the criterion. There may of course be good reasons why the truth theory should exhibit the asymmetry that would legitimise this criterion; but if these reasons in any way tacitly appeal to the notion of rigid designation, we cannot appeal to them at *this* point.

We can coherently quantify into the context governed by "$\vdash_{T_L}$" if the quantifiers range over expressions. So, letting $\alpha$ be a variable over expressions, we might offer as a third attempt

$$\exists \alpha(\text{for all sentences } \underline{G(t)} \text{ of } L, \vdash_{T_L} T(\underline{G(t)}) \equiv \langle\alpha\rangle \text{ sats } \underline{G(\xi_1)}).$$

The problems with this are at least twofold. Provided $T_L$ is cast in a free logic, it is possible to write out a truth theory for a first-order extensional language that evaluates definite descriptions directly (as *terms*), and which contains as theorems sentences of the form

$$T(\underline{G(\imath x)Fx}) \equiv \langle(\imath x)Fx\rangle \text{ sats } \underline{G(\xi_1)}.$$

(Cf. in particular Grandy [1972], Scott [1967], and for discussion of some (but not all) philosophical issues surrounding direct evaluation of descriptions, Lambert and van Fraassen [1972].) The appropriateness of such truth theories in this particular area can be rejected only on some substantive grounds. The second problem concerns the natural way of writing out $T_L$ which would make this criterion plausible; that is, of applying Russell's theory of descriptions everywhere, so that definite descriptions simply do not occupy singular term position in the metalanguage of the truth theory, and so certainly will not feature as values of "$\alpha$" in the criterion in a fashion that would count definite descriptions as rigid designators. The trouble is that, even if we presume underspecification in the description adequately accommodated, Russell's theory seems to be unsatisfactory as an account of the *truth conditions* of sentences containing definite descriptions in some of their uses; for definite descriptions on some occasions of their use seem to function quite legitimately in the language as rigid designators. The matter is worth some discussion, *inter alia* simply because one's stand on it affects one's final criterion and one's attitude to direct evaluation in this field.

There is a relatively clear criterion for picking out historic uses of definite descriptions that are, as then used, rigid designators; if, in an utterance of "the F is G", what is strictly and literally said would equally and appropriately be said by an utterance of "*that F is G*", then "the F" functioned as a rigid designator. I shall label this an *entity-invoking* use of the description. The criterion is unsurprising; for when "that F is G" is appropriately uttered, there is an answer to the question "Which object is the one of which the speaker is saying that *it* is G?" The criterion, unlike some other accounts, is not stated in terms of factors that can bear at most upon the issue of what the speaker *meant* by uttering a sentence, as opposed to what he said; and the fact that there are such uses seems to be one way of making Strawson's original point against Russell's theory of descriptions.

Underspecification—the fact that in an utterance of "the F is G" there is not strictly just one object in the universe that is F, even relative to a fixing of the referents of demonstratives—is not sufficient and not necessary for entity-invoking uses of descriptions. If you and I visited the Casino at Monte Carlo yesterday, and saw a man break the bank, and on the same day saw a man break the bank at Nice, and it is common knowledge between us that this is so, then the description

"The man who broke the bank at Monte Carlo yesterday"

as it occurs in a particular utterance *today* of

"The man who broke the bank at Monte Carlo yesterday had holes in his shoes"

may well be satisfied by just one object in the universe; but it is here entity-invoking both intuitively and by our criterion. That underspecification is not sufficient is shown by the case of two school inspectors visiting an institution for the first time: one may say to the other, on the basis of the activities around him, "The headmaster doesn't have much control over the pupils." Here there is no object such that the inspector said of it that it doesn't have much control over its pupils. One cannot say the headmaster is such an object, since what this inspector (*actually*) said would be true even if someone else were headmaster. Moreover, the features that, as Strawson has taught us (Strawson [1964a]), are important *in concreto* in entity-invoking uses are absent from this example; the speaker does not invoke stretches of his audience's *identifying* knowledge.

The whole topic bristles with complexities we can only ignore here; but we have enough before us to conclude that any criterion of rigid designation stated in terms of truth theories must embrace whatever expressions in the input to the truth theory that are taken as representing entity-invoking uses of definite descriptions. The close tie between such uses of "the F" and that of "that F" supplies a hint of how to do this.

## III

It is not hard to expand our intuitive criterion of rigid designation to cover demonstratives, the paradigm rigid designators. Suppose person p utters a complete sentence A at time t. We form an expression $A\#$ thus: we omit all demonstratives, syntactically identified (I, that, this, that F, you, here, . . .) from A, replacing the i'th by the i'th placeholder $\xi_i$ until all are replaced. So

(that man stole the money from me)$\#$

is the expression

$\xi_1$ stole the money from $\xi_2$.

Let $d(p,t)$ be that sequence of objects whose i'th member is the object *demonstrated*[4] by p at the i'th occurrence of a demonstrative in the sentence p uttered at t if the demonstrative is non-complex; let it be the demonstrated F if the demonstrative is "this F" or "that F". (This is only rough.) So, if you say "that man stole the money from me" at noon today, then $d$ (you, noon today) is the sequence consisting of the man you demonstrate and you, in that order. Now, that demonstratives are rigid designators in a sense not very distant from that of our original criterion is brought out by this fact: we can say that if $d(p,t) = s$ then *whatever* sentence A p in fact uttered at t, the truth-condition of his utterance is that the sequence s (of *objects*) satisfy $A\#$. Whereas previously, our criterion started: there is an object $x$ such that for all sentences. . ., it now starts (in effect): for any given historic occasion of utterance, there

---

[4] Some important remarks on the relevant notion of demonstration are contained in Appendix VIII of Kaplan [1973].

are objects (there is a sequence of objects) such that for any sentence
... Thus the two crucial and related features of the old criterion, its
existential-universal character and the idea that the truth-conditions
for the (uttered) sentence concern certain objects directly, are retained.

By arguments essentially parallel to those given earlier, we would
not expect demonstratives to interact with modal and other operators to produce scope distinctions; and this does indeed seem to be
the case. The truth-conditions for an utterance of

It might have been the case that: that man is not bald.

are one and the same as those for

Concerning that man: he might not have been bald.

provided that the same man is demonstrated and the same time
indicated. The same applies to the following pairs:

In the past: I lived in Russia.
I am such that I: lived in Russia in the past.

It is possible that: it rained yesterday.
Yesterday is a day such that: it is possible that it rained on that
day.

Demonstratives, like other genuinely referential singular terms, are
essentially scopeless. It is interesting that even Frege conceded that
(certain) demonstratives are rigid designators in the sense of the
intuitive criterion; in "Der Gedanke" he remarks that the very
same *thought* can be expressed by uttering on Wednesday a sentence
containing "today" as by uttering a certain sentence on Thursday
containing the word "yesterday" (Frege [1918]). Here a particular
*day*, a certain Wednesday, directly enters the truth-conditions of the
uttered sentence.

It is illuminating, and important for our later development of a
criterion of rigid designation or genuine reference, to see how a
truth theory for a language containing demonstratives might be
written out. Let us consider a simple extensional first-order language
containing the demonstratives "I", "here", "now", and "that".
The following theory is meant to cover only those historic uses of
"that" unsupplemented by a substantival expression that can be
said to be used as rigid designators of an object on their occasion of

utterance. Not all unsupplemented uses of "that" are such uses, but some are: if we are to give the most plausible explanation of the soundness of the argument (on a particular occasion of utterance)

> That is the Radcliffe Camera
> The Radcliffe Camera was built in 1737
> ∴ That was built in 1737

the first premiss must be taken as an identity statement, and "that" as then used as referential. "$L(p,t,c)$" is to be read in the sequel as "c is the location of p at time t" and "$D(n,p,t,x)$" as "$x$ is an object demonstrated by p at the nth occurrence of a demonstrative in the sentence uttered by p at t".[5] "$\tau_1$", "$\tau_2$",...are variables over terms of the given language. We suppose given a finite stock of atomic predicates and relation-letters and some standard axioms about sequences of objects and about expressions. "$s_i(k)$" denotes the kth element of sequence $s_i$, and '$s_i \underset{k}{\approx} s_j$' is an abbreviation for the formula that states that sequences $s_i$ and $s_j$ differ in at most the kth place. "var(i)" denotes the ith variable; there are also place-holders $\xi_1, \xi_2, \ldots$ A# is defined as we defined it earlier, except that now we do not replace occurrences of "I", "now", and "here" by placeholders. For simplicity, we consider the case in which translation is homophonic.

We define the evaluation function (of terms with respect to sequences) thus:

$$(\text{D1}) \quad \varkappa(s_1, s_2, s_3, \tau_1) = \begin{cases} s_1(i) \text{ if } \tau_1 \text{ is the i'th variable} \\ s_2(i) \text{ ,, ,, ,, ,, ,, placeholder} \\ s_3(1) \text{ ,, ,, ,, } \underline{\text{I}} \\ s_3(2) \text{ ,, ,, ,, } \underline{\text{now}} \\ s_3(3) \text{ ,, ,, ,, } \underline{\text{here}}[6] \end{cases}$$

(The motivation for this will be given by the definition of "A is true as (potentially) uttered by p at t.") Finally we can give the satisfaction axioms:

$$\text{sats}(s_1, s_2, s_3, \underline{P_j^n \tau_1 \ldots \tau_n}) \equiv P_j^n \varkappa(s_1, s_2, s_3, \tau_1) \ldots \varkappa(s_1, s_2, s_3, \tau_n),$$
$$\text{for each atomic predicate } P_j^n;$$

[5] For full generality, this relation should have a sentential, and perhaps even a (token) event, argument; on the relevant notion of utterance, a man may utter two sentences at once. They might even be utterances of the same sentence type.

[6] With a little loss of perspicuity, the evaluation function could be compressed so as to have the usual two arguments; and similarly for the satisfaction relation.

$$\text{sats}(s_1,s_2,s_3,(A \vee B)) \equiv .\text{sats}(s_1,s_1,s_3, A) \vee \text{sats}(s_1,s_2,s_3,B)$$

$$\text{sats}(s_1,s_2,s_3,\overline{(\sim A)}) \equiv .\sim\text{sats}(s_1,s_2,s_3,A)$$

$$\text{sats}(s_1,s_2,s_3,\overline{\exists\text{var}(i)(A)}) \equiv .\exists s_4(s_4 \underset{i}{\approx} s_1 \ \& \ \text{sats}(s_4,s_2,s_3,A))$$

"A is true as (potentially) uttered by p at t", "T(A,p,t)", is given by the following definitional schema, for the case in which A contains n occurrences (n > 0) of "that":

(D2) $T(A,p,t) =_{\text{df}}.$

$$\exists x_{i_1}\ldots x_{i_{n+1}}\left[\bigwedge_{j=1}^{n} \forall z(D(j,p,t,z) \equiv z = x_{i_j}) \ \& \ L\ (p,t,x_{i_{n+1}})\right.$$

$$\left. \& \ \forall s_1(\text{sats}(s_1,\langle x_{i_1},\ldots,x_{i_n}\rangle,\langle p,t,x_{i_{n+1}}\rangle,A\#))\right]$$

In the case in which A contains no indexicals at all, we set

$$T(A,p,t) =_{\text{df}}. \forall s_1(\text{sats}(s_1,\langle-\rangle,\langle-\rangle,A))$$

in classical fashion; and the case in which A contains no occurrences of "that" but some of "I", "here", or "now" is equally straight-forward.

It is an illusion to think that we could accommodate singular terms of the form "that F" (where $\overline{(\text{that } x)\ldots x\ldots}$ is a singular term forming operator on one-place predicables) by simply altering the relevant occurrences of "$\forall z(D(j,p,t,z) \equiv z = x_{i_j})$" in this defini-tion of truth to a formula having the force of: $x_{i_j}$ is the unique thing that is both demonstrated and satisfies $F(\xi_1)$. For this involves the suspect view that "is the demonstrated $\overline{F}$" splits up logically into "is uniquely both demonstrated and an F". Whatever the correct analysis of the notion of demonstration, there is every reason to think that the role of F in "that F" in fixing the demonstrated object is more intimate than that of just adding an extra condition which picks out one of a number of demonstrated objects. In the general case of utterances of sentences of the form $\overline{G(\text{that } F)}$, there is no such "first-stage" initial fixing of a *number* of objects.

The given truth theory largely implements our naïve exposition of the truth-conditions of sentences containing indexicals. A simple example shows its operation. Suppose a person $p_0$ located at $c_0$ at time $t_0$ then utters this sentence of the language for which the truth definition is given:

$$\exists z(Bz \ \& \ N(I,z,\text{now}) \ \& \ W(z,\text{that},\text{now}))$$

or, as we would say, "I am now north of some building which is west of that"; and suppose the object $p_0$ demonstrates while uttering "that" at this time is $z$. Given as hypotheses that these are the circumstances of the utterance, we can conclude in the truth theory from definition (D2) that the utterance is true iff

$$\forall s_1(\text{sats}(s_1,\langle z\rangle,\langle p_0,t_0,c_0\rangle),\exists z(Bz \ \& \ N(I,z,\text{now}) \ \& \ W(z,\xi_1,\text{now})))$$

Working through the clauses of the truth definition in the usual way, we conclude that the last displayed sentence is equivalent to

$$\forall s_1\exists s_2(s_2 \underset{3}{\approx} s_1 \ \& \ Bs_2(3) \ \& \ N(p_0,s_2(3),t_0) \ \& \ W(s_2(3),t_0))$$

and with the help of the theory of sequences this in turn reduces to

$$\exists x(Bx \ \& \ N(p_0,x,t_0) \ \& \ W(x,z,t_0))$$

This is of course just the desired truth-condition.

With such a treatment of demonstratives in the truth theory, it seems appropriate to suggest that entity-invoking (historic) uses of "the F" be treated at the level of the input to the theory of truth as occurrences of "that F", the truth of utterances so employing the F requiring the existence of a unique demonstrated F (with respect to that occurrence of "the F"); while, modulo the problems of underspecification, those historic uses that are not entity-invoking be treated by Russell's theory of descriptions. I shall presume, in the development of a criterion of rigid designation, that some such divided treatment is correct.

Pursuing this policy leaves no role for direct evaluation of definite descriptions, even in relation to the entity-invoking uses. But there seems to be the following argument against so using it, in any case.

It is a constraint on any truth theory that, if $\alpha$ is the term that is used to represent entity-invoking uses of "the F", it should be provable in the truth theory (without additional hypotheses) that

$$\underline{T(G(\alpha),p,t)} \supset \underline{T(\exists y G(y),p,t)}$$

for some variable $y$ not occurring in $\underline{G(\ )}$. Pretheoretically, the reason for the constraint is clear: if "the F" is used entity-invokingly, then if the utterance is true, there is an object $x$ such that the truth-condition for that utterance is that $x$ meet condition $G(\ )$; and so if it *is* true, $x$ will meet condition $G(\ )$. Thus $\exists y G(y)$ will be true.

The simple truth theory given above meets this constraint with respect to demonstratives. It follows in fact from (D2) plus the satisfaction axioms that

$$T(\underline{G(that)},p,t) \supset T(\underline{\exists yG(y)},p,t)$$

for arbitrary one-place predicables G and F.

Let us consider, in the homophonic case, what would result if this constraint were fulfilled in a theory that evaluated entity-invoking uses of definite descriptions directly, as terms. To give such a theory a run for its money, we must suppose it employs a free logic in the metalanguage. For if it did not, we would have as a theorem

$$T(\underline{G(\imath x)Fx},p,t) \equiv G(\imath x)Fx$$

where F and G are one-place predicables free of indexicals; hence we would also have as a theorem

$$\exists y(T(\underline{G(\imath x)Fx},p,t) \equiv G(y))$$

But this last "theorem" is not even *true*; a quick way to see this is to observe that if everything is G and nothing is F, it would follow that a (putatively) entity-invoking utterance of "the F is G" is true. So let us grant the use of free logic.

Such a theory will contain as theorems

$$T(\underline{G(\imath x)Fx},p,t) \equiv G(\imath x)Fx$$

and

$$T(\underline{\exists xGx},p,t) \equiv \exists xGx$$

Thus if we fulfilled our constraint by having as a theorem

$$T(\underline{G(\imath x)Fx},p,t) \supset T(\underline{\exists xGx},p,t)$$

we would also have as a theorem

$$G(\imath x)Fx \supset \exists xGx$$

given only that the theory contained the weaker parts of the sentential calculus. But this effectively reinstates existential generalisation; even if there is no such rule of inference in the theory, we can secure the effect of any given application by using other theorems and modus ponens. By the observations of the preceding paragraph, we find ourselves again with the unacceptable theorem

$\exists y(\text{T}(\underline{\text{G}(\imath x)\text{F}x},\text{p},\text{t}) \equiv \text{G}y).^{7}$

This objection is not answered by having as theorems sentences of the form

$$\exists y(y = (\imath x)\text{F}x) \supset (\text{T}(\underline{\text{G}(\imath x)\text{F}x},\text{p},\text{t}) \equiv \text{G}(\imath x)\text{F}x)$$

for again from this would follow in the truth theory

$$\exists z[\exists y(y = z) \supset (\text{T}(\underline{\text{G}(\imath x)\text{F}x},\text{p},\text{t}) \equiv \text{G}z)]$$

and since it is a theorem of classical and free logic that

$$\exists z[\exists y(y = z) \supset \text{A}(z)] \equiv \exists z\text{A}(z)$$

the last but one displayed sentence implies in the truth theory the already rejected

$$\exists z(\text{T}(\underline{\text{G}(\imath x)\text{F}x},\text{p},\text{t}) \equiv \text{G}z).$$

This argument might be rejected on the ground that we had shown only that "$\text{G}\imath x(\text{F}x) \supset \exists x\text{G}x$" is a theorem of such theories for predicables not containing semantical vocabulary used to implicitly define truth for the object language. But other questions crowd in if the argument is blocked this way. Since we are concerned with the homophonic case, terms of the form $(\imath x)\text{F}x$ are as much entity-invoking in the metalanguage as the object language; how then can "$\exists x\text{G}x$" fail to follow from "$\text{G}(\imath x)\text{F}x$" for an *arbitrary* predicable G? And how can the truth theory fail to include some theorems that are, at very least, not true, viz. any theorem of the form $\text{G}(\imath x)\text{F}x$, where nothing is in fact F? If the theory is adequate only if we restrict the range of predicables for which

$$\text{G}(\imath x)\text{F}x \supset \exists x\text{G}x$$

is provable in the theory, why does this not provide an objection to that treatment if no non-circular reason can be given for the restriction?

I conclude, though tentatively—for there may be technically ingenious ways of fulfilling these constraints—that any direct-evaluation treatment of entity-invoking uses of descriptions is less satisfactory than their partial assimilation to demonstratives proposed above. This being so, the way is now open to a rather different

---

[7] Reservations about this step will be given later.

ontologically acceptable criterion of rigid designation based on the theory of truth. We again abstract from ambiguity, but not now from indexicality:

> truth theory T treats expression $\alpha$ of language L as a rigid designator iff for any sentence $G(\alpha)$ of L containing $\alpha$, given as premisses specifications of the objects demonstrated by person $p$ at time t, then: in any maximally short derivation in T from those premisses of a target biconditional of the form
>
> $$T(\underline{G(\alpha),p,t}) \equiv A,$$
>
> where A does not contain *sats*, the evaluation function of T is applied to some expression $e$ (e.g. $\alpha$ itself or a placeholder) which occupies the place of this occurrence of $\alpha$ via the application of the satisfaction axiom for the atomic predicate in which the given occurrence of $\alpha$ features as argument in the original sentence $G(\alpha)$; where the evaluation is such that *either* given p,t, and the fixing of the indexical referents, there is a sequence of objects $s_0$ such that evaluation of $e$ only with respect to $s_0$ occurs in maximally short derivations, *or* $e$ is such that the result of evaluating it with respect to *any* sequence of objects is always the same.

(Variables fail the hurdles in the last two clauses of this rough criterion.) Proper names, demonstratives, and correspondingly entity-invoking uses of definite descriptions will all be treated as rigid designators by any adequate truth theory for their language: such has been our argument so far. What a rigid designator $t$ is a rigid designator of, relative to adequate truth theory T, will be further relative to an occasion of utterance, but we have the resources for defining the notion: for it will be the object which is the result of the evaluation of any expression functioning in relation to $t$ as $e$ does to $\alpha$ in the above criterion, this evaluation occurring in a maximally short derivation in T of a target biconditional giving the truth-conditions of the uttered sentence, from premisses specifying the demonstrated objects on that occasion of utterance.

I should note two points. First, the intended account of a truth theory T treating an expression as a rigid designator makes use of denotation relations for singular terms of the *metalanguage* of T: for the only sort of "evaluation" that literally takes place in a truth theory is that of writing function *symbols* next to other symbols. Second, the plausibility of the whole account rests upon a certain conception of singular term position; for I would say about genuine singular terms what Quine so clearly states about names:

"What distinguishes a name is that it can stand coherently in the place of a variable, in predication, and will yield true results when used to instantiate true universal quantifications."

(Quine [1970c])

It is in a clear sense true to say that our final criterion, though demarcating the right class of expressions, and for the right reasons, presupposes that the argument over whether any *particular* expression is a rigid designator will come over how we are to treat it in the regimented language that we feed into an adequate truth theory. But it seems to me that this is, or should be, the actual situation.

## IV

It may be objected that if proper names were rigid designators on even our intuitive criterion of rigid designation, non-relational readings of sentences in which a proper name falls within the scope of a propositional attitude verb would be impossible. For if proper names are rigid designators on that criterion, then the truth-condition for

John believes that Cicero was bald

is that

⟨Cicero⟩ satisfies "John believes $\xi_1$ was bald";

and that simply *is* the relational reading of that sentence.

My response is to insist that our criterion be applied not to surface structure sentences, but to those that are the input to the theory of truth for a language; and then to follow Davidson (Davidson [1968]) in holding that "John believes that Cicero was bald" is to be regimented as two sentences, the first, on an occasion of utterance, containing a demonstrative reference ("that") to an utterance of the second. Our problem now dissolves; "Cicero" occurs only in the sentence

Cicero was bald.

We are committed to saying that the truth-condition for *this* sentence is that Cicero satisfy $\underline{\xi_1 \text{ was bald}}$, but that is fine.

We may feel reassured that this is somewhere near the truth by the observation that if *n* and *m* are proper names, for the non-relational reading it is a *sufficient* condition for the move from "John believes that G($n$)" and "$n = m$" to "John believes that G($m$)" be to a *non sequitur* that $n$ and $m$ be distinct *expressions*. But matters are slightly more complex than this happy confirmation suggests.

The problem is that if the semantic contribution of a proper name $n$ to the truth-conditions of G($n$) is simply to fix an object $x$ such that the truth-condition for G($n$) is that $\langle x \rangle$ satisfy $\overline{G(\xi_1)}$, then if proper names $m$ and $n$ denote the same object, G($n$) and $\overline{G(m)}$ have identical truth-conditions; how then can a pair of such sentences fail to *samesay*? But since fuller analysis of the "believes" that occurs in

John believes that. Cicero was bald

must make reference to the samesaying relations of the demonstrated utterance (and perhaps make reference *only* to that aspect of the utterance), and since an utterance of "Tully is bald" will samesay with an utterance of "Cicero is bald", the objection arises that on this account it is hard to see how "John believes that Cicero was bald" could be true without "John believes that Tully was bald" also being true.

It is important that this objection should have no tendency to incline one to assign senses, modes of presentation, or anything else to names to explain the phenomenon it adduces: for it remains, as noted, a sufficient condition for *non sequitur* that the *names* used in the report of the propositional attitude be distinct.

A pragmatic explanation may be in order. If we are to follow the conversational policy of being maximally informative on relevant matters, when reporting the beliefs (desires, hopes,...) of a being who speaks the language we ourselves speak, we should actually use in our report of the belief a name the believer might use in expressing it; so we cannot expect what is conversationally implicated to be preserved under substitution of a co-denoting proper name, and this might be held to explain the appearance of *non sequitur*. It might seem to support this explanation that we are able to imagine nothing that would make it appropriate to report in English a native, with whom we share no language nor even proper names with a common history, as believing that G($n$) but not G($m$), where $n$ and $m$ are distinct co-denoting proper names; but of course this fact, if it is a fact, is also explained on a view which makes the putative believer's relation to the *name* "Cicero" feature in the truth-conditions of

John believes that Cicero was bald

read non-relationally. Moreover, in a sense the pragmatic explanation does not explain but explains away the original datum; for
according to it, strictly speaking, in the matter of what is *said* as
opposed to what is conversationally implicated, there are no such
non-relational propositional attitude sentences containing proper
names after all.

We need not choose here between the pragmatic account and
some different story altogether which brings "Cicero" rather than
Cicero into the truth-conditions of the problem sentences. For in the
case of any latter such theory, which will of course deny that if
utterances $x$ and $y$ samesay, $\langle x \rangle$ satisfies the Davidsonian predicate
John believes $\xi$ iff $\langle y \rangle$ does, "Cicero" will be mentioned and not,
as a *component* of the relevant sentence, used in the regimented sentences that are the input to the truth theory. In saying this I have
in mind a theory of quotation endorsed by Davidson (in his third
John Locke lecture at Oxford in 1970) according to which quotation
marks themselves have a demonstrative force akin to that of:

the expression with the shape here pictured.

On this theory, one may say that the occurrence of "slowly" within
quotation marks in the sentence

"slowly" is an English adverb

contributes to what is strictly and literally said in an utterance of that
sentence; but it does so by being the referent of a demonstrative, not
by occurring as a truth-significant part of the corresponding regimented sentence. So again we have no counter-example to the
thesis that proper names are rigid designators.

We have in this reply an instance of a general strategy that it is
natural for the defender of the view that names are rigid designators
to adopt; that is, of explaining any apparent difference in truth-
conditions of surface structure sentences differing only in the occurrences of distinct proper names $\alpha$ and $\beta$, where $\alpha$ and $\beta$ denote
the same object, by the difference between the *expressions* $\alpha$ and $\beta$
themselves.

## V

There are, among others, three issues each worthy of extended
separate treatment that are closely connected with the question of

whether proper names are rigid designators in our sense; I will briefly comment on positions on them that support or enlarge the claims so far made.

(i) There is the question of positive and negative existentials containing proper names. It is important to see that what has been claimed *already* implies that a general uniformity of treatment of both denoting and non-denoting names in both existentials and other contexts is impossible. For while the truth-condition of

Uranus has a satellite

is that a certain object have a satellite, there is no object, actual or possible, such that one can reasonably claim that the truth-condition of

Vulcan does not exist

is that that object satisfy "$\xi$ does not exist". Yet "Vulcan does not exist" is a *true* sentence. The impossibility of uniformity is especially clear when we ask how to treat negative existentials containing denoting names. If we treat

Uranus does not exist

along the lines of "Vulcan does not exist" we make the contribution of the denoting name "Uranus" differ with the context in which it occurs; but if on the other hand we assimilate it to contexts like "$\xi$ has a satellite", we have to say that the truth-conditions of

$\alpha$ does not exist

vary with whether $\alpha$ is a denoting name or not. So, if we accept the earlier arguments, uniformity is a chimaera, and non-uniformity is no objection to a theory of these contexts.

If we accept that the name "Uranus" is used and not mentioned in a regimented version of "Uranus does not exist", then it follows from our criterion and the assumption that "Uranus" is a rigid designator that the truth-condition for this negative existential is that a certain object not exist; and correspondingly for "Uranus exists". It is sometimes thought that this makes all such assertions of existence pleonastic, and such denials self-contradictory. Now it is certainly true that if, as it is, "Uranus" is a genuine singular term, on which existential generalisation is valid, we can prove in first-order classical logic that Uranus exists, and also that the literally self-contradictory

> there exists an object such that it does not exist,

i.e. $\exists x \sim y(\exists y = x)$, follows from "Uranus does not exist". But this does not show that an utterance of "Uranus exists" to be pleonastic in the sense that one who utters or hears it *knows* that the utterer is repeating himself (or, more carefully, saying something that, properly regimented, is derivable in first order logic); all we have is that *if* a man knows the logical form of the sentence, then he knows that it is true (or false in the negative case). But in situations where existentials are of interest to us, the antecedent of this conditional is untrue. Why should we not say that there are some sentences such that only when we know whether the names in them denote do we know their logical form? (One has, however, to agree that these considerations do show that the rule of Necessitation, if ⊢A then ⊢□A, needs restriction in any system we use for regimenting these existentials; for it would take us to the false $\Box\exists x\ (x = \text{Uranus})$ as a theorem from $\vdash\exists x(x = \text{Uranus})$.)

This argument against an argument is essentially permissive: it *allows* us to say that in "Uranus exists" we have a first level predication of an object, but we need further reasons actually to take that step. Some strong reasons can be found in terms of the occurrence of existentials, positive and negative, inside other operators. In

> $\Diamond\sim(\text{E!}(\text{Uranus}))$

or

> $(\lambda x . \Diamond \sim\text{E!}x)\text{Uranus}$

i.e. "Uranus might not have existed", we seem to have a statement that says of an object that it is possible that *it* does not exist; existential generalisation holds; and the context is transparent when substitution is properly carried out: if Hesperus might not have existed, and Phosphorus is the very same object as Hesperus, Phosphorus might not have existed. For the case of the positive existential, similar arguments can be applied to

> $\sim\Box(\text{E!}(\text{Uranus}))$.

There is no commitment here to any particular account of negative or positive existentials containing *non*-denoting names; on these I shall make only the remark that every adequately precise account of the matter I have seen or constructed has been open to more or less obvious objections.

(ii) The objects which the truth-conditions of sentences containing ordinary proper names concern are genuine continuant particulars; they are objects of which it is true to say that they can have a property at one time and, remaining one and the same object, lack it at another. Now Dummett, among others, has claimed that "any verbal specification [of the sense of a proper name]...must... include a stipulation of the criterion of identity for the object which is the referent of the name". (Dummett [1973] p. 545.) Will this thought, if correct, prompt us to assign something else besides an object to a name in giving its semantic role in a language?

Here we must distinguish sharply between these two claims:

(a) for every object, there is an associated criterion of identity
(b) when specifying the referent of a proper name, we must actually specify a criterion of identity (perhaps in the form of a sortal predicate) for the referent of the name.

(a) seems undeniable; to say it is to say that for every object, there is some biconditional of the form

$$x = y \text{ iff } \phi(x, y)$$

whose variables range over that object, that does not contain the identity sign on its right-hand side, that is a necessary (which is not to say *a priori*) truth, and that guarantees that whatever is true of $x$ is so of $y$ (and conversely).[8] But (a) does not commit us to (b); on the contrary. The thought that is commonly offered in support of (b) is that if we fix the referent of the name $\alpha$ by some complex description "the F", one will not thereby have specified what object one refers to in using $\alpha$ in a sentence with a time reference other than that to which the description F relates. This is a confusion. Either the predicable $F(\xi_1)$ is satisfied by only one object, or it is not. If it is, the instruction "trace *that object* through space and time" is perfectly intelligible, even if "the concept under which" it is to be traced (as David Wiggins would say) can only be discovered by investigating the world to discover what kind of object it is that uniquely satisfies $F(\xi_1)$. If $F(\xi_1)$ is not uniquely satisfied, then the referent-fixing procedure in this case was *already* inadequate, and the absence of a specification of a criterion of identity is not to the point.

---

[8] For examples of such criteria, see for the case of material objects, Wiggins [1968], and for one account for the case of events, Davidson [1969].

(iii) We are naturally driven to enquire whether there is any close connexion between the utility we derive from having proper names in our language and the fact that proper names are rigid designators. The conditions under which we may expect to find that a proper name for a spatio-temporal particular has useful currency in a group have been investigated by Strawson;[9] he reaches the conclusion that these conditions are that that group has frequent need to refer to that particular, in virtue of its being that particular (as opposed to a need based on the fact that it always happened to satisfy a description of interest), and finally that the group has no short description of the particular always available or natural to all the members of the group. The name will be useful, approximately, just because it preserves the same "referential force" through its referent's changes of relations to other things and because it has the same referential force for speakers who encounter the referent in different connections.

It is hardly to be conceived that any expression that meets these needs fails to be a rigid designator on our intuitive criterion; for any departure from the paradigm that criterion represents is a departure from the idea that the truth (fulfilment, ...) conditions for a sentence $F(\alpha)$ containing the name $\alpha$ require a certain object to be $F( )$. In so far as there is a departure, the needs are not being fulfilled in the best possible way, for a departure involves the truth-conditions for some sentence $G(\alpha)$ not simply being a matter of the object which the need concerns being $G( )$. But we can say more than this.

Could any other sort of rigid designator, of the kinds we currently possess, fulfil these needs? Demonstratives are no help if the object cannot be relied upon to be literally present, or if the speaker cannot rely upon his audience to have the sort of knowledge enabling him to work out the speaker's referent in a less direct use of "that F", for some F; similar remarks apply to entity-invoking uses of "the F", and Strawson's plausible conditions seem designed to ensure that speakers in a group where there is such a need cannot rely on such factors. I conclude that only rigid designators in our sense can meet the needs Strawson's conditions express, and that among rigid designators, only proper names can meet them in a way that allows us to do what we wish to with language with maximum efficiency.

[9] In a seminar at Oxford in 1973.

# 5

## Conversational implicatures

### RALPH C. S. WALKER

In a recent article, L. J. Cohen criticises a theory about the logical particles "if...then...", "or", "and", and "not" as they occur in ordinary language (Cohen [1971]). This theory he calls the Conversationalist Hypothesis and ascribes—though with important reservations—to Grice. It is an application of the notion of a conversational implicature, which Grice put forward in his article "The Causal Theory of Perception" (Grice [1961]) and developed in his William James lectures.[1] The theory maintains that the sense or meaning of these particles is truth-functional, the appearance that it is not being due to our mistaking conversational presumptions for features of their meaning, these presumptions being generated by the conversational conditions under which these words are used. It is only with very serious reservations that this theory can be ascribed to Grice, however; firstly, because he puts the theory forward only very tentatively, and produces what he takes to be a substantial objection to it; secondly, because in the lectures his principal concern is with indicative conditionals—he does not try to establish the truth-functionality of "if...then..." in subjunctive conditionals, and treats of the other connectives only incidentally. Cohen is attracted to the Conversationalist Hypothesis, but feels himself bound to reject it in favour of what he calls the Semantical Hypothesis. This does not rely on conversational presumptions (or not in the same way), holding instead that the logical particles in question are non-truth-functional in sense. It admits that there are occasions when they do seem to work truth-functionally, but accounts for these by saying that on certain occasions the context may indicate

---

[1] At Harvard in 1968. These lectures are unfortunately not yet published, but some of the content may be gathered from the discussions by Cohen [1971] and by J. L. Mackie [1973] pp. 74–81.

that some elements of the sense of an expression are to be deleted.[2]

The Conversationalist Hypothesis and the Semantical Hypothesis thus agree in each ascribing a single sense to (for example) the "if... then..." of ordinary language. They differ in that on the Conversationalist view this sense is the logically weak one of material implication, while on the Semantical view it is some stronger and non-truth-functional kind of implication. Each theory explains apparent divergences from the standard sense by an appeal to contextual considerations, and each theory takes it as a virtue that it can thereby avoid "multiplying senses beyond necessity" (Cohen [1971] p. 46, quoting Grice). They are both, therefore, to be contrasted with a third theory, which would hold that such expressions do have more than one sense: that the "if...then..." of ordinary language is ambiguous, sometimes expressing material implication and sometimes expressing something stronger. On this third view it is doubtless contextual considerations which enable us to determine with what sense the words are being used on a particular occasion, but their role is confined to that.

What I want to discuss is the difference between these three theories, and how we can decide between them. This seems to me an interesting question, not only because one would like to know what the truth is about the logical particles of natural language, but also because an investigation of the differences between these theories promises to cast some light on the notions of sense and of a conversational implicature. This latter notion looks likely to be of enormous value in the resolution of philosophical disputes, so the more light that is thrown on it the better.

I

To discover the difference between the Conversationalist Hypothesis and the Semantical Hypothesis, the obvious place to look is of course Cohen's article. Cohen believes that the Conversationalist Hypothesis does not work, and he tries to show this. What he does is to consider in turn ordinary-language examples involving "not", "and", "if...then...", and "either...or...", arguing in each case

---

[2] For Cohen as for Grice, both the linguistic context of an expression—the context created by the other words and sentences around it—and the non-linguistic context of utterance are to be taken into account. He mentions the former on p. 56; the latter on p. 60.

that what we normally understand by these examples could not be generated by conversational means from the truth-functional assertions which, on the Conversationalist view, constitute their actual content. What are "conversational means"? The Conversationalist Hypothesis relies on a general principle, due to Grice, which participants in a conversation are normally expected to observe; this is (roughly) "Make your conversational contribution such as is required, at the stage at which it occurs, by the accepted purpose or direction of the talk-exchange in which you are engaged" (Cohen [1971] p. 53, again quoting Grice). We assume a speaker to be observing this principle, and he knows that we as hearers will assume this; he is therefore able to communicate more to us than the strict sense of his utterance. To take an example which Cohen accepts as "relatively uncontroversial" ([1971], p. 56), if one professor is asked his opinion of another and replies "He is a very competent bicyclist", he thereby communicates—"conversationally implicates"—his low opinion of his colleague's academic capacity, though that is no part of what his sentence means. For if he had been able to express a charitable view of the other's competence in matters with which the questioner may be presumed to have been chiefly concerned, then by Grice's principle he ought to have done so—and we may therefore take it that he has no such charitable opinion. We may take it, also, that he expects us to reason in this way and so intends to convey his poor opinion to us. In this he is relying on a presumption, and the presumption can be defeated; he can defeat it by adding that his colleague is a brilliant academic as well—thereby, as Grice would say, cancelling the conversational implicature that he is not. Much if not all of what is conveyed by hint or suggestion relies in this way on the general principle just given, which Grice calls the Co-operative Principle, and can thus be said to be conversationally implicated. Metaphors also rely upon the same device: it is clear from the context that the speaker does not intend what he says to be taken literally, so that we are led to adopt some more appropriate alternative interpretation. In each case the speaker gets across more than he actually says by relying on the audience's expectation that he is adhering to the Co-operative Principle: for this expectation leads them, when faced with an utterance *prima facie* in violation of that principle, to interpret it if possible in such a way as to bring it into accord with the principle. to give it point in the conversation.

Grice also mentions certain more specific conversational maxims, such as "Make your contribution as informative as is required", "Don't say what you believe to be false", "Don't say what you lack evidence for", "Be relevant", "Avoid obscurity, ambiguity or unnecessary prolixity", and "Be orderly" (Cohen [1971] p. 53). But these are not independent of the general Co-operative Principle; in fact, so far as one is normally entitled to assume that a speaker will observe them, it seems to be because obedience to them is required by the general principle.

Conversational implicatures, then, are generated by the presumption we all share that the speaker is conforming to the Co-operative Principle. Besides conversational implicatures Grice thinks it is also possible for an utterance to carry conventional implicatures which, while not dependent on the Co-operative Principle, are at the same time not strictly part of the propositional content, the sense and reference, of what is said.[3] "$p$ but $q$" and "$p$ therefore $q$" provide examples: the contrast or connectedness between $p$ and $q$ does not belong to the sense of what is said, according to Grice, but is conventionally implicated. At present, however, the notion of a conventional implicature need not concern us; nor need the possibility, for which Grice also allows, that there may be implicatures of other types still. It is with conversational implicatures that the Conversationalist Hypothesis is concerned. It tries to explain why we understand what we do by utterances containing the logical particles, by saying that although their sense is truth-functional they may conversationally implicate very much more than they strictly say. Cohen maintains that this hypothesis does not work. But it seems to me that he does not succeed in showing this, mainly because his arguments presuppose that the conversationalist holds a principle to which in fact he could not possibly subscribe.

Let us consider "and" first. According to the conversationalist account "and" is always truth-functional in sense, though on occasion a speaker may convey more by an utterance of the form "$p$ and $q$" than he could by its propositional content alone. The conversational maxim "Be relevant" leads us to expect the two clauses to have some bearing on one another; so that by saying "The king came forward and the shouting ceased" one can convey that the two events were connected. Again, the general expectation that the

---

[3] Instead of talking about sense or propositional content Grice talks about what is *said*, in a special sense of "said".

speaker will obey the conversational maxim "Be orderly" enables him to convey, in cases like "The old king died of a heart attack and a republic was declared", which of the two events happened first.[4] However, Cohen considers that the conversationalist account cannot handle an utterance like the assertion in a normal context of

(1) If the old king has died of a heart attack and a republic has been declared, then Tom will be quite content.

For here it seems that the "and" in the antecedent cannot be truth-functional: the truth of the conditional may depend on the order of the events related in the antecedent. "Tom might not be at all content," Cohen points out, "if a republic had been declared first and then the old king died of a heart attack." (Cohen [1971] p. 58.)

The conversationalist has a reply to this. He can start with something Cohen does not dispute: it is by no means *always* the case that an ordinary-language assertion of the form "If *p* and *q*, then *r*" conveys that *p* and *q* are related in this or any other way. Indeed, there are circumstances in which even an utterance of (1) would carry no such suggestion: for instance, if the speaker goes on to add (or if it is already clear from the context) that the old king was king of Prussia, that the country declared a republic was Burgundy, and that no other connection was intended than that these occurrences were amongst the things which would not dissatisfy Tom. In the case of the more normal assertion of (1), then, the relevance of the temporal order must be indicated contextually; and it is communicated, on the conversationalist view, through the presumption of obedience to the Co-operative Principle. Cohen does not claim to have any decisive objection to that part of the conversationalist thesis which says that by uttering "The old king has died of a heart attack and a republic has been declared" in fairly normal circumstances we conversationally implicate that the death of the old king happened first (Cohen [1971] pp. 55–7). And if this be granted, it would seem highly natural that the same assumption about ordering

---

[4] An alternative way of following this maxim would of course have been to obey a convention to the effect that of two events thus mentioned by conjoined clauses the later should always be mentioned *first*. But this would be an unnatural order, which is why it would require a special convention; in the absence of such a rule the speaker may be assumed to follow the order which is most natural to us (and this is the order he will expect to be assumed to follow). Provided, of course, there is some reason to suppose he *knows* the order; if there is not the situation gives rise to no implicatures.

should carry over to the case where this sentence appears not by itself but as the antecedent of a conditional; so natural, indeed, that to ignore it and reverse the order of clauses would be very misleading, and would thus violate the Co-operative Principle by serving badly the purposes of the talk-exchange. There is no reason why the antecedent of a conditional should not carry implicatures of its own, or at any rate contribute to the implicatures of the whole conditional. And it would be hard to deny that in the normal conversational context of (1) the order of the events is as important to the purposes of the talk-exchange as it is when "The old king has died of a heart attack and a republic has been declared" is asserted by itself.

Cohen recognises that the conversationalist might make a move of this sort. He replies that if he does he is conceding that the "if... then..." in (1) cannot be construed truth-functionally. For the truth-value of the conditional is now being said to depend not just on the truth-values of antecedent and consequent, but on something else: the order of the events mentioned in the antecedent (Cohen [1971] p. 58). At this point there are two strategies open to the conversationalist. He might insist that despite all appearances the truth-value, though not the acceptability, of (1) must be the same as that of

(2) If a republic has been declared and the old king has died of a heart attack, then Tom will be quite content;

the truth-value of the whole conditional depends solely on the truth-values of the three clauses involved, though obviously (2) will be seriously misleading and inappropriate where (1) is appropriate. If he takes this line he will cut himself off from the ordinary everyday ascriptions of truth and falsity made by people without an axe to grind. Alternatively, he might avoid doing this by conceding that the order of events does make a difference to the truth-value; but then add that it need be no part of his claim that it should not.

It may seem obvious that this second strategy is not available to the conversationalist; for after all he is trying to maintain that "and" and "if" are truth-functional. How can they be truth-functional unless, when they occur as principal connectives in complex utterances, the truth-values of these are completely determined by the truth-values of their sentential constituents? But this objection is not well taken. The hypothesis is that the *sense* of these expressions is truth-functional, not that what they serve to convey on a particular occasion of utterance is; that, indeed, can be freely admitted not to be. So what the hypothesis requires is that the truth-values of the complex utterances *would* be completely determined by the truth-values of the component sentences *if* conversational conditions could be abstracted from: *if* we had to deal with propositional content, sense and reference, and cannot depend in any way on the con-that the truth-value of an utterance must be fully determined by its sense and its reference, and cannot depend in any way on the conversational conditions in which it is uttered; his argument against the Conversationalist Hypothesis depends on the assumption that moves like this second strategy are not open to his opponent. But by calling these particles truth-functional the conversationalist does not wish to claim that what we should normally, in everyday talk, think of as the truth-value of the complex utterance is determined truth-functionally by the truth-values we should ordinarily and naturally assign to the constituent sentences. If he were to claim this the Conversationalist Hypothesis would be so wildly implausible as not to require the lengthy treatment given to it by Cohen; for it is quite obviously *false*, in any normal acceptation, that if I stop writing this essay now the Queen will abdicate, though on a narrowly truth-functional account it would be true. But on the contrary the conversationalist claims that "and", "if...then...", and so on do *not* function in this way in ordinary conversation, and he offers a reason why they do not—a reason which involves saying that they have a truth-functional *sense* on which conversational conditions operate.

By saying this he commits himself to talking about the truth-value an utterance would have if its sense and reference alone were considered, and conversational conditions left aside. Philosophers have sometimes found it convenient to think of this as the truth-value the utterance really has; and so in effect to adopt the first strategy mentioned above. There is no harm in this, so long as one recognises that the ascriptions of truth-value one now makes for technical reasons are liable to diverge substantially from those that people ordinarily and unreflectively make. It is not necessary to hold that either side is using "true" and "false" wrongly in these divergent cases, or to hold that different senses of these words are involved; rather one must recognise that ascriptions of truth and falsity are themselves context-relative and can be made for different purposes.

As Austin points out, whether one says that "France is hexagonal" is true will depend on what one's purpose is: "It is good enough for a top-ranking general, perhaps, but not for a geographer." (Austin [1962] p. 142.) "It is true (false) that *p*" carries its own implicatures, and can be more or less appropriate in a context, just as "*p*" or "Not-*p*" can. Normally our interests are such that the order of clauses in the antecedent is crucial to our understanding of what is conveyed by a remark like (1), and so we are not prepared to call (1) false if the republic is declared first and Tom is far from pleased.

The extent to which we are prepared to take into account what a speaker conveys conversationally, as well as the sense and reference of his remarks, in determining the truth-value of what he says, is not a question to which there is any sharp answer: it will depend very much on the context. No doubt there are extremes beyond which we will not go; we will not describe as *false* the professor's statement that his colleague was a competent bicyclist, however much it may have been designed to induce a false belief about the man's other abilities, provided he can indeed bicycle satisfactorily. This is because it seems likely that the professor chose this form of words in order to try and convey his message without being held committed to it: our inclination to let truth depend on what is implicated varies with the likelihood that the speaker will want to be committed to it. But there is an area of shading. Does one speak falsely if one calls Frege the father of modern logic, or describes General Amin's hands as bloodstained? Or if, in reply to someone who defends the use of napalm by saying that war is war, one says "It needn't be"? What we say will depend on how exacting, how pedestrian the context is. In such cases we find it natural to indicate the more pedestrian answer by saying that of course it is not *literally* true that logic has a father or that the General has not washed since his latest murder; and it is this notion of literal truth, carried as far as it will go, which is used by those who wish to exclude everything but sense and reference from the determination of truth-value. Our intuitions about literal truth are often unclear, which is not surprising since it is not a notion we normally use much; but it is a notion of considerable utility for the theory of meaning. A theory which sets out to assign truth-conditions to the sentences of a language may be expected to assign conditions for literal truth. What matters here, though, is that the Conversational Hypothesis is not committed to holding that what we ordinarily and naturally take to be the truth-value of an utterance depends on its sense and reference alone: if it were it would be too implausible a theory to be worth considering.

Cohen's alternative Semantical Hypothesis claims of "and" that

In addition to expressing the conjunction of two truths it also indicates that the second truth to be mentioned is a further item of the same kind, or in the same sequence, or of a kind belonging to the same set of commonly associated kinds of item, or etc. etc., as the first truth to be mentioned.

(Cohen [1971] p. 55)

On occasions where it does not appear to carry this full meaning, as when it is made clear that no such connection is intended, the Semantical Hypothesis holds that the context *deletes* for the occasion certain elements in the full lexical meaning: just as (to take an example which Cohen hopes, perhaps wrongly, to be fairly uncontroversial) a context in which imitation flowers are under discussion serves to delete from the full meaning of "flower" those elements which make it impossible for flowers to be made of plastic (Cohen [1971] p. 56).

Cohen's hypothesis treats "if...then..." similarly: it holds that

a dictionary entry for the particles 'if . . . then . . .' should state that they indicate a connection between antecedent and consequent as well as performing the purely truth-functional role of ruling out the conjunction of the antecedent's truth with the consequent's falsehood, though the Hypothesis is quite consistent with finding certain occurrences of these particles where the context is such as to delete the connexive aspect of their dictionary meaning . . .

(Cohen [1971] p. 59)

Certainly it is usually the case that an utterance of a conditional conveys some sort of implication of connection between antecedent and consequent, and for this reason the Conversationalist Hypothesis is intuitively less plausible for "if" than it is for "and", where the implication is by no means so standard. But to take account of this there is an important difference between the treatment Grice offers for "if" and the conversationalist account of "and", which is that with "if" the conversational implicature is *generalised*: the adoption of that form of words, that mode of expressing the propositional content rather than some other, itself gives rise to the implicature; which therefore *normally* holds when that form of words is used—though contextual features may delete it on occasion. For "and" this would not, I think, be maintained. But Grice's suggestion for indicative conditionals, at least, is that the speaker's choice of the words "if...then..." (or just of "if", with the conditional form) normally conveys that he has non-truth-functional grounds for accepting the material conditional. It is not that he relies on his audience's familiarity with the practice of using the words to convey this, but just that in any ordinary circumstance his choice of this peculiar way of expressing himself gives rise to this presumption. If his grounds were simply that he knew the antecedent to be false, or the consequent to be true, it would be puzzling why he should choose so cumbersome and evasive a form to express the information; except in the presence of very special circumstances his utterance would be misleading, or at best less informative than it might have been, and would therefore violate the Co-operative Principle. So his choice of words, together with the assumption that no such violation of the Co-operative Principle can be intended, entitles us to infer that he has other grounds than these for his assertion; and because a speaker can rely upon his hearers reasoning in this way, he can use the utterance to convey to them that he has such other, non-truth-functional, grounds. Moreover, the choice of the conditional form "If $p$ then $q$" rather than a truth-functional equivalent like "Either not-$p$ or $q$" suggests that what the speaker is interested in is the possibility of arguing from $p$ to $q$: the conditional form is particularly well adapted for use in inference. It is convenient and natural to have such a form, just because we all do find modus ponens a more natural way of arguing than modus tollendo ponens. And this provides a further reason why it would be conversationally inappropriate to use "If $p$ then $q$" where one knew just that $p$ was false or $q$ true, or generally where one's purposes in no way involved the possibility of inferring $q$ from $p$. (Mackie [1973] pp. 76f.)

Cohen feels that what is conveyed by "If...then..." is rather the connectedness of antecedent and consequent than the existence of further evidence than would be required for a truth-functional conditional. It is not clear to me whether there is a genuine issue here, because of vagueness in the notions of connectedness and of the availability of evidence; if there is, and it is to be resolved in Cohen's favour, one would still expect a conversationalist account, pretty similar to the one just given, to be plausible. People are usually interested in connected antecedents and consequents, not just in material implications, and the Co-operative Principle requires one's contribution to be relevant to the purposes of the conversation. Similarly, if it were to be resolved in the other direction, Cohen's Semantical Hypothesis could easily be amended appropriately. Now that the conversationalist account is framed in terms of generalised conversational implicature it looks a little more like the semantical account; but the crucial difference remains—that what the latter assigns to sense is on the former generated from the sense by the assistance of the Co-operative Principle. Although the words used help to produce the implicature, it is still the circumstances of the particular occasion of utterance which have to be considered on the conversationalist view; by calling the implicature generalised Grice in no way means to deny this, but only to point out that a speaker's choice of words is amongst the things that may be important.

As with "and", Cohen thinks that although his own theory can handle whatever is necessary the Conversational Hypothesis breaks down. And as with "and" he feels that the real difficulty for the latter arises when the connective occurs in a subordinate position, inside the antecedent of another conditional. His argument here has the same structure as before. He gives the example

(3) If it is the case both that if the government falls there will be rioting in the streets, and also that the government will not fall, then the shopkeepers will be glad.

The difficulty here is that although the conversationalist can explain why the truth of the consequent of (3) is felt to *depend* on the truth of the antecedent, he is also (according to Cohen) obliged to hold that the truth of the antecedent is fully determined by whether or not the government will fall. If the government will not fall, and the antecedent of (3) is taken truth-functionally, then it must be true; for the contained conditional will have a false antecedent. If on the other hand the government will fall, then the antecedent of (3) must be false, since one of its conjuncts is. (Cohen [1971] p. 63.)

We can again reply that when the contained conditional, "If the government falls there will be rioting in the streets", is asserted by itself, its sense is truth-functional, but what it conveys is not truth-functional at all; if in analogous types of context it were expected to convey only its truth-functional sense when it appeared in the antecedent of a more complex conditional, it would be confusing and misleading not to indicate this and would thus violate the Co-operative Principle. And when Cohen says that this involves making

(3) "not wholly truth-functional—contrary to what the Conversational Hypothesis asserts" ([1971] p. 63), we can point out that he is again supposing that the conversationalist takes truth to depend on sense and reference alone. But the conversationalist is perfectly well aware that conversational factors help determine what truth-value we should naturally and intuitively assign to a conditional, whether it stands by itself or inside a subordinate clause. It is only the sense of the connectives that he holds to be truth-functional.

Mackie [1973] in his discussion of Grice also rejects the conversationalist account of "if . . . then . . .", though for different reasons. He feels that it cannot be plausibly extended to counterfactuals or to "even if" statements, and that it cannot be extended at all to conditional questions and commands. Yet one would like if possible to give a single account of the meaning of "if" which will cover all of these. I am a little puzzled why Mackie feels the doubt he does about counterfactuals and "even if" statements, for he sketches highly promising conversationalist treatments of them which he then dismisses. But it is the incapacity to deal with conditional commands and questions which he considers the decisive objection.

Commands like "See to it that if the French attack we can defend ourselves" offer no great difficulty to a truth-functional account of "if"; nor do questions like "Will the grenade make a nice bang if I throw it?" For here the conditional occurs wholly within the specification of what is asked or commanded—within what Hare calls the phrastic (Hare [1952] Ch. 2).[5] And although the phrastic is not being asserted, but instead commanded or enquired about, we can intelligibly assign truth-values to it and to the subordinate clauses within it, for it and they are perfectly capable of being asserted. Thus there is no evident bar to a truth-functional account of the "if", or of any other connective that may be involved in such examples. To the objection that the order is to ensure a dependence between French attack and our ability to resist, and not merely to make true a material conditional, the conversationalist can make a reply of his usual sort: the speaker's choice of this form of words in this conversational context generates an implicature of connectedness between antecedent and consequent. The words suggest an

[5] See also Hare [1971] pp. 89–93 and *passim*. The sense-and-reference, or propositional content (as I am using these unreliable terms), of course includes more than the phrastic and cannot be identified with it, for it is part of the *sense* of "Will the grenade make a nice bang?" that it is a question.

affinity with the assertive case and with the implicatures one might there expect; in a typical context of utterance, the indicative sentence describing the state of affairs which the command is concerned to realise would carry just such an implicature. And we can also apply directly to the imperative case Grice's argument that if the speaker is interested only in the material conditional he could have expressed himself more naturally. Parallel considerations will apply in the case of the other propositional connectives.

But it is not with these cases that Mackie sees a difficulty; it is with cases where the command itself, or the question, appears to be conditional upon the antecedent. He gives as examples "If it rains, stay indoors" and "If he comes, what will he do?" (Mackie [1973] p. 79.) Here the connective cannot be thought of as simply occurring within the phrastic, for what follows it is a command or question and not just a phrastic. This does create a difficulty for the truth-functional account of "if", since it does not seem plausible to suppose that commands or questions have truth-values. But it does not seem to be an insurmountable difficulty.

Even setting plausibility aside, the expedient of assigning truth-values in some technical and unnatural sense to questions and commands does not look promising. The most natural thing would be to give them the truth-values of their phrastics, but that will not do; the difficulty arises from examples where in the consequent more than the phrastic has to be considered. The alternative suggestion that the truth-value in question should be that of the statement that there *is* such a command or question, or that such a command is operative, runs up against the objection that this does not seem to be what we are saying. This proposal does its best to forget that commanding and asking questions are speech acts. But once we recognise that they are we are faced with a problem: how can one perform a speech act in a conditional way, any more than one can stand on one's head in a conditional way? A speech act may of course have conditional effects, but that is another matter. This suggests a quite different way of handling examples like Mackie's: to hold that they are not really conditional questions or commands after all, because there can be no such thing.

This approach attempts to handle every apparent case of a conditional question as really a question about the truth of a conditional, and every apparent conditional command as a command to bring about the truth of a conditional. So accustomed are we to making scope distinctions of the sort thus dismissed that the dismissal sounds like a sheer confusion: so much so that Rescher has called it Mally's Perplex, after Mally, who committed it (Rescher [1966] p. 40n). But it is not so obviously a confusion. It fits in with our intuition that the whole of "If it rains, stay indoors" is a command, and the whole of "If he comes, what will he do?" a question. The usual objection is that if the antecedent of the conditional is unfulfilled no command has been given, or no question asked; and this seems comparatively persuasive with imperatives of the form "If you want to do *x*, do *y*", and with questions like "If you were born before 6 April 1799, are you receiving a pension?" But even to these our intuitive reaction is more likely to be that the command or question does not apply than that nothing has been asked or ordered. And in any case such examples are not decisive, particularly against a conversationalist. He can say that on the basis of sense an affirmative answer to this question would strictly be quite correct, though in the circumstances highly misleading; which is just what he would say of an affirmative answer to "Is it the case that if there were women fellows of Magdalen in 1973 they would all be blonde?",[6] though here the question is explicitly about the truth of a conditional. Similarly he can hold that even complete inaction on my part would constitute literal obedience to the command "If you want to get up early, buy an alarm clock", given what my predilections are, while admitting that it would be conversationally odd to *describe* me as obeying the imperative by sleeping on; just as he would consider it inappropriate, though strictly and technically correct, to describe the pre-emptive nuclear destruction of France as a way of obeying the order "See to it that if the French attack we can defend ourselves."

As a proposal for handling apparent occurrences of conditional question and command in ordinary language, I think this suggestion will do; at any rate it deserves to be considered seriously. But Dummett has argued ([1973] pp. 339, 341ff.) that we can find more room than this allows for the idea of a genuinely conditional command or question: not holding that the speech act of commanding or asking would be performed in a conditional way, but taking the view that the occurrence as consequent of an imperative or interrogative clause *could* function to indicate that the complex sentence was typically used to perform a new and logically complex

[6] There are no women fellows of Magdalen in 1973.

kind of speech act: "conditional-commanding" or "conditional-asking". There would be point in conditional-commanding if, for example, it was our practice to reward obedience to an order as well as to punish disobedience, but wished to do neither of these things where the antecedent of the conditional turned out false.

So far as this is a claim about what might happen, and not about what does happen in ordinary language,[7] the conversationalist can reply that he is concerned only with the uses we actually do make of the connectives. But though arguably conditional-commanding and conditional-asking are speech acts which we do not perform, we do perform other speech acts which stand to one another in relations it is very natural to call logical and to symbolise by means of particles in which the conversationalist has an interest; though doing so means applying these particles to things which cannot be said to have truth-values. The permissive "may", for instance, indicates that an imperative is not being given; though admittedly we do not ordinarily express it by using "not" with an imperative (and appropriate indications of scope). But we do quite normally use "and" to concatenate speech acts; as Dummett points out ([1973] p. 337), we are using it like this in such conjunctive questions as "Has she gone away, and has she stolen all the teaspoons?"—to which two answers are required, for two questions have been asked.

In reply, the conversationalist might concede that "and" does have a special sense in such cases; rather as it would if one performed two non-verbal acts saying "and" in between, to show that they were to be thought of together. But he could say that it was a natural extension of the truth-functional use; and that the same applied or would apply to similar uses of the other particles. It is a natural extension because of the striking analogy between the logical relations which can obtain between propositions and the relations which can hold between speech acts; an analogy so striking as to make it natural to call the latter relationships logical as well. Nevertheless, he can say, it *is* an extension of the sense of "and"; an extension to which the Conversational Hypothesis does not apply. But nothing important is lost if the claims of that Hypothesis are so restricted as to make a specific exception of this extended use.

Alternatively, however, he might tentatively suggest that even here the sense of "and" may still be truth-functional. This would

---

[7] Dummett considers that we do ask genuinely conditional yes/no questions, but that we do not give genuinely conditional commands.

mean that there was something very odd, something categorially absurd, about the literal meaning of "Has she gone, and has she stolen all the teaspoons?"—an impropriety which would constitute a breach of the Co-operative Principle unless the speaker were trying to communicate something other than the senses of his words. And since there is so striking an analogy between the logical relations between propositions and the logical or quasi-logical relations in which speech acts can stand to one another, would it not be natural to infer that the speaker must be trading on this analogy, rather as in a case of metaphor, and that he is conversationally implicating a connection, not between two propositions, but between two acts?

I think, then, that Mackie has not established the inadequacy of the Conversational Hypothesis by showing that it cannot handle conditional questions and commands, or analogous phenomena. We can deal more briefly with his claim that it cannot accommodate counterfactuals or "even if" statements, because as I have said Mackie himself provides us with the start of an account of how it can. Every material implication with a false antecedent is true; yet ordinarily we discriminate amongst counterfactuals, considering some true and others false, and the hypothesis has to explain how we can do this. Now if a speaker takes the trouble to assert one counterfactual rather than another, his hearers may naturally be expected to look around for an explanation, for by uttering so evident a truth he violates the Co-operative Principle—in a normal conversation, his remark taken literally would be pointless. Therefore, as Mackie says,

> Since the second conjunct in 'Not-$P$ and if $P$, $Q$' would, on this assumption, be redundant, there will be a conversational implicature of the use of this (or of anything with the same meaning) that there is some special point in saying 'If $P$, $Q$' over and above its being made true by not-$P$, and hence that there is some connection between $P$ and $Q$ which would rule out the conjunction of $P$ with not-$Q$ even if that were not ruled out simply by the falsity of '$P$'.

> (Mackie [1973] p. 78)

We can add that this implicature will be much strengthened by the speaker's choice of the "if...then..." form, which with indicative conditionals carries a generalised conversational implicature of connectedness (or of something similar) and is specially suited for use in inference. Mackie's objection to this account of counterfactuals is that it is "so fantastic as to be implausible", since an analogous view would be that an utterance of "The baby has a head" will conversationally implicate that the baby has two heads. For the speaker "could hardly call it a baby unless it had at least one head" (Mackie [1973] p. 78). Waiving any doubts on this last score, the speaker's utterance is here again devoid of conversational point (except in very unusual circumstances) because so trivially true. But the difference is that this remark is baffling as a counterfactual conditional is not. Without further information from the context—which might or might not help—one just does not know what the speaker might be getting at in Mackie's example, and that is why he fails to implicate anything conversationally. Whereas with counterfactuals this is not so: the adoption of the "if...then..." form, whose use we are familiar with from other contexts, and indeed usually the singling out of a $p$ and a $q$ which are obvious candidates for this sort of connectedness, are clear pointers to what the speaker is trying to convey.

Finally, "even if". On behalf of the conversationalist Mackie suggests that the sense of "Even if $p$, $q$" is "And equally, $p \rightarrow q$". So far as "and equally" differs from ordinary "and" Grice might wish to account for it by conventional implicature rather than sense, but let us leave that aside. Produced in a context where it is natural to assume that not-$p \rightarrow q$, an utterance of "And equally $p \rightarrow q$" may well suggest that it is to this that "$p \rightarrow q$" is being conjoined: and in this way it can be used to convey "$(\sim p \rightarrow q)$ & $(p \rightarrow q)$"—together, presumably, with whatever further implicatures this in turn may carry—"the second conjunct being asserted, the first merely suggested". Having given this account Mackie says "This is all a bit forced, but it is possible." ([1973] p. 79.) It is indeed possible. But in any case a conversationalist failure to account for "even if" would not be disastrous, since it might be held that "even" produces conventional implicatures which account for any difficulties.

So much, then, for "if". The Conversational Hypothesis accounts for the apparently non-truth-functional uses of "or" along similar lines. Again Grice suggests that a generalised conversational implicature attaches to the use of the word. If someone says "Either Amin will soon be overthrown or the Israelis will withdraw from Rwanda", in the absence of special circumstances he conversationally implicates that he has non-truth-functional grounds for his assertion, or at any rate that there is a connection between the disjuncts. If his grounds had been rather that he knew the truth of (at

least) one disjunct, he would have violated the Co-operative Principle by giving us less than he might of information in which we
may be presumed interested. (In normal circumstances, that is: no
violation need be involved if he were a freelance intelligence agent
who would charge us more for more precise information.) Grice
adds that just as "if. . .then. . ." seems naturally designed for use in
inference, "or" seems naturally designed for answering W-questions
(who. . . ? where. . . ? etc.), to which the best answer is the most
specific we can give.

Cohen's strategy is the same as before. His Semantical Hypothesis
builds into the sense of "or" the element that Grice holds to be conveyed conversationally, though admitting that on occasion it can
be deleted by the context. His objection to the conversational
account again arises from considering conditional assertions, in
which the connective occurs within the antecedent; he offers the
example

(4) If the prize is either in the garden or in the attic, and in fact
it is in the attic, the gardener will be glad. (Cohen [1971] p. 66.)

Once again, if the antecedent were taken in a purely truth-functional
way, the disjunction would be strictly irrelevant; the truth-value of
the antecedent as a whole would be determined by that of "The
prize is in the attic", being true if it is true and false if it is false. The
conversationalist's reply, as before, is that we can accept that (4) is
truth-functional in *sense* without accepting that it is sense (and
reference) alone which determine what we normally and naturally
take to be its truth-value.

In each of these cases, with "and", with "if", and with "or",
Cohen has argued that the Conversational Hypothesis fails because
it considers only simple cases, and forgets about cases where the
connective occurs within the antecedent of a conditional. In his
last paragraph he explicitly draws the parallel with speech-act
analyses of truth, goodness, etc., to which it has been objected that
such accounts cannot cope with certain occurrences in unasserted
clauses.

Such theories gain what support they seem to have from the consideration
of relatively simple examples. Their weakness becomes apparent when more
complex sentences are examined—especially sentences where the locution
in question occurs within the antecedent of a conditional.

(Cohen [1971] p. 67)

Now this objection to speech-act analyses of concepts like truth and goodness is far from obviously insurmountable. (Cf. Hare [1970]; Dummett [1973] pp. 351ff.) But what matters more here is that the parallel is not close. The difficulty in the speech-act case arises because the speaker cannot be performing the relevant act— commending, confirming, or whatever—in a subordinate clause like the antecedent of a conditional. But there is no analogous problem for the Conversational Hypothesis. This holds that by a particular utterance on a particular occasion the speaker can convey more than his utterance strictly means through relying on a general recognition of Grice's Co-operative Principle. It is therefore concerned with utterances, whether they constitute self-standing speech acts or not; an utterance of a subordinate clause, as in the antecedent of a conditional, is still an utterance, and therefore may convey conversationally more than it literally means. It may convey, for example, a further condition on which the consequent is to be taken to depend.

One should also mention Cohen's remarks on "not", though he puts no great weight on them. A truth-functional account of the sense of "not" does seem very plausible, and it is hard to think what alternative account Cohen's Semantical Hypothesis might give. He makes no attempt to tell us, and confines his remarks to whether the conversationalist can handle the double negative of Cockney— "You won't get no beer here"—and its counterpart in various other languages; for if the sense of the negative particle is truth-functional a double negative ought to cancel out (Cohen [1971] pp. 52–4). He points out that it would not be very plausible to treat these cases as instances of irony. However, as he in part sees, the conversationalist should not bring on implicatures here at all; so far as Cockney is concerned it is not the word "not" which should be said to be equivalent in sense to truth-functional negation, but whatever linguistic device in that dialect performs the negating function served in standard English by "not". If the thesis were solely about the standard English word it would be highly parochial; but it is not; it is about that word and its counterparts in other natural languages. And the Cockney counterpart of "not" is not "not" (or not simply).

It may be that someone ignorant of the practice of using a negative particle emphatically could understand what was meant by "You won't get no beer here", using a process of reasoning rather similar to that which the conversationalist depicts us as subconsciously following when faced with an apparent violation of the

Co-operative Principle. For it may be clear from the context both that no beer is available and that the speaker is not trying to be funny or ironic. Hence the most likely interpretation of the remark is that it is intended to mean "You won't get any beer here." In this case it would be wrong to say that the Cockney conversationally implicates anything, however, for his expectation that the hearer will grasp what is said to him is based not on a confidence that the latter will apply the Co-operative Principle satisfactorily but rather on a (misplaced) belief that he is familiar with the conventional meaning of the sentence in Cockney.

Much more important are certain further remarks Cohen makes about negation and "if...then..." (Cohen [1971] pp. 64–5). Grice considers the Conversational Hypothesis to run into a serious difficulty, a difficulty he has no way of surmounting, over negated conditionals. In a case like "It is not the case that if the Liberals win the next election Mr Wilson will retire", what is denied seems to be not the material conditional but rather what the conditional was supposed conversationally to implicate. The speaker is not saying that the Liberals will win and that Mr Wilson will not retire; he is denying a connection between these things. Grice feels that the denial clearly ought to negate the sense, rather than the conversational implicatures. But unlike Grice, Cohen considers this rather a weak objection to the Conversational Hypothesis. There are, he says, plenty of cases in which denial of an assertion is also denial of what it implicates; whether it is in any particular instance "must depend on the nature of the assertion and the nature of the implicature". It does, indeed, seem fairly obvious that if I negate an assertion (and the context remains the same) I may thereby cancel the implicatures which the assertion set up; and my new negative assertion may carry implicatures in its own right which conflict with them.

Grice is aware of this. His own illustration is "She is not the cream in my coffee", which because of the absurdity of its literal interpretation must in most contexts—outside, for example, a contemporary Greek myth—be interpreted as denying just what would be implicated by "She is the cream in my coffee." But he does not regard the difficulty as solved. If I understand him (which I may well not) his point is that here the sense is negated as well as the implicatures; it is the fact that the negative utterance would violate the Co-operative Principle if intended literally that gives rise to the new implicatures, implicatures negating those an affirmative utterance would have in the same context. Whereas with negated conditionals this is not so. For one thing, the supposed sense does not seem to be negated at all. For another, if the speaker did negate it, asserting something tantamount to "The Liberals will win and Mr Wilson will not retire", in most contexts there would be nothing conversationally odd or pointless about this; nothing to give rise to the necessary implicatures.

The Conversational Hypothesis is certainly committed to holding that the sense of "It is not the case that if $p$ then $q$" is the same as that of "$p$ and not-$q$". Cohen too goes on to make this an objection to it (Cohen [1971] p. 65). But it is an objection somewhat similar to his previous objections. "The Liberals will win and Mr Wilson will not retire" may be false when we would describe the negated conditional as true, but we have seen it is wrong to suppose implicatures do not help determine our ordinary ascriptions of truth-value. The conversationalist will hold that the sense of what I say is given by "The Liberals will win and Mr Wilson will not retire", but that I may well consider this false and yet be using it to convey something I believe true. If the conversationalist were not allowed to distinguish the truth-value of an utterance from the truth-value it would have if one were to consider only its propositional content, his Hypothesis would be a non-starter, since he would have to admit "If I stop writing this essay now, Amin will conquer Kenya" as true when it is palpably false (unless we jettison intuition and import a technical notion of literal truth). Presumably it is no objection to the conversationalist to say that I am not *aware* of the sense of my negated conditional when I utter it, or again the Conversational Hypothesis would be a non-starter—for when I utter an affirmative conditional I am generally not aware that "if" has a truth-functional sense. Nor is it an objection that I do not regard it as *committing* me to "The Liberals will win the next election" or yet again the Hypothesis would be ruled out from the start: I do not regard "I shall not stop writing this essay now" as committing me to "If I stop writing this essay now, Amin will conquer Kenya."

There remains the objection that the supposed implicature carried by the negated conditional cannot be generated by conversational means. But this hurdle looks superable. Frequently when I assert something of the form "It is not the case that if $p$ then $q$" it would be out of place for me to assert "$p$ and not-$q$", and known by my audience to be so. They may know that I am now in a position to say whether $p$ and whether $q$. Or the recognised purpose of the talk-exchange may make it clear enough that what is of interest is the connection, if any, between $p$ and $q$. Even where this is not so the hearer's interest is very often less in $p$ than in the truth-value of $q$, and if I know that $q$ is false I ought simply to say so. More importantly, even where none of these circumstances obtain, it remains true that we generally find "$\sim(p \to q)$" a good deal less perspicuous than "$p$ & $\sim q$" as a way of conveying the same information; so it is offending against the Co-operative Principle if, in a normal conversational context, I wantonly use the ordinary-language equivalent of the more cumbrous formulation without meaning to indicate anything thereby. If I do use it, my use of the negative will naturally call to mind the affirmative "If $p$ then $q$", which I am negating; and if in the context an utterance of "If $p$ then $q$" would carry a conversational implicature, is it not reasonable to suppose that I want to make some allusion to this—and in fact to negate it?

## II

That the Conversational Hypothesis appears capable of overcoming these objections does not show that it is right; nor does it show that there is anything wrong with Cohen's Semantical Hypothesis, or with the alternative theory which is prepared to multiply senses for the logical particles in a way that neither Grice nor Cohen will tolerate. As yet we have no method of telling which of the elements in what is conveyed by an utterance are due to its sense, and which if any are conversational implicatures. In order to be able to determine which of these hypotheses is correct we shall need to examine more closely the notion of a conversational implicature and the notion of sense.

A conversational implicature is produced by the use of a particular utterance-token in a particular context; and generally an utterance carries conversational implicatures because the speaker (or writer, *vel cetera*) intended it to. There are, admittedly, cases where an utterance conveys to its audience a suggestion or nuance even though this was not intended—just as it may convey a sense which the speaker did not intend because (for example) he was misusing his words. And so we may, if we wish, allow the class of conversational implicatures to include not only those intended by speakers but also those carried by utterance-tokens in contexts where the audience would naturally suppose such a thing to be intended. But these latter cases are in a sense secondary; the implicature arises only through a misunderstanding; what gives rise to it are the hearer's expectations about what the speaker must *intend*. Thus, by praising someone's bicycling I might not in the least wish to disparage his other abilities, but in the circumstances it might be natural for my audience to take me to be doing so—by relying on the consideration (in this instance misplaced) that the Co-operative Principle would have prevented me from saying what I did unless I wanted to convey this further message.

A speaker's intention to convey something by conversational implicature must be what Grice calls an M-intention (Grice [1969b]), as must his intention to convey something in virtue of the commonly-accepted senses of his words. Each is part of what he *means* by his utterance, in a broad but intuitive sense of "means". It is a matter of some difficulty to give a precise analysis of this broad sense of "means", and thus to make quite clear what it is for a speaker to M-intend to convey something. But roughly, what is required is that the speaker intend to produce a certain effect in his hearer (often the acquisition or what Grice calls the activation—the bringing to consciousness—of a belief, [1969b] p. 169); and that he also intend this effect to be produced at least partly in virtue of the hearer's recognition of his intention to produce it. Moreover, the hearer must also be intended to recognise this second, higher-order, intention; and to recognise the third intention, of even higher order, just mentioned; and so on. In fact, the speaker must intend his intentions to be "wholly overt" to his audience. (Grice [1969b] p. 169; Strawson [1964b] p. 454; Schiffer [1972] Ch. 2.)[8] This would require some

---

[8] Various modifications are made by Schiffer, of which the most important is his attempt to handle this iteration of intentions by using the concept of what he calls "mutual knowledge*"—more or less the same as Lewis's "common knowledge" (see below, n. 15). Two people "mutually know*" that *p* iff each knows that *p*, knows that the other knows, knows that the other knows he knows, etc. etc. Schiffer tentatively requires that the speaker intend it to be "mutual knowledge*" between speaker and hearer both that he intends to produce the effect in his hearer by means of recognition of intention, and that he intends to produce this mutual knowledge*. This is neat, but too strong, as Schiffer recognises: a speaker who does not know who, if anyone, will hear him does not intend to bring about a state of mutual knowledge* between himself and the unknown hearer. Rather, his intention is that anyone who hears him should recognise his intentions; and Schiffer modifies his account in this direction ([1972] pp. 74 ff.). It is not clear to me, however, that there is now any work for the notion of mutual knowledge* to do in this context. The speaker, *S*, must intend that anyone who

amendment before it was quite right; but it is not necessary for our purposes at present to go into that. Let us suppose the amendment accomplished, and just say that conversational implicatures are among the things that speakers M-intend to convey.

So we can perhaps say that a speaker, *S*, conversationally implicates φ by an utterance-token, *U*, only if *S* utters *U* M-intending thereby to convey φ to his audience in virtue of his audience's expectation that he is both conforming to the Co-operative Principle and expecting to be taken to be conforming to it. Or—to put the same thing slightly differently—*S* conversationally implicates φ by *U* only if in uttering *U S* M-intends to convey φ to his audience, and intends this intention to be recognised in part because the audience expects *S* to be conforming to the Co-operative Principle and because the audience also expects *S* to anticipate this expectation and to act accordingly. It must of course be granted that *S* is unlikely to be aware of the exact form that his intentions take; nor will his audience be conscious that its expectations can be characterised in this way. But many of our expectations and intentions are such that we do not or cannot formulate them consciously to ourselves, not least the complex ones connected with linguistic rules and practices. That we have such intentions and such expectations is shown in what we do, not in what passes before the mind's ear.

This gives us only a necessary condition for the truth of "*S* conversationally implicates φ". Not everything that is M-intentionally conveyed with the help of the Co-operative Principle is to be accounted a conversational implicature. For one thing, in ordinary cases of ambiguity we rely on that principle to determine which sense is intended; if I say "The bank is mossy" I can usually rely

---

hears him should know what his intentions are, but it is not necessary that *S* should intend to bring about a state of affairs in which he himself knows, or even believes, any proposition about what anyone who heard him would know; though it is a consequence of Schiffer's amended account (pp. 75 f.) that this is required. Someone might hear him who did not understand him; it is no part of *S*'s M-intention to induce in himself the belief that this will not be so. Even where *S* is addressing some particular person he does not have to intend to make himself *believe* that that person will recognise his intentions; if *S* can speak only English, and he is addressing a Bulgarian police officer, he may be well aware that this recognition is unlikely. So *S* is not concerned with bringing about anything that can be called, even by extension, a state of mutual knowledge*; his intentions concern only what his hearer should recognise, and not what he himself should know. This seems to leave us where we were before the idea of mutual knowledge* was introduced.

on the accepted purpose of the talk-exchange to disambiguate my remark (we might, for example, be talking about the buildings on some street). Here the intended sense of my remark is conveyed only in virtue of the presumption that I am obeying the Co-operative Principle; yet one would not say that the intended sense was conversationally implicated. To accommodate this we can stipulate that an utterance-token which carries a conversational implicature must carry it partly because of its sense: the implicature cannot determine the sense, because the sense must be already understood. So we get: $S$ conversationally implicates $\phi$ by $U$ iff in uttering $U$ $S$ M-intends to convey $\phi$ to his audience, and intends this intention to be recognised partly because of the audience's recognition of the sense of $U$ (together with its expectation that $S$ also knows the sense of $U$); but partly also because the audience expects $S$ to be conforming to the Co-operative Principle, and expects $S$ to anticipate this expectation and to act accordingly. This legislates out the possibility of a conversational implicature being carried by an utterance which lacked a sense, but that may be no bad thing.

A further restriction seems called for to deal with certain common cases of reference. The Co-operative Principle often helps to determine to what item a speaker is referring when he uses a proper name or a definite description, because there is more than one bearer of the name, or more than one object in the world which satisfies the predicate from which the description is formed. It is the Co-operative Principle which enables the speaker to convey that the Tom he is talking about is the Tom we have both just left, and that by "the candle on the dresser" he means the one we can both see and not some other candle on a dresser in Timbuctoo. In such cases, where the item referred to is a bearer of the name or does satisfy the relevant predicate, we should normally take the successful reference to be determinative of what is "strictly and literally said"; so I shall stipulate that the speaker does not conversationally implicate what item it is. The case is different, of course, if he M-intends to refer to something which does not bear the name or satisfy the description, as if he refers to an incompetent subaltern as Alexander the Great or to Queen Victoria as the grandmother of Europe.

With this qualification, then, something along the lines suggested above may be sufficient as well as necessary for the presence of a conversational implicature, at any rate when extended to cover those secondary cases where we might say that an utterance-token carried an implicature even though it was not M-intended by the speaker. But it is not immediately clear how this helps us to decide whether the Conversationalist Hypothesis is right. The Conversationalist Hypothesis may be able to show that what we ordinarily understand by the logical particles *could* be conveyed by conversational implicature if their senses were truth-functional, but it does not follow that that *is* what happens; it may still be that their senses are not truth-functional. Since the failure of the arguments against the Hypothesis does not show that it is correct, it begins to look somewhat difficult to discover whether it is or not. To appeal to the speaker himself would not be very satisfactory, since he is unlikely to have a clear idea of what belongs to the sense of his utterances and what he conveys by conversational means.

We could avoid this difficulty by insisting that whenever it is *possible* to explain the fact that $\phi$ is communicated by saying that it is conversationally implicated, and not part of the sense of the utterance, it *should* be explained in this way. In other words, we could take very seriously the recommendation not to multiply senses beyond necessity, and hold that an adequate account of communication would give as small a part as possible to sense and differences of sense, and as large a part as possible to the Co-operative Principle. But the adoption of this rather attractive recommendation leads to undesirable consequences. For it seems quite possible for a word to develop a new *sense* as a result of the operation of the Co-operative Principle: a conversational implicature gets crystallised into the standard meaning. That this happens is recognised by Grice. It is least controversial where an expression like "grass roots" or "head of school" gets so worn out as a metaphor that people may even forget the old meaning; but the borderline between a frozen metaphor and one that is not yet frozen is one of degree, and where the frozen metaphor occurs it may be quite possible for someone unfamiliar with it to work out what is being conveyed by means of his understanding of the old sense and the presumption that the speaker is obeying the Co-operative Principle. The same thing can happen with irony: in East Germany the word "Heldentat", used in talking about American action in South-East Asia, has acquired a new sense and no longer means 'heroic deed'. Moreover, it could be suggested that if we disregarded altogether our intuitions about sense, and really took as seriously as we could the idea of minimising the role of sense, we might find ourselves led to adopt a theory which assigns the same sense to *every* utterance and accounts for every difference conversationally—leaning heavily on the idea of generalised implicature, and saying perhaps that although "It is nearly bedtime" actually *means* "Hail to the sacred Mushroom!" the speaker's choice of these words rather than others on this occasion, together with other features of the context, indicates to a hearer who expects him to make appropriate, sincere, and helpfully expressed remarks what his real message is.[9]

The case of metaphor suggests that perhaps we should not hope to find any very sharp distinction between the sense of an utterance and what it conversationally implicates. Yet there does seem to be one very important difference between the two. For its sense belongs to it as a token of an utterance-type—as a member of a class of tokens of a shared physical form. Conversational implicatures, however, are generated by the circumstances in which this particular utterance occurs: and it may be that no other token of the same utterance-type ever occurs in a conversation with quite the same accepted aims, or under quite the same conditions. This difference, however, is not very helpful in giving us a *test* to settle whether a given implication is conversational or due to sense alone; for it will not do to say that we can test by seeing whether other utterances of the same type carry the same implication. An utterance might be the only token of its type ever produced with that *sense*, or indeed the only token of its type ever produced at all; we can still call it a token of a type, and speak of a sense as appertaining to it as such. And although it may happen that a particular conversational implicature is carried only once by an utterance of a given type, it may also happen that it is carried often or even normally by such utterances: for it may be that the appropriate conversational conditions for generating the implicature often or normally occur. This is what the Conversationalist Hypothesis holds with regard to words like "if...then...".

It might be thought possible to devise a test by appealing to the notion of truth, on the grounds that truth-values are determined by senses and not by conversational implicatures; but we have already seen reason to reject this suggestion. We may decide to say that the "literal" truth-value of an utterance is fixed by its sense and reference alone, but then our ordinary intuitions about truth and falsity

---

[9] This was suggested by David Bostock, in conversation.

are no guide to the "literal" truth-value of an utterance, in this technical usage.[10]

Grice puts forward two other tests for the presence of a conversational implicature: is the implication cancellable, and is it non-detachable? The more important of these tests is the former. According to this, if an utterance carries a conversational implicature in a certain context, the speaker can always find or create another context in which he can use a token of the same utterance-type with the same sense and reference, but without the implicature. One way of creating such a context is simply to add an explicit disclaimer of the implication that would otherwise be carried; this is generally enough to defeat the presumption that the speaker regards the utterance as produced in accordance with the Co-operative Principle, which is what gave rise to the implicature. Alternatively, he can make sure that the context in which the utterance is now made is such that, although the presumption remains, it no longer makes it necessary to suppose he must be trying to convey some unstated message. Thus, to take the familiar example, if one says in reply to a question about a colleague's academic work "McFiggis is a competent bicyclist" one implicates that he is less than adequate professionally; but one can use the same sentence, with the same sense and reference, without implicating this, either by adding "but I do not mean to imply that he is no good at his work", or else by producing it during a conversation about cycling.

Grice does not consider that his cancellability test gives us a sufficient condition for the presence of a conversational implicature. For even where an implication is part of the sense of an utterance, he thinks it may be possible to find contexts in which the utterance is used loosely without carrying it. Thus, it may be part of the sense of

---

[10] Conceivably the conversationalist might try to support his position with the help of a correspondence theory of truth: he might argue that an empirical statement can only be properly described as true or false if there is or could be some fact for it to correspond to, and that the only *facts* available for "If it is sunny they will play cricket" are the facts about whether it is sunny and whether they play cricket. There is (he might say) no place for a further fact in the world, the fact that *if* it is sunny they will play cricket (the "if" being interpreted non-materially); perhaps because non-material hypotheticals purport to describe "merely possible" situations, and "simple truth, truth in the strict sense, can belong only to descriptions of what is actual" (Mackie [1973] p. 106). But it is not in the least clear what entitles anyone to cut down on facts in this way, unless it be an antecedent conviction that it is only so far as it states a material conditional that "If $p$ then $q$" can be accounted true (or false).

"It is light green now" that the thing in question really is and does not merely seem to be light green now; yet this sentence can be loosely used to make the lesser claim, when it is clear to those conversing what is intended. Moreover, on any occasion when we try to apply the cancellability test, someone prepared to multiply senses can hold that the original utterance—the one said to carry the implicature—differs in *sense* from the inscriptionally similar utterance which no longer carries the implication; he can say that by adding "but I don't mean to imply..." or by otherwise altering the circumstances of utterance the speaker has provided a context in which it is natural to expect a different sense from the one expected before.

So cancellability can at best be a necessary condition for the presence of a conversational implicature. And Grice does hold that every conversational implicature is cancellable. That it should be so is indeed a consequence of what a conversational implicature is; for it is conveyed contextually, by means of the Co-operative Principle, and therefore it must be at least logically possible that there should be contexts in which it is conveyed no longer; if only because it must be possible for a speaker on occasion to make it clear that he is simply not doing his best to further the purposes of the talk-exchange—that he is being deliberately irrelevant, unnecessarily elusive, or long-winded and obscure. But this is still very far from giving us a test which we can use in practice. If the claim that a conversational implicature must be cancellable were the claim that it must be possible to find some *natural* set of circumstances in which someone could produce the utterance without either conveying the implicature or violating the Co-operative Principle, then indeed it would provide us with a test which many putative conversational implicatures might fail; for example, it is not clear that there is any natural situation in which it would be conversationally pointful to say "If it had rained they would not have played cricket, though I don't mean to suggest that there is any sort of connection between the antecedent and the consequent." But this is not what is claimed. No such claim would follow from the consideration that such implicatures are generated contextually by the Co-operative Principle, though Grice occasionally talks as though it would (e.g. [1969a] p. 131). All that is required is that there should be no *incompatibility* between the cancelling clause "though I don't mean to suggest that..." and what precedes it, as there would be if what were cancelled were part of the sense. (An incompatibility which is close to contradiction, for when $p$ entails $q$, "$p$ but not $q$" is a contradiction, and although "$p$ but I do not mean to suggest that $q$" is not precisely self-contradictory it is not far removed from being so.) An implicature can be cancelled consistently; and if "$p$ but not $q$" is consistent there will be some logically *possible* context in which it can be asserted as an acceptable and pointful part of a conversation, even if we should find no such context natural. For we can include among logically possible contexts those in which the speakers have quite different interests and purposes from ours, and quite different ideas about acceptability and point. So in the long run the cancellability test leaves us simply with the question "Is '$p$ but not $q$' consistent?"; for if it is the implicature of $q$ will be cancellable.[11]

Disappointingly, then, cancellability does not provide us with a workable test for conversational implicatures; it does not advance matters, for we already knew that if an utterance of $p$ conversationally implicates that $q$, "$p$ but not $q$" will be consistent. This is indeed a theoretical distinction between conversational implicature and entailment, but it gives us no way of applying the distinction in particular cases. To do that we should have to be able to test for consistency remarks which do not bear their logical structure on the surface. Grice seems to rely largely on intuition here, and it does give us tolerably unambiguous deliverances in certain cases. It does tell us that "It seems to me that I see something red—not that I mean to say I am in any doubt on the matter" is free from any incompatibility. It is much less reliable on "If $p$ then $q$—but I don't mean to suggest that there is any connection between them"; and in general it is useless as a guide in just those cases where we need help—those cases where we are in doubt whether an implication is a conversational implicature or not. One would prefer not to rely too heavily on intuition, in any case.

What then of the non-detachment test? For our purposes at least, this turns out also to be disappointing. Grice does not consider it to provide either a necessary or a sufficient condition for the presence of a conversational implicature. The cancellability requirement said, in effect, that if an utterance of $p$ conversationally implicates $q$ it must be possible in some context to utter $p$ without this implica-

---

[11] Strictly this is not quite right, because $p$ itself might be self-contradictory; so we should really ask whether the addition of "not-$q$" adds any new element of inconsistency.

ture; what is now claimed is that so far as the implicature is borne by what is literally said (the sense and reference) and not by the manner in which it is expressed, it will not be possible to find any alternative way of saying the same thing in *that context* without also carrying the implicature. We could of course alter the context, verbally or by other means, and cancel it thus; the non-detachment "test" amounts to the remark that if the manner in which $p$ is expressed is *not* responsible for the implicature, the latter must be generated by the context together with the meaning of $p$ (which it would share with any other synonymous utterance). But it is obvious that this does not give us the test we are looking for. In any disputed case, it is unclear to start with how much is to be included in the meaning of $p$; and as Grice himself points out if $q$ is entailed by $p$ it will be entailed by any synonym of $p$, so that entailments are as non-detachable as conversational implicatures are.[12]

So these suggestions do not advance us beyond the point we had already reached. This was, roughly and with one important reservation, that $S$ conversationally implicates $\phi$ by uttering $U$ iff he utters it M-intending thereby to convey $\phi$ to his audience, and intending this M-intention to be recognised partly because of the audience's recognition of the conventional sense of $U$; but in part also because the audience expects $S$ (i) to be conforming to the Co-operative Principle, (ii) to anticipate that it will expect (i) and to act accordingly. The reservation was, that where $S$ conveys by contextual means which of the bearers of a name he is referring to, or which of the items satisfying the predicative component of a definite description, we shall not call these cases of conversational implicature. And no doubt there are other reservations to be made. But unless we already have some way of determining what the sense of an utterance is, none of this enables us to tell whether something conveyed by it is a conversational implicature or not.

### III

So far, at least, we have not discovered how to determine whether the Conversationalist Hypothesis is true. Is it easier to decide

---

[12] The non-detachment test is really meant to separate conversational implicatures from conventional ones, not to distinguish between conversational implicatures and entailments; and I do not wish to suggest that Grice himself ever considered it suitable for the latter purpose. I mention it here only because a casual reading of his work might suggest that it might be.

whether the Semantical Hypothesis is? The Semantical Hypothesis appears to differ in two ways. Firstly, of course, the Conversationalist Hypothesis builds as little as possible into the sense of an expression, and lets the context generate the rest of what is conveyed; the Semantical alternative builds as much as possible into the sense, and lets the context of the particular utterance delete unwanted elements as required. Secondly, the Semantical Hypothesis as Cohen states it places no limitation on the ways in which context can be invoked for this purpose; the Conversationalist Hypothesis is more precise and requires it to work by means of the Co-operative Principle—which is, indeed, a principle on which we are clearly entitled to rely in conversation.

I don't think this *second* difference is a very serious one. The Co-operative Principle places no restriction on the *types* of context which can be invoked, for any type of context can help to determine what the accepted purposes of a conversation are and how a speaker may be expected to achieve them; it only explains how it is that the context can bear on what an utterance conveys, without requiring us to suppose that we have to learn a lot of special rules about the ways in which context can affect what is communicated. Cohen seems to leave it open whether his Hypothesis requires a lot of special rules of this sort—extra rules, which can be learnt in learning the meaning of words or sentences, about the conditions under which elements of the full sense are deleted—or whether the job can be done by some general rule like the Co-operative Principle, which one learns practically automatically in learning how to converse. If special rules were necessary on the Semantical view, it might be reasonable to prefer the Conversationalist Hypothesis on grounds of simplicity, other things being equal; but in fact special rules are not required, and the Semantical Hypothesis can employ the Co-operative Principle itself.[13] On the assumption that "The king came forward and the shouting ceased" includes as part of its sense the claim that there is a connection between the two events, "The king came forward and the shouting ceased; but there is no connection between the two events" is actually self-contradictory, and indeed blatantly so. If someone utters a blatant self-contradiction, then the Co-operative Principle suggests that he cannot intend to convey quite what he says; as in "Florence isn't Florence nowadays",

---

[13] "Semantical Hypothesis" is not really a very appropriate name, for the theory relies on context as much as does Grice's, although at a different place.

or "I'm not myself." Where the whole sense of what is said is cancelled, as in these latter examples, we must look to the context to see what can be intended; but where only part of it is one would naturally suppose that what is to be conveyed is simply the rest of the sense. Similarly, if an element in the sense is deleted not in this explicit way but by the context, it will be because the context makes it clear to the intended audience that what the speaker says would if taken literally be false—or at any rate unsupported by evidence, or otherwise conversationally unsound. Thus in an example of Grice's which Cohen quotes (Cohen [1971] p. 59), a bridge convention might be set up whereby "Five no trumps" was to mean (besides the normal commitment to make five no trumps) "If I have the king of hearts, I also have a black king." This conditional sentence, uttered in explaining the convention, appears to be truth-functional; for in the context it would be very odd to suppose that the speaker is talking about any connection between antecedent and consequent. We can also, incidentally, deal in this way—without invoking any special pragmatic rules—with the sort of case in which Cohen takes a "semantic" account to be most intuitively plausible: where one says "That is a plastic flower", or "That is a sabre" when pointing to part of a picture (Cohen [1971] p. 56). In the former case the linguistic context, in the latter case the non-linguistic context of utterance, make clear that what is said would be patently false if taken literally; so the speaker is interpreted as deleting those elements in the sense which require a sword not to be part of a picture, or a flower not to be made of plastic.

The Conversationalist Hypothesis would be falsified if it could be shown, as Cohen and Mackie tried to show, that our ordinary understanding of the logical particles of natural language *cannot* be accounted for in the way it suggests. Now if the Semantical Hypothesis were to allow *special* contextual rules to operate in deleting elements of the customary sense, it would be very difficult to see how it could possibly be falsified until these rules were made specific—and difficult also to distinguish it from what might be called the Third Hypothesis, the one whereby the context serves not to qualify a single sense for "if", etc., but to pick out which of several related senses is intended.[14] But if the Semantical Hypothesis were to employ only the Co-operative Principle, and thus to hold

[14] This Third Hypothesis has really more right to be called "semantic" than Cohen's.

that elements in the full sense of an expression are deleted only when the speaker *conversationally implicates* that they are to be set aside, then it would be falsifiable by showing that the Co-operative Principle cannot effect the required deletions. What would make a keen defender of the Third Hypothesis abandon it is again not clear, for the only considerations apparently available here are those of economy and it is not obvious how these should be assessed. The proponents of the Conversationalist and Semantical Hypotheses believe in cutting down on senses and increasing reliance on context, increasing the number of conversational implicatures; and although intuitively they seem right to economise in this way if they can, it might be maintained that only a curious prejudice could make us prefer cutting down senses to keeping to a minimum those curious entities, conversational implicatures.

Each of the three Hypotheses appears at least *prima facie* to be capable of explaining what we convey by logical particles like "and", "if...then...", etc. In fact there are more than just the three of them; what I called the Third Hypothesis has a variety of possible versions. It might be held for instance that "if...then..." has *two* senses, a truth-functional sense and a very strongly non-truth-functional sense, uses apparently diverging from these being conversationally explained; or it might be held that it has three senses; and so on. If the Conversationalist or the Semantical theory, or both of them, can explain the observable facts about what we M-intentionally convey, it seems that the Third Hypothesis (in at least some of its versions) can hardly fail to: for wherever they claim that something is communicated conversationally by relying on a contextual principle, it can assert that this same principle shows which of the various possible senses of the expression was intended in the circumstances.

But the Hypotheses are distinct theories; so one of them presumably must be right. The differences between them are not merely verbal, for even though each appears capable of dealing with the logical particles there are other cases in which a hypothesis of one of the three types would clearly be right and the others wrong. There are differences of sense which cannot be explained by any conversational or contextual means, as with the two distinct uses of the word "bank". There are cases which can be handled by a hypothesis of the conversationalist sort, for which it seems clearly wrong to multiply senses and for which no corresponding semantical hypothesis would do; the implicature carried by "McFiggis is a competent bicyclist" could not be handled by building "incompetent academic" into "competent bicyclist" and allowing it to be deleted contextually. Similarly, "That is a sabre", said when pointing to part of a painting, can be dealt with by a hypothesis of the semantic type, but the situation could not be explained conversationally by generating all the more ordinary uses from a very minimal sense for "sabre", in which a pictured sabre literally is a sabre.

The difference between the Hypotheses is in the role they assign to sense. But an appeal to our ordinary intuitions about sense is not a satisfactory way of deciding between them, at least until it is made clearer what we are supposed to be intuiting about; and it is just not intuitively obvious what belongs to the sense of "if" and what does not. The "cancellability test" offers in effect to bolster our initial intuitions about sense with a further set of intuitions about whether "$p$ but not $q$" is self-contradictory, but again this does not help, for in the difficult cases it is not obvious what is self-contradictory and what is not. Nor, as we have seen, are we helped by appealing to a distinction between what is "literally true" and what is not; we ordinarily consider a judgement true if the message it conveys is correct, and we have no firmer intuitions about its "literal" truth than we have about what constitutes its sense and reference and thereby determines its "literal" truth-value. And we have also seen that we cannot decide the matter by an appeal to economy, unless some reason can be given why we should not multiply senses rather than multiplying conversational implicatures (or the other way about). Moreover, to demand that we should postulate as few senses as we can get away with, and account for as much as possible by relying on the Co-operative Principle, would if taken strictly conflict with our intuition that a conversational implicature can be gradually frozen into the sense of an expression—as with a metaphor like "grass roots".

Various further suggestions may be put forward. Some of these do cast light on what we *mean* by "sense", but unfortunately without giving us any way of deciding, within broad limits, what belongs to sense and what does not. It would be clearly unhelpful, for example, to say that within the realm of what is M-intended the sense is what the hearer is supposed to understand, rather than to infer from the context. For he is intended to grasp all that is M-intended, and the problem of separating what he can "strictly" be said to understand from what he gathers from the context is just the problem we started with. Similarly it would not help to say that the sense of an utterance is what it conveys independently of context, for it is not clear what "context" is supposed to include; and we have also seen that the context is frequently required to determine which of a variety of possible senses is intended. It would also not be of much practical help to say that the sense of an utterance is what one has to learn concerning it in order to learn the language to which it belongs; for here "knowing the language" is thought of as knowing the senses of the expressions of that language. In any disputed case the disputants will disagree over what is required to understand the language: over whether someone understands English or not if he thinks that in a normal context "If you strike this match it will light" conveys nothing stronger than a material conditional.

This last suggestion, of course, reminds us that sense is primarily a property of utterance-types. We have seen that this fact by itself does not help to settle whether "if...then..." has one, two, or several senses, or what they may be. But the sense of an utterance seems to be more a matter of convention that its conversational implicatures; what one conveys by virtue of its sense one conveys because one's hearer recognises the type to which the utterance belongs, knows the appropriate convention, and thus recognises the intended sense. And it might be felt that a closer examination of the sort of convention involved here would help us towards a decision between the three Hypotheses. Unfortunately, however, when the examination is done the practical difficulties seem to remain.

Obviously, to hold that the sense of an expression is conventional is not to hold that it was ever explicitly agreed on by the speakers of the language. It is rather to hold at least that it is common practice among them to use a particular expression in a particular way. But if we say that it is common practice, we do not mean that they necessarily ever *do* use this expression in this way; they may never use it at all. There are plenty of complex expressions which possess a sense and which nobody ever uses. What is meant by calling the use of such expressions common practice among the speakers of the language is that they *would* use them in this way if they used them at all. Though even this is not quite correct; complex utterance-types which are never used no doubt include many that are ambiguous, and for such expressions there are possible worlds in which they are used, but used with only one of their senses. In learning a language we learn rules which will enable us to construct the meanings of new utterance-types from the meanings of expressions already familiar to us. These rules are themselves regularly followed by the users of the language, which is what makes them rules; and it is this which entitles us to speak of the use of a complex expression that is never actually produced as "common practice": it is assigned this use by the operation of rules which are themselves regularly practised.

But it is not enough that an expression should be regularly used in a certain way, or that its use should be generable by rules which are regularly followed. It must be common knowledge[15] among the speakers of the language that it is so used, or at least the rules which generate its use must be commonly recognised: they must expect one another to follow them, expect to be expected to follow them, and so on. Not, of course, that they must be able to state such rules, for the precise formulation of them is notoriously difficult; but besides following them they must recognise and seek to avoid lapses by themselves or by others. Moreover, it must be *because* it is common knowledge that the common practice obtains; a speaker uses an expression in the way he does because he expects his hearers to expect him to use it in that way. It is the fact that the practice is regularly adhered to which makes it desirable for each person individually to adhere to it.

We can put this briefly by saying that in calling the sense of an expression conventional we mean at least that this use of it is common practice amongst the users of the language; that it is common knowledge that it is common practice; and that it is common practice because it is common knowledge.[16] But now the question arises whether in that case conversational implicatures are not equally conventional. For it is a common and generally recognised practice

---

[15] In something like D. K. Lewis's sense. Lewis's conception of common knowledge is substantially the same as Schiffer's mutual knowledge*: the intuitive idea behind both is that each person should know that the others know, know that the others know he knows, and so on. As Lewis defines common knowledge, however([1969], p. 56), it is essential that some state of affairs obtain which provides a *basis* for the common knowledge by indicating to all concerned what it is that is commonly known and that they all have reason to believe it. I prefer if possible not to incorporate this requirement, and so to admit as common knowledge a case in which people just knew these things about one another —perhaps by intuition or without any grounds at all.

[16] This is very rough, of course. See further D. K. Lewis [1969], esp. p. 78; and the modification by J. F. Bennett [1973].

to follow the Co-operative Principle in making utterances, and to rely on one's audience's consequent expectation to convey more than one actually says; this principle generates the conversational implicatures an utterance carries, rather as other linguistic rules generate the senses of complex utterance-types. These senses are called conventional because the rules which generate them are; so if the Co-operative Principle is itself conventional, it ought to be equally proper so to describe the use of "He is a competent bicyclist" in certain contexts to disparage a man's academic worth. Now it may be said that although it is a common and generally recognised practice to obey the Co-operative Principle when one is conversing, nevertheless obedience to this principle is not really conventional since speakers do not obey it *because* they expect their hearers to expect them to obey it: it is common knowledge among speakers that the principle is generally adhered to, but it is not adhered to *because* this is common knowledge. It is adhered to rather because there is no alternative; and it is this which provides the basis of our common knowledge that each of us will obey it and expect others to. But this does not seem to me correct. There are alternatives.

One alternative would be not to talk at all. That we have a language at all for communicating with one another is a matter of convention, and a matter which might have been otherwise. To make sounds or other marks with the intention of inducing propositional attitudes in a hearer is a common and generally recognised practice, and it is a practice we each stick to because we know that others will stick to it, expect us to stick to it, expect us to expect them to stick to it, and so on. There would be no point bothering to talk if a policy of silence was universally adhered to and expected of one. And it might be; people who preferred solitude might have a convention whereby nobody ever tried to communicate with anybody else. Still, it may be held that no further element of conventionality is involved in our obedience to the Co-operative Principle and in our recognition of the implicatures it gives rise to; on the grounds that an acceptance of this principle is a necessary condition of being able to talk at all. The conventionality of the Co-operative Principle, and of the implicatures to which it gives rise, would thus be at least of a different order from that of the meanings of words, which require special conventions which vary from language to language. But this still seems wrong. We may find it difficult to imagine taking part in a conversation without feeling any obligation to "make your

conversational contribution such as is required, at the stage at which
it occurs, by the accepted purpose or direction of the talk-exchange
in which you are engaged", but there is no obvious contradiction in
supposing a people who could talk to one another but who felt no
such obligation. No doubt their talk-exchanges could not be said
to have any accepted purpose or direction at all (though individual
remarks could have); they would simply consist in series of dis-
connected remarks which speakers and hearers did not attempt to
tie together. In the circumstances we might perhaps say that these
people lacked the notion of conversation; and we might think also
that they would have to be very stupid, or very limited in what they
could do with their language, to be unable to see how much more
they could achieve by conversing, as we do, in accordance with the
Co-operative Principle. But we have no reason to deny that they
can talk; they do possess a language, which they can use to communicate beliefs and other propositional attitudes. Moreover, the
mere recognition by a community of speakers that one ought to
obey the Co-operative Principle is not by itself enough to ensure that
apparent breaches of the principle are treated as giving rise to conversational implicatures; for in a society of very literal-minded men
it might be held that if one's conversational contribution were not
obviously and straightforwardly appropriate to the context it was
to be dismissed as out of place. In such a community an individual
would gain nothing by trying to suggest more than he said, or trying
to understand others as doing this. There might in other words be
an alternative *convention* even among people who did recognise
that they ought to subscribe to the Co-operative Principle: a convention to the effect that subtleties are not to be looked for, that a
speaker means no more than he says, and that if he says the wrong
thing his remark must be censured as out of place and as violating
the Co-operative Principle.[17] We can, of course, agree that for most

[17] To show that the practice which gives rise to conversational implicatures is
conventional in my sense, it is not strictly *necessary* to show that it has alternatives
which would themselves be conventions; it is sufficient that there should be
alternatives—that there might, for example, have been no common practice at
all in the area in question. What is important is that the practice be followed
because of the general expectation that it will be. D. K. Lewis, however, does
not count a practice as a convention unless it has alternatives which are conventions. I therefore include as conventions certain practices which Lewis calls
"social contracts" and not conventions (though not those in which the agent's
first preference is that others should follow the practice while he does not).
(Cf. D. K. Lewis [1969] 9. 95.) (*Continued overleaf*)

purposes it is much better not to have this pedestrian and unimagina-
tive convention, though people like mathematicians, lawyers and
scientists perhaps come close to adopting some such rule in certain
circumstances; but it does represent an alternative to the practice of
looking for hints and concealed suggestions, which enables us to
recognise and to employ conversational implicatures. And if this
practice has alternatives which people might have adopted, without
being any the less able to use language or even to converse with one
another, the basis of our expectation that others will follow it and
not an alternative practice cannot be so very different from the basis
of our expectation that they will use the word "goat" to mean
'goat': it must be something we learn by seeing how the people
around us use language, for we might have found ourselves in a
society which did things differently.

I admit one is inclined to feel that our practice of looking for
hidden suggestions is very *natural*; more natural to us, no doubt,
than the alternative of treating every failure to say what is literally
appropriate as a straightforward failure to live up to the Co-
operative Principle. And substantially more natural than is the
practice of using the word "goat" to mean 'goat'. We tend to assume
that everyone we come across, whatever language they speak, will
be familiar with the device of communicating by conversational
implicature; legal or technical contexts in which the alternative
literalistic convention seems to be followed have to be very carefully
set up. Now if a practice is one that human beings find natural, or
more natural than any available alternative, there is some point in
distinguishing it from any purely artificial convention; for the basis
of one person's expectation that others will conform, expect him to
conform, etc., need now be only the knowledge or feeling that this is

That is merely a verbal point. A more serious difference is that according
to Lewis it must be common knowledge that alternatives are available ([1969]
pp. 73 ff.). Now I agree that it may not be common knowledge among most
people that there are alternatives to our using the Co-operative Principle in
the way we do. Equally, however, it may not be common knowledge among
certain groups that there are alternatives to the grammatical rules they use—
or even to the rules that assign meanings to their words, for they may not realise
that languages other than their own are possible. I am interested in a sense for
"convention" which will make their linguistic rules conventional despite this;
and it is in this (rather natural) sense of the word that I want to call our use of
the Co-operative Principle equally conventional. What matters is that the
participants in the practice act as they do *because* it is common knowledge
amongst them that they do act in that way; it is compatible with this that it
may never occur to them that they could do things otherwise than as they do.

the natural thing to do. Unfortunately, however, this distinction cannot be used to mark any very fundamental difference between the implicatures and the sense of an utterance; for though it may turn out that the practice which gives rise to implicatures is in some sense more natural to us than any of the linguistic rules involved in the assigning of sense, this is very far from obvious and has often been denied. And if we found that it was equally natural for human beings to use the word βεκός to mean 'bread', or to make use of cyclical transformation rules in their grammars, we should still speak of the sense of the word βεκός, and still think of the grammatical rules in question as determinant of sense. There might be a man or a race of men who possessed innately a complete knowledge of how to speak Phrygian, and to whom all the linguistic rules involved seemed perfectly natural; but the problem of distinguishing sense from implicature would be the same with respect to them as it is for us. (It scarcely matters, of course, whether we call their linguistic rules conventions, and say that they find that certain conventions come naturally to them, or whether we so define "convention" as to exclude this;[18] though the former course seems to me preferable since the other features of conventions are present. These differ from purely artificial conventions only in that it does not have to be learnt by agreement or from precedent what the rules are.)

We cannot, therefore, rely on the naturalness of using the Co-operative Principle as we do to give rise to implicatures, to provide us with any essential difference in kind between that practice and the rules which assign to expressions their sense; or with any very adequate ground for refusing to call that practice conventional. So it does not seem that we can exploit any difference in conventionality between implicatures and sense to give us a practical test to apply in dubious cases.

When the Co-operative Principle is used to generate an implicature, it is very often the case that the context in which it is applied, and the implicature it is used to produce, are of a new and unfamiliar kind; but as we have seen this does not make the principle itself, or the practice of using it to generate implicatures, any the less

---

[18] It would be excluded by D. K. Lewis's definition only if they also failed to envisage the possibility of other, less natural, ways of talking. It is excluded by Schiffer, who does not allow the common knowledge involved in a convention to be based on the presumption that everyone will adopt the most natural practice—Schiffer [1972] pp. 130, 150.

conventional, and it is a consequence of these things that in just these circumstances such-and-such an implicature will be carried. In a quite similar way those linguistic conventions which determine the senses of complex semantical units (like sentences), given the senses of their constituent parts, may determine the sense of some quite new and unfamiliar sentence. What makes us think that conversational implicatures are not conventional, or not conventional in the way that senses are, is perhaps the fact that there is no definite limit to the things that tokens of a single utterance-type can be used to conversationally implicate, since there is no definite limit to the varieties of context that can occur or be created.[19] But as we have seen this does not help us to tell in any particular case whether something is conversationally implicated or not. It seems that all we can usefully say to distinguish conversational implicatures is that they depend, not on any further special conventions about particular pieces of language, nor even on more general conventions about the dependence of the senses of complexes on the senses of their constituents, but on the contextual convention regarding the use of the Co-operative Principle. The sense of an utterance is certainly one of the factors which gives rise to its conversational implicatures, but what is conveyed goes beyond the sense: and the point of saying that it goes beyond the sense is that there is no convention other than this Co-operative convention which associates with the utterance-type the actual message that this token of that type is M-intended to convey. We have seen that the Co-operative Principle can function not only to produce conversational implicatures but also to determine which of the senses of an ambiguous utterance is intended: the difference between the two sorts of case is that in the latter there are other separate conventions which assign the reading in question to the utterance-type—and the only part played by the context is to determine which of its readings is appropriate in a given instance. The question we have to ask ourselves therefore, when faced with any particular example, is whether the speaker is relying on the existence of some such separate convention or just upon the usual conventions of sense together with the Co-operative Principle. If he conversationally implicates something,

---

[19] It is this open-endedness of what any given utterance-type can be used to convey, in different contexts, that in general distinguishes contextual conventions like the Co-operative convention from those conventions which are determinative of sense.

he intends the basis for the common knowledge that the utterance is meant to convey this not to be some extra rule concerning the utterance-type, but rather to be the shared expectation that the Co-operative Principle will be observed despite any appearance of the contrary. The gradual process of hardening an implicature into a new sense, as when a metaphor becomes frozen, is thus the process of developing a special new convention for the word which speaker and hearer can make use of in communicating, instead of relying any longer on the machinery of implicature.

Now this does justify what might possibly be called an appeal to intuition to help decide, in the more extreme cases, whether something is conveyed by conversational implicature or not: for as users of the language we can reflect on whether we rely on some special new convention for the word, or whether we rely only on the old conventions of sense and the Co-operative Principle. And we may come up with a pretty decisive answer.[20] It is quite implausible to suppose that "competent bicyclist" has acquired the new sense of 'incompetent academic', not because a hypothesis to that effect would not explain how the phrase is used but because it is clear to us that we have no special rule to that effect; it is similarly implausible to suppose that a broadcaster talking about the grass roots of the Labour Party is employing only the original sense of those words in conjunction with the Co-operative Principle. On must ask oneself what one's grounds are for the expectation that one will be understood: is one relying upon general familiarity with that employment of the Co-operative Principle which generates conversational implicatures?

It is clear from this what is wrong with the very extreme suggestion, mentioned above, that all our words have but one sense and that whatever else we use them to convey is conveyed conversationally. The suggestion strikes us as highly implausible, because we are aware that in communicating we do not rely on the Co-operative Principle to the extravagant degree that this would require. It may perhaps be conceivable that there should be a people all of whose

---

[20] Not that our beliefs on this score are infallible, of course. I may believe I am relying on a certain convention when in fact I am not; in that case, the discovery that there was no such convention to rely on would not affect my practice. But more usually, if I believe I am relying on a particular convention in making some remark, I would not make just that remark (or make it in just that way) unless I did believe there was such a convention; and here my belief that I am relying on that convention is correct.

utterances had the same sense, though they used different words to express this sense on different occasions, and relied on this difference in mode of expression to generate enough implicatures to get across a fair variety of messages. Conversational implicatures can certainly be generated by the speaker's choice of words, as in Grice's account of "if...then...". The difference between such a "generalised conversational implicature" and a special convention governing the use of the form of words is that the expectation speaker and hearer share concerning the use of the expression is differently grounded in the two cases. The implicature is conversational, and not part of the sense, so long as they rely on the Co-operative Principle in the way we have become familiar with; it ceases to be a conversational implicature when they base their expectations instead upon common knowledge of the conventions governing the utterance-type involved. But although there is thus a theoretical difference between the two cases, and though they can sometimes be told apart, it is not always easy or even possible to tell them apart in practice, for the basis of our shared expectation may not be clear to us; and if there were a people like those just imagined they would probably find themselves gradually assigning different senses to different forms of words and so reducing the extent of their reliance on the Co-operative Principle, perhaps without noticing it.

Thus sometimes we do know what the basis of our shared expectation is. But not always; and not in the problematic cases. They are problematic just because they cannot be so easily resolved. They fall within an area in which as speaker and hearers we have no very clear idea what conventions we are using. We get no definite answer if we ask ourselves whether it is in virtue of any special convention that an utterance of "If it is sunny they will play cricket" conveys a connection between antecedent and consequent, or whether this is conveyed conversationally. For normal purposes, indeed, it does not in the least matter; what matters is to get the message across, and for that it is necessary that there should be common knowledge between the speaker and his audience of what he intends to convey by his utterance—but how this common knowledge is achieved, which conventions are actually involved, is a matter of indifference. What is surprising is not that there should be cases in which we do not know what conventions we are using, but that there should be any cases in which we do. Normal speakers and hearers, after all, have no very sophisicated notion of a convention or of a linguistic rule; not even linguists are at all clearly aware what conventions they rely upon to communicate.

All we need to know is how we shall be understood; the notions of a convention and a linguistic rule are brought on to explain how we can know this. Besides our linguistic practice, and such intuitions as we do possess about why we expect to be understood, there is *nothing more* that determines the application of these notions. It should be remembered that we cannot find additional evidence by appealing to what people think they understand initially by an expression when they hear it, or to whether they are aware of making any recourse to the Co-operative Principle; for such recourse may be made without thinking (and standardly is). While, as Mackie says ([1973] p. 80), speakers of English do not generally think of "if" as meaning '⊃', this may only be because they naturally associate it with the conversational contexts in which it normally occurs, and in which, by an automatic and unconscious application of the Co-operative Principle, they interpret it non-truth-functionally. So all we have to go on is our use of language and such knowledge as we may possess about the conventions on which we rely; and if in a given case these considerations leave it indeterminate which of two or more accounts is appropriate, then the matter simply *is* indeterminate. There is no further evidence to be adduced; no new consideration to be discovered which will settle the question. This appears to be the case with the logical particles, and with other examples that give us trouble in a similar way: to the question whether or not there is a special convention of sense for "if...then ..." to the effect that antecedent and consequent are connected, there is no definite answer. Either theory will do; indeed any of the three Hypotheses or their variants. For an affirmative answer to that question would still leave us to choose between the Semantical Hypothesis and the Third Hypothesis, where the issue is again one of how much is to be handled by an appeal to difference of sense and how much by contextual means.

## IV

Choice between alternative theories is an aesthetic matter; and the tastes of some may decide the present issue for them, perhaps in favour of having as few senses as possible, perhaps in favour of minimising reliance on the Co-operative Principle. Others may wish to bring on considerations of convenience within some more general theory about the character of language: considerations which might well include a close connection between the sense of an utterance and its logical form. There is something very attractive about the Leibnizian idea that the propositional content, the sense and reference, of what we say can be expressed in a formalised language for which all the legitimate inferential moves are precisely determined by syntactical means; someone who considers himself to have independent grounds for holding that this formalised language must be truth-functional will naturally adopt the Conversationalist Hypothesis. To someone who thinks that it must admit (for example) modal operators, and so cannot be purely truth-functional, the Conversationalist Hypothesis will be inadequate. However, no consideration we have come across here lends positive support to either of these views about the logical form of natural language. There are, of course, general arguments in favour of the truth-functional view, usually to the effect that there would be something unintelligible—or at least radically confused—about a language the logical form of which was not extensional; but to assess such arguments would take us far afield. However, the consideration that in cases like that of "if...then..." there may be no determinate right answer to the question what belongs to the sense suggests that there may equally be no determinate right answer to the question what belongs to the logical form of what is said. For is there any other way of determining the logical form of an utterance than by deciding what its sense is? Indeed, does determining its logical form *differ* from determining its sense? To discover its logical form we have to investigate what part it plays in entailments—what its logical relationships are; but what *logical* relationships it bears is fixed by its sense. If we hold that the sense of "If $p$, then $q$" is truth-functional, we shall say that it follows from "Not-$p$", whereas if we hold that it is not we shall deny this; if instead we adopt the Semantical Hypothesis we shall say that from it follows something like "There is a connection between $p$ and $q$", which otherwise we might not admit. The difference, of course, is not over what people normally understand by and infer from "If $p$ then $q$", but over how much of what they understand belongs to the sense and which of their inferences are licensed by the logical form. So if the evidence underdetermines what is to be accounted to the sense of "If...then...", it under-determines what is to be taken as the logical form of hypotheticals in ordinary language.

Not that this is regrettable or surprising. What it suggests is merely that instead of looking for a single logical form for "If it is sunny they will play cricket", and instead of trying to find a single formalised language in which the moves we want to treat as logic-ally valid are all systematically expressed, we should recognise that questions about propositional content and about logical form can be answered differently depending on what our purposes are. Sometimes, as in mathematical contexts, our interests are best suited by treating the senses of the logical particles truth-functionally; for other purposes it may be more satisfactory to repre-sent the logic of natural language as making use of strict implication, or conceivably as having the properties of some such system as that of Anderson and Belnap, or that of Geach and von Wright. But perhaps none of these alternatives should be looked on as more correct than any other; only as more or less useful for certain purposes.

What has been said above does require a slight modification. All along I have been contrasting sense with conversational implicature, and leaving out of account what Grice calls conventional implica-tures. He says very little about conventional implicatures; but it has now become possible to see what role they might play. It might well be that two words like "and" and "but", or "dog" and "cur", differ in what they convey in a manner not plausibly to be ex-plained by appeal to the Co-operative Principle; and that one might nevertheless want to hold that they differ not at all in respect of their part in legitimising inferences. In that case it would be natural to say that they had the same sense, because they have the same logical role; and then there would be a difference between them, not to be explained conversationally, but due to a difference in the specific semantic conventions governing them. As I was talking earlier, any such difference would have to be accounted a difference of sense. But if it is convenient to work with a narrower concept of sense, in order to facilitate the close connection between sense and logical form, then we can say that what we have here is not a difference of sense but a difference in what is conventionally impli-cated. (How close this may be to Grice's account of conventional implicatures I do not know.)

It seems, at any rate, that perhaps we should not regard either the Conversationalist Hypothesis or its rivals as definitely right or wrong. Certainly, more would be needed to establish definitely that the Conversationalist Hypothesis can account for the linguistic facts of natural language, though it seems very likely that it can; and the same applies to Cohen's Semantical Hypothesis. Some version of what I have called the Third Hypothesis, the theory which postulates several different senses for each particle, is bound to fit the facts of *usage*, provided the hypothesis itself can be clearly stated; though at the cost of supposing us to rely on a perhaps counterintuitively large number of special conventions. But what seems likely to be true for the logical particles will hold in other instances as well, and perhaps in other instances of considerable philosophical importance.

The conception of a conversational implicature promises to be very fruitful in a wide range of philosophical fields. In some cases there can be little doubt that it provides the proper way of explaining what is conveyed, as in the bicycling example. No account of how we communicate can omit conversational implicature; the Cooperative Principle gives us a way of conveying new messages in new contexts indefinitely, and no multiplication of senses could account for this. Still, there are other cases of philosophical interest where it seems that the linguistic evidence, and the evidence of our intuitions as to what conventions we rely on, could be handled equally well by a theory ascribing something to the sense of an expression and by a different theory which treated it as conversationally implicated. It is of course hard, if not impossible, to find an uncontentious example of this, but a possible candidate would be furnished by definite descriptions: here one theory treats it as part of the sense of "the F" that there should exist one and only one F, whereas another theory might regard this not as belonging to the sense but as something that is conversationally implicated in very many circumstances by utterances of "the F". Intuition may be consulted, but here, as with the logical particles, it yields no clear reply; so here again perhaps the matter should be regarded as indeterminate. We do of course require to carry out a thorough investigation before we are entitled to affirm such a conclusion in any particular case; for we have to show that the alternative theories are capable of accounting for the facts of our linguistic practice, and we have to consider, for what they are worth, our intuitive beliefs about what conventions we rely on in communication: beliefs which are not usually sharp or clear-cut, since we are more interested in communicating successfully than in the character of the rules which enable us to do this, but which at least place limits on the plausibility of otherwise acceptable theories.

# 6

# The identity of propositions

## SIMON BLACKBURN

Hostility to propositions is common; taking the philosophical community as a whole it is probably orthodox. At its weakest it is expressed in the view that we can permit talk of propositions, but since propositions are abstract entities an empiricist ought to understand and preferably paraphrase such talk in terms of more concrete notions. By philosophers' standards this counts as friendliness and I shall not be concerned with it, although I shall have some incidental remarks about certain attempts to follow the idea through. Next we have the view that we can permit talk of propositions, but must remember that they are of no value in clarifying any problems in the theory of meaning. I shall not be concerned with that either, although I might record my opinion that not talking of them has proved of great value in obscuring many problems in the theory of meaning. Finally there is the view that we cannot permit talk of propositions at all, even as a prelude to analysis or paraphrase, because the notion is itself infirm. It is this view which I wish to discuss.

There are two different demands which the notion of a proposition is introduced to meet. Firstly we want a noun to stand for that which two people who believe the same thing both believe, two people who doubt the same thing both doubt, two sentences which say the same thing both say, and so on. Secondly we want a noun for that which is identifiable, because of the meanings of its words and its syntax, as the particular truth or falsehood that a sentence of a language is used to put across. I shall discuss in section III whether the same thing can play both roles. For there is no immediate reason why the thing which is believed, doubted, and so on should be identical with the thing introduced by the theory of truth. It requires, we shall see, some sort of proof that their identity conditions are the same, and this is not easily found. But quite independently of these internal stresses in the notion, blunter considerations threaten to destroy it.

## I

Is it proper to introduce something—the proposition—as that which two people who say that same thing both say, that which two people who know the same thing both know, and so on? A philosopher with ontological scruples might already protest. Admitting the phenomenon of synonymy, whereby two people, two utterances, or two sentences can express the same thing, he might nevertheless query the propriety of talking about a thing which they each express. The fact of synonymy between two items, he would say, should not be presented as each of those items expressing the same *thing*. For we should not inflate our ontology more than we can avoid, and without some more compelling reason for it than the mere existence of synonymy relationships the introduction of propositions does just that. At first sight this reaction is weak: it is quite general for us to allow the formation of a noun once we have a feature which things share. A disposition is what all similarly disposed things share, a direction is what all parallel lines point in, and a quartet is what all similar sequences of sounds render. So once we have relations of synonymy we are only true to form in talking of a proposition as that which synonymous sentences all express. The abstract noun stands for exactly what its name implies: the harmless but useful abstraction from some similarity between concrete items.

So at least it might seem. But whilst such abstraction is common, and whilst common sense urges that it cannot be philosophically dangerous, it does introduce a problem. For the purpose of the abstraction appears to be pure abbreviation. It enables us to be brief and neat where without it we would be long and cumbersome. But it introduces no new truths into the world, for the abstraction is itself no new thing, and what is said by using it ought to be sayable at greater length referring only to the concrete items out of which it is constructed. But it proves extremely hard to analyse out reference to the things which people believe, doubt, etc., and to replace them by ways of expressing the same facts without such reference.

This might make us suspect that we should not after all let the notion in purely because of the propositional attitudes. If the truth about a person X when X says that $p$ is a matter of X's relation to words or utterances then there may be no need to countenance the thing which X says—the proposition—at all. Many writers have followed this path. Carnap [1956] and Geach [1972], for example, claimed that the only reference made in "X says that $p$" is to X and to the words which occur after the "that". X is therefore related to some particular English words. The classical obstacle is that X might have said that $p$ without having any relation to the English words which we have used in reporting him. But the reply is that if we construct a complicated enough relation this will not be so. Thus it is admitted on all hands that X could have said that (for example) the earth moves without having spoken, understood, or been aware of the existence of, just those English words. It is also not contested that X could have said that the earth moves even had the course of events been such that English had never developed at all as a language, so that the particular sequence of words "the earth moves" did not exist, at any rate as a sequence with a meaning. So the relation to those words which, in the theory, X bears when it is true that X said that the earth moves, needs to survive X's apparent independence of them.

It is not at all clear what these writers hope to gain by reliance on such a relation. It is not that it is obscure, but rather that the only clarification introduces the very abstractions the relation is designed to avoid. We can see this by considering an instructive parallel. What relation to the numeral "12" does someone bear who is thinking of the number twelve, remembering that he could do that in ignorance of the meaning of that numeral, or even had it never existed? The only evident answer is: he is thinking of that thing which is in fact denoted by the numeral. The relationship to the numeral is there sure enough, but it is indirect, and only exhibited by mention of the number and of the linguistic contingency. It can therefore be no substitute for a theory which demands explicit reference to numbers. Likewise: what relation to the words "the earth moves" does someone bear who said that the earth moves? He said what (the proposition that) they express in English. Again the relationship is only naturally exhibited by mention of the proposition and of the linguistic contingency, and whilst our understanding of it remains at that level it affords no real alternative to reference to propositions.

A similar theory of a propositional attitude, also hoping to avoid reference to propositions, is given by Davidson [1968]. Davidson conceives the problem as that of giving an adequate display of what makes true, sentences of the form "X said that *p*". An adequate display would make clear how it is possible for beings who have a finite vocabulary and have been through only a finite learning process to understand the limitless number of predicables on X made by different substitutions for *p* in "X said that *p*". Regarding each as primitive would not do, for example. An adequate display would also show how the original sentence possesses its logical relations; by displaying what makes something true we display what it entails and what entails it.

The theory is that the word "that" occurring in "X said that *p*" is to be regarded as a proper demonstrative. The object demonstrated is the utterance following it, i.e. the utterance of "*p*" which anybody saying "X said that *p*" must make after he has pronounced the demonstrative. To avoid the objections we have already mentioned the word "said" is construed as introducing the relation of samesaying, where one samesays an utterance by making one synonymous with it. The important equivalence then is between:

(S) X said that the earth moves; and
(D) X samesaid this: "the earth moves";

where the quotes indicate that it is the utterance made which is the object of the preceding demonstrative.

If the theory is adequate then it does block introduction of propositions by simple abstraction of what X said when X said that something. For apparently X's relations are fully captured by his relations to utterances, and the noun phrase *what he said* should only be regarded as proxy for a samesaying utterance. And the theory does capture the nature of indirect speech in one respect. It is obviously right that to truly report someone in this way what is needed is "X said that..." followed by an utterance which is synonymous with X's original. But this fact by itself is as easily accommodated by any theory which makes the object of the demonstrative some function of the succeeding utterance; there is no argument from this alone to a semantics in which the object of the demonstrative is the succeeding utterance itself. It might, for example, be the proposition which it expresses. How are we to decide?

There is no logical equivalence between (S) and (D). For I cannot now make an utterance such that (S) entails that X samesaid that utterance. At least two different classes of possibility rule that out. Firstly (S) doesn't entail that there were any utterances at all ever made after X said that the earth moved, since it is possible that the utterance made by X was the last one ever. Secondly of any utterance I now make it will be possible that X should have said that the earth moved and not samesaid that, since that utterance might have failed to mean what X said. Even if it does mean it, there is a possible world in which it does not. So (S) does not entail (D). But neither does (D) entail (S). For as well as the possibility that my utterance should have failed to mean what X said there is the possibility that it should have meant something different. And then it might have been true that X samesaid it, but false that he said that the earth moves.

If (S) and (D) are not logically equivalent, can they nevertheless stand in the sort of equivalence which is demanded for the theory of truth which Davidson is seeking? Obviously not if, as described, a purpose of that theory is to display the logical relations of the sentences with which it deals. For far from displaying the logical relations of (S) in a more perspicuous form, (D) is in no way logically equivalent to (S) itself. But this is not easily remedied, for unless it generates logical equivalences the theory of truth will not give the truth-conditions of the sentences put into it either. Nor will it give us a theory of how people's understanding of the input sentences arises, since if the logical relations are different then people are taking the sentence differently from the way in which the truth theory presents it. A symptom of all this would be that when it comes to deal with those constructions of the language which contain modal concepts, a theory which has not generated logical equivalences will break down altogether. Thus eventually the theory of truth for natural English will need to consider the sentence "Of any utterance of English it is possible that X should have said that the earth is round and not samesaid that." But no account of the truth-conditions of that can incorporate the equivalence of (S) and (D).[1]

---

[1] It might be thought that this argument can be evaded by pointing out that the left-hand side of the equivalence in a Tarski type of truth-definition would not be (S) itself, but rather a sentence mentioning (S) and saying that it is true. Then the modal arguments which show that there is no interesting equivalence between (S) and (D) may not work in the same way to distinguish this related sentence from (D). This is true, but not to the point. For the purpose of the theory is to exhibit the truth-conditions of (S) itself, not of any related sentence which mentions it, and our argument remains that those truth-conditions cannot be found in X's relation to a particular utterance.

Three further aspects of the matter present themselves. Firstly if we wish to preserve the sensible view that the demonstrative in (S) really is functioning as a demonstrative, we have as I earlier remarked a choice of functions of the succeeding utterance to serve as its reference. But in the light of the arguments governing the choice we need a candidate (and corresponding relation R for X to bear to it) such that X R that: f("the earth is round") corresponds in truth-value to X said that the earth is round, in all possible worlds. The only natural solution is to take the demonstrative to refer to the thought or proposition which X in fact expressed. It will only be possible to avoid this by contorting R to give the right result over the whole range of possibilities, and as I have already argued the understanding of R will then, in effect, be in terms of *that which* some sentence/utterance/concrete item does actually express, and propositions are brought in by the back door.

The second point is that it is no transgression of Davidson's demand of finitude to admit propositions as referents for the demonstrative. There are indeed a limitless number of predicables "... said that $p$" generated by the limitless number of things to be said. But if we can exhibit our understanding of which proposition is meant by any sentence put for $p$ in a finitary way then each of these predicables is equally intelligible. So there is no new problem here for the finitary theory of truth.

The third aspect of the matter is more interesting. For our discussion could be applied to other cases of abstraction than that of propositions. Colours for example might be taken to be abstractions from relations of matching between ordinary physical objects. Since Frege directions are thought to be abstractions from relations of parallelism between lines. But exactly parallel modal arguments to those above would block any attempt to remove colours or directions in favour of objects and their relations. For example, "X is coloured red" and "X matches that pillar-box" are not equivalent because concerning any pillar-box, X might have been red but not matched it, and concerning any pillar-box, X might have matched it and not been red. These are true because concerning that pillar-box and concerning what is in fact its colour, the first might not have been the second. There is no mystery about this: any pillar-box might have been a different colour from that which it in fact is. It seems then that in each case—propositions, colours, directions— the abstraction is not quite so innocent as at first appears. We cannot simply elide it in favour of the objects and their relations because in each case it is contingent that an object has that relation with others which is intended to define the abstraction. Furthermore that contingency is itself one whose expression needs mention of the abstract item. It is because two expressions each express whichever proposition they do that they are synonymous, because two objects each have the colour they do that they match, because two lines each have the direction they do that they are parallel. So the abstract item seems doubly immune to reduction: a contingency prevents any reductive analysis or equivalence for the purposes of the theory of truth, and the nature of the contingency, its own involvement with the abstraction, makes it unlikely that any gain in understanding could be made by pursuing such reductions.

It appears then that we can quite properly start from the propositional attitude constructions "X says/thinks/knows...that *p*" and go to the abstraction "what X says/thinks/knows": the proposition. At any rate there exists no plausible semantic theory of the that-clauses which can block the move.

## II[2]

Deep hostility to propositions ought then to query the propriety of the that-clauses from which they are generated rather than the mode of generation. In effect this is exactly what has happened. By casting doubt on the possibility of synonymy Quine and others have cast doubt on the possibility of true reportage of propositional attitudes, for as we have seen such reportage demands the insertion, after the "that" of indirect speech, of an expression synonymous with the original. If this is a demand that could not possibly be met, perhaps even an unintelligible demand, then no truths are made by such statements, and they need not be considered by scientific semantic theory. Nor would they license the introduction of any abstractions. Of course the price is high: nothing less than the abandonment of all reports and beliefs about what anybody else says, thinks, believes, hopes, fears, means, argues, understands.

The attack on synonymy of individual sentences gains its stature almost entirely because of the work of Quine, and Quine's critique of it is almost entirely concentrated in the doctrine of the indeter-

[2] This section owes much to an unpublished paper by D. Bolton, read at Cambridge in 1970.

minacy of radical translation. Quine has residual doubts that even if this doctrine were rejected, even within classical theory of meaning, there is a formidable problem of individuating sentence-meaning in a satisfactory way. This problem arises from the demand that propositions should remain the same under various transformations whereas the attitudes of which they are supposed to be the objects do not: it comes to full flower in the cluster of variants of the paradox of analysis, and will be the subject of section III. But Quine says: "The difficulties...are merely by the way. The very question of conditions for identity of propositions presents not so much an unsolved problem as a mistaken ideal" ([1960b] p. 206). So it is appropriate to consider these difficulties only when we have deflected Quine's principal attack.

The arguments surrounding the indeterminacy of radical translation are easy to criticise, but difficult to criticise well. To supporters they form an interlocking, stable, metaphysic; to opponents they resemble the partnership of a shifty mutual support society, particularly in that it is never clear which one is responsible for which element of the doctrine. For my purpose—the purpose of showing that constructions relying on synonymy, and the abstraction of propositions, is legitimate—it is necessary to distinguish just three elements of Quine's thought. Two of these are conveniently named already: they are the argument "from above" and the argument "from below" (Quine [1970b] p. 183). The third needs christening. I shall call it the pragmatic argument for allowing selective transcendence of indeterminate origins, or pragmatic selection for short. Although it is a relative latecomer to the partnership it is easy to see that it bears a great deal of weight. It alone denies to intensional concepts all the respectability that the concepts of science retrieve from the other two arguments. But before we reach that conclusion it is necessary to investigate the others. They have a definite ranking, for although the argument "from below"—the argument which starts with the "gavagai" example—is prominent in *Word and Object* [1960b], Quine himself later says of it, "This whole effort was aimed not at proof...The argument for the indeterminacy is another thing." (Quine [1970b] p. 183.) What then, is the argument from above?

Quine believes with Peirce that "the very meaning of a statement consists in the difference its truth would make to possible experience" ([1968a] p. 78). So, for the meaning of a statement to be a respectable item, it must be possible to identify the difference its truth would make to possible experience. If this is possible then it carries with it an epistemology: to determine what a speaker's statement means we must simply map the states of affairs which prompt his assent to it or dissent from it, and then we have identified its meaning. But, the argument continues, why suppose that there *is* such a thing as *the* difference which the truth of a statement would make to possible experience? There are some sentences, which Quine calls occasion sentences, for which a fair substitute for such a thing can be found, but this will not support even limited application of the idea of a proposition, because identity of stimulus-meaning falls short of synonymy. For the rest however the situation is much grimmer. For if there were such an item as *the* difference which the truth of a statement would make to experience, then the occurrence or non-occurrence of that difference in experience would afford a conclusive verification of the statement. But reflection on the structure of our beliefs shows us that experience does not have this potency. For the tribunal of experience is faced not by individual statements but rather by networks of statements, or theories. Faced with an experience which, we recognise, demands a modification of our network of beliefs, there is always choice what to hang on to and what to give up. Therefore one theorist may hold a statement when confronted by the experience which prompts another to give it up.

We might put this down to mere finitude, to the fact that at any time our experience forms only a fragment of the totality of possible experience. But this is not Quine's view. If this were the diagnosis of the choice which we have, no conclusions about indeterminacy of meaning would follow. For we could still hold that a statement puts a definite constraint on all possible experience, while admitting that at any time the experience already encountered leaves a choice whether to regard it as true or not. If we pursue this line into the epistemology of meaning it would be seen to merge with the merely inductive scepticism about meaning which Wittgenstein drew from Hume: after parallel experiences two theorists might appear to hold the same network of beliefs but at any later time they might suddenly diverge (Wittgenstein [1953] §185). For the current agreement in response would be no guarantee against one theorist actually holding his sentences responsible to a different set of possible experiences from the other—this difference emerging only in some future circumstance. But on this view sentence-meaning and sentence-synonymy remain perfectly determinate and respectable, it is just that there are inductive difficulties in knowing about them. This is not Quine's position.

For Quine believes that a choice of theories, or networks of beliefs, is open, even in the face of all possible experience, not just in the face of the limited experience any one person, or any scientific community, has at any time. The consequence can be presented vividly like this. Imagine two omnipresent omnitemporal entities of limitless intelligence and capacities of memory. They are supposed to have sated themselves with all the experience which a physical world can provide—past, present, and future. (If the notion of such a being is thought suspect, it doesn't matter: its defects are just those of the notion of the totality of all possible experience.) Suppose a linguist finds that as a result of all this experience one of them has a total structure of beliefs about the nature of the world, which we can christen A, and the other has a similar structure of beliefs, amounting to a theory B. Then the doctrine which Quine espouses cautions us that there is no guarantee that A and B are in any way identical; these beings may have made different choices and may hold different views about the world they have experienced. Furthermore, *ex hypothesi* there is no crucial test awaiting them: the observational basis of their beliefs is complete in a way that that of a finite being never is. It follows that the linguist has no right to identify A and B, but it equally follows that, if he does so, nothing in the reaction of either of the beings to an experience would show that he is wrong to do so.

This seems to leave the linguist with something of a problem, and Quine claims it to be insoluble: "The question whether, in the situation last described, the foreigner *really* believes A or believes rather B, is a question whose very significance I would put in doubt. This is what I am getting at in arguing the indeterminacy of translation." ([1970b] p. 181.) The linguist is in this trouble precisely because his favourite device of varying the situation and seeing how the theorists vary their assent and dissent is already played out: he already knows precisely what the two beings assent to, and it is apparently too blunt to tell which of A or B it is.

The natural response to this argument is puzzlement about the criterion of theory-identity which is behind it. The criteria are evidently tighter than mere identity of consequence of all possible experience, but what are they? Doubt then focuses on two distinct issues: firstly whether there exist any such tight criteria of theory identity, and secondly whether if there do, they are available to Quine. For Quine is frequently thought of as having moved onto total theories the semantic crown which in his view fitted sentences but badly. From "Two Dogmas of Empiricism" [1951] onwards Quine has emphasised that it is a network of beliefs, or theory, which is vulnerable to experience and which places a determinate constraint upon it. Combine this with the view that determinate meaning consists in placing a determinate constraint upon experience, and theories immediately seem to usurp the place of sentences as the smallest things with determinate meaning. This gives rise to *an* argument for indeterminacy of sentence-meaning: in one of Quine's papers it is indeed simply the contrast between the single sentence, which has "no fund of experiential implications to call its own", and a block of theory, which does, which works to the indeterminacy of the former, and "seals the fate of any general notion of propositional meaning..." ([1968a] p. 81). But this is not the present argument, for it makes no mention of the possibility of different theories with identical experiential consequences.

I do not intend to discuss whether this is indeed a possibility; for a decision on that, it seems to me, must be a consequence of a full theory of meaning rather than one of its premises. Nor do I wish to pursue further the question of whether it is consistent with Quine's other writings. What I do want to point out is that it is a futile starting point for an attack on sentence-meaning or synonymy. For the possibility arises, if it arises at all, because of some difference in the content of the theories—we are not talking about inscriptional or phonetic differences in their expression. But if difference of content does not entail difference of experiential consequences it must at least entail some difference of component semantics or syntax. The theories must say different things; they must either be talking of different things or saying different things about them. But then all we have to do is to investigate the semantics and syntax of the components of each theorists' speech, and what differences there are in their thought will make themselves plain. (See R. Kirk [1973].)

This reply can also be made to a natural weaker version of Quine's premiss. Rather than say that there *is* a possible world in which there are two distinct theories with identical experiential consequences Quine might argue that the unverifiability which, in his

view, this suffers, establishes its meaninglessness and the conse-
quential meaninglessness of classical theories of meaning which
allow it. But again the reply is that the unverifiability is unproven
because by investigating internal structure we have a perfectly good
technique for separating or identifying bodies of belief.

It is plain then that Quine's position needs some injection if it is
to neutralise this counter. It must cast doubt on the adequacy of
these methods to the task of individuating bodies of belief. Now it
could readily seem that this is easy. Because theories, in the light of
Peirce's doctrine, seemed the best bet for determinacy. But now it
appears that their determinacy will only be assured if we can locate
the meanings of various components of them, as well as the semantics
of the various devices for combining those components. So attention
switches to the view that whatever we think about total theory
identity, no method can isolate the meaning of a sentence within a
theory. But is this plausible?

It is fairly easy to establish that unless the range of considerations
which starts with "gavagai" can be taken as decisive, there is not
the slightest reason to believe it. Any sentence which occurs in my
expression of my total body of belief about the world commands my
assent not as an unstructured quantum of noise, but because it has a
semantics which I can recognise as a function of its structure and of
the semantics of its component parts. In plain terms it is made up
of words which it is open to an interpreter to identify, and whose
part in my linguistic reaction to the passing show can be plotted.
It is quite true that in following this method the linguist is not concerning himself directly with the verification conditions of the
individual sentence. He is looking on it as a structure whose identity
is a function of the identity of its parts. But since, as I mentioned, I
assent to it or dissent from it only in virtue of my own recognition of
its structure, this is perfectly to the point. It is true that by paying no
attention to verification conditions, directly, the method may seem
to conflict with Peirce's doctrine, but it is not therefore mentalistic
or unempirical. It accords perfectly well with the sort of naturalistic
approach to language which Quine applauds in Dewey; it may even
be said to find meaning in assent/dissent conditions, with the pro-
vision that we also look at assent to or dissent from other sentences
in which individual terms of the sentence under consideration also
occur.

Now if this method is inadequate it must be because behaviour does not identify the semantics of the terms and sentences of a person's speech. That is precisely the point which Quine attempts to prove with the argument "from below", the "gavagai" argument, and we have here shown that all the later work, the "different, broader and deeper" ground rests squarely upon it ([1970b] p. 178). If this whole effort was not aimed at proof, then we have no reason to believe in the indeterminacy of translation.

Quine is quite right that the argument "from below", the argument, that is, which hopes to unsettle our belief in the semantic determinacy of things like predicates, quantifiers, numerals, is suggestive rather than compelling. It starts with the reflection that if a native utters a particular sound, say "gavagai" when and only when a rabbit is visible to him, then although the visiting linguist can make a respectable entry in his notebook about the noise regarded as a sentence, he has various choices when he thinks of regarding the noise as utterance of a predicate. Does it mean "rabbit", or perhaps "undetached rabbit part"? If he could ask "How many gavagai?" he would settle the problem, but he does not know how to ask this when starting on an alien language. Similarly if he could ask "Is this the same gavagai as that?"

The linguist then starts to search for items in the natives' vocabulary which correspond to "Is this the same... as that?" or "How many...?" It would be natural to think that he has a good empirical method of identifying such items, particularly by conducting his observations in banks, markets, warehouses. This is not Quine's view. He thinks that however natural it might be for a linguist to think he has the answer, it is always a question of the projection of our "domestic" apparatus of reference, identity, and number onto the native, and this projection being testable for rightness or wrongness by no empirical evidence, the question of whether it is right or wrong does not arise.

It is of the utmost importance to clear our minds of one type of case if we want to properly assess this claim. Suppose we search for a native analogue, say, of the numeral "three". It could be that we can detect no phonetic modification of native noises which corresponds to our introduction of "three" into a sentence. If the natives appear to bother about number, say in buying apples, their way of communicating this concern would be opaque to us. It could be that whilst they apparently carry on commercial concerns there simply exists no phonetic disposition which we can isolate as expressing demands for or truths about three apples as opposed to some different number of apples. This peculiarity would stump a linguist. The natives have no disposition which is identical with our disposition to use numerals: we might concede outright that their semantics is straightforwardly mysterious to us. Some of Quine's remarks about the domesticity of our apparatus of reference, and some of his remarks about the possibility of achieving the same over-all effect with individually distinct means, might encourage us to think of such a case. But in fact it is not to the point. Because Quine's thesis is not that there is indeterminacy of translation where there is lack of correlation of linguistic disposition, nor where there is paucity of linguistic disposition; his thesis is that there is indeterminacy *tout court*. If we follow the argument through then at best the type of case I have described might encourage us to restrict the application of synonymy and propositional identity to cases where we have a correlation of linguistic disposition. We could agree with Quine that the question "Does he mean the same as him?" might have no answer where the phonetic variations in speech fail to map at all. We would restrict sameness of meaning and propositional identity to speakers whose phonetic dispositions can be mapped onto each other—and that means all people in whose utterances structure *can* be discerned and identified with mine. The concept still has plenty of scope.

This is one of the reasons why Quine gets no help from his example of the difficulty of choice posed by "ne...rien", and by the Japanese oxen counting case ([1968b] pp. 30–6). In these examples it is just because the overall locution has an apparently different structure that difficulty arises in identifying the function of one part within the structure with that of one term in ours. Similarly Harman's example of the indeterminacy of the set theoretic transla-tions of arithmetic is beside the point because here it is the paucity of the mathematicians' linguistic dispositions, arising no doubt from the nature of mathematics, which allows the indeterminacy (Har-man [1969]). The other reason Quine gains no support from his examples is, as he notes, that they trail no indeterminacy of total sentence-meaning in their wake.

To make his thesis, then, Quine needs the case where the terms can be isolated and found to play the same part in behaviour that mine do. The native is now perhaps a fellow English speaker. What we now need is an indication of how, say, the term "three" can play the full role in a person's linguistic responses that the term does in mine, yet be equally translatable as doing something different. In the case of "gavagai" Quine gave us some indication of what the possible alternatives are. We reply that with the identification of numerals and other locutions we can decide between the possibilities. Quine nowhere offers suggestions about how the indeterminacy continues: he contents himself with reiterating that the empirical evidence cannot provide determinate meaning, and that the search is therefore in pursuit of a mistaken ideal. But this awaits proof, or even plausibility.

But do we want to say that sufficiently rich behavioural evidence will actually entail the truth of just one semantic theory of a speaker? Or is there not always the logical possibility of some devious alternative interpretation? The question has intrinsic interest, of course. But it cannot possibly feature in an attack on the concept of meaning. For if the logical possibility of choice about meaning in the face of evidence were taken to discredit that concept, then the logical possibility of choice about almost anything in the face of evidence would discredit virtually all concepts. In particular there would be an exact parallelism with the concepts of physical science, where most philosophers, but especially Quine, believe that there is not logically conclusive evidence for the truth of theories containing them. Quine has often appeared unsatisfactory on this to critics. Faced with the charge that an exactly parallel argument to this would discredit the concepts of science, be replies that the indeterminacy of meaning is "parallel but additional". But the point is that the position *is* parallel, not that it isn't additional. (See for example, Alan Reeves [1973] p. 323.)

It is here that the third partner which I mentioned comes in: the pragmatic argument for allowing selective transcendence of indeterminate origins. We need scientific concepts. Perhaps we don't need semantic concepts. In that case, although nothing worse can be said about the relation of the latter to evidence than can be said about the former, it might be prudent to limit our acceptance of concepts to the bare minimum, and refuse to accept that there are any truths other than those about which we have to think.

There are two comments to make about this. Firstly there is no argument here against the intellectual reputability of the concepts of the theory of meaning. The idea that a speaker is saying something determinate which it is open to us to identify has survived the two specific arguments brought against it exactly as well as the concepts of science, so the present ground of discrimination has a purely take-it-or-leave-it character. But secondly the pragmatism itself is breathtakingly myopic. The ongoing theory of physics seeks descriptions of what are taken to be facts behind the appearances of things. The ongoing theory of translation seeks descriptions of what it takes to be facts underlying and explaining the blocks of noise and writing human beings make to each other. What use or value attaches to the one enterprise which lacks in the other? It is difficult to imagine a more valuable intellectual goal than removal of the fear that there is no fact of the matter which explains and interprets the human signs which are such an important component of everyone's experience.

## III

This leaves the way clear for propositions as perfectly respectable theoretical items: the notion of the sense of a single sentence can survive the radical empiricist doubts which we have so far discussed. But we now face the difficulties which stand in the way of producing identity-conditions for such items, and therefore of producing a respectable theory of them. The description of the method by which a linguist is able to identify a native's belief seems at first sight to give unproblematic identity-conditions. The semantics of the component terms and structure whereby they give a sentence with determinate truth-conditions are identified: if we are strict in reporting him we put into our *that* clause an item having synonymous terms and identical structure with that used. No obvious importance would attach to the question of how far we could let lapses from this ideal count as proper reportage. The slogan "no entity without identity" is quite wrong if taken to imply that we need to be in possession of decision procedures for all questions of identity; nobody knows, for example, how far one may alter orchestration or tempi and still count as playing the same symphony. Any decision would be purely pragmatic, yet the concept of a symphony is entirely proper. For since we have an ideal for the same sequence of sounds we know that we *can* be as strict as we like, and then how strict we like to be is simply a matter of our purposes. In the same way, if sameness of semantics of components and sameness of structure in the creation of determinate truth-conditions can function as an ideal, nothing of theoretical importance will hinge upon how far we let ourselves depart from it.

The real difficulty lies elsewhere, with the tensions inside the ideal itself. For the notion of a proposition, or the sense of a sentence, has two separate aspects which, like most writers, I have so far tacitly run together. It is to serve as the object of the understanding: what the subject believes, thinks about, doubts, asserts, and so forth. And it is the thing whose truth puts an objective constraint upon the way the world is: it is the determinant of a set of truth-conditions. To develop the second aspect for a moment: since Frege, propositions have been seen as constructed out of the senses of the terms used in their expression, and the senses of such terms are the contributions they make to the truth-conditions of any whole sentence incorporating them. I shall, for reasons which will become clear, prefer to use only sentences which do not put a term inside a propositional attitude context to determine sameness or difference of sense; we may call the identity-conditions fixed by this means "simple semantic identity". This ties well with the epistemology of identifying sentence-meaning which we used against Quine, for to determine the native sense of a term was precisely to map which features of the world the speakers take as crucial to determining the truth or falsity of sentences involving it, and to identify the sense of a particular sentence is then to recognise which set of truth-conditions it creates out of the senses of the component terms. Naturally this approach can give a heavily intensional criterion for sameness of sense. There is nothing to prevent us seeing that a native speaker needs different features of things to determine the applicability of each of a pair of terms, even although they end up applied to just the same things. This will be obvious in the case of complex terms, "having a heart" and "having a liver", for example. In the case of semantically simple terms (and ones which are not just abbreviations of complex terms), we could still know that different features contribute to the truth-conditions of sentences involving them, if the native needs different sensory modalities for their application, for example. With ordinary proper names the precise nature of their contribution to truth-conditions is controversial, but if we see them as serving simply to introduce an object as the item which is the focus of the truth-conditions, and deny that the features of the object which we actually use when deciding if it is the bearer of the name enter into those truth-conditions, then co-referentiality will give simple semantic identity.[3]

The criteria of identity which this approach generates can, then, be fairly clear in outline. It is worth noticing that it can give a strong criterion of identity in cases in which holistic views, concentrating solely upon the truth-conditions of the overall sentence without regard to its internal structure, give a weak one. Thus "this has a physical shape" and "this has a physical size", said of the same object, will necessarily have the same truth-value, and the notion of "truth-condition" is not yet definite enough to rule them out as synonymous. But once we concentrate upon the creation of their senses, we immediately perceive that "shape" and "size" are entirely distinct in meaning, contributing as they do to the truth of most sentences in entirely different ways (contrast: this has changed shape, this has changed size; has a nice shape, has a nice size). Clearly there is room for much further theory about this sort of identity, particularly about cases where an otherwise respectable set of components and an otherwise respectable structure combine to give unverifiable truth-conditions. But the problem that concerns us lies in a different direction.

In simple cases the Fregean theme I have developed plays in harmony with such intuitions as we have about the objects of the understanding. "Procrastinates" and "puts things off" are semantically identical, and to know, say, realise, doubt, etc. that a person procrastinates is to know, say, realise, doubt, etc. that he puts things off. This harmony seems so inevitable that most writers, including Frege himself, use interchangeability *salva veritate* within propositional attitude contexts as criterial for sameness of sense. Yet if sense is constructed as simple semantic identity, described in the way which we have outlined, it is fairly easy to generate difficulty. For it is not at all obvious that a true reportage of what someone said, knew, believed, etc. will be preserved under substitution of simple semantically identical components. We can anticipate trouble simply by reflecting that although two linguistic expressions may actually make the same contribution to truth-conditions, it may not be at all obvious, even to the reflective and competent native speaker, that this is so. Then where there is this ignorance it seems possible that true reportage of what the speaker is

---

[3] The point of view defended in C. A. B. Peacocke, "Proper Names, Reference, and Rigid Designation", Ch. 4 in this volume.

wondering, or thinking about, might need to pay attention to the way the object of his understanding is presented, and not merely to its simple semantic identity.

We can best develop these points, and give force to the possibility I have suggested, by elaborating a straightforward version of the classical paradox of analysis. (See e.g. Mates [1950]).

Substitution of simple semantically identical (hereafter s.s.i.) components must, of course, preserve the semantic identity of a complete sentence in which they are contained. Thus we have the following principles of conservation; for the case of predicates:

If "F" is s.s.i. with "G" and $a$ is any name:
(i)   "$a$ is F" is s.s.i. with "$a$ is G"
(ii)  "$a$ is not F" is s.s.i. with "$a$ is not G"
(iii) "$a$ is F and H" is s.s.i. with "$a$ is G and H"
(iv)  "$(x)x$ is F" is s.s.i. with "$(x)x$ is G"

These are self-evident, and without them no account could be given of how the truth-conditions of the sentences generated could be recovered from knowledge of the senses of the component predicates.

Now suppose we adopt the view that the criteria of identity of objects of the understanding—what is said, known, doubted, etc.—should be tied to simple semantic identity. Using the notation "[understand]" to stand for any of the list of propositional attitude verbs, we then have corresponding principles:

If "F" is s.s.i. with "G" and "$a$" is any name:
($i_u$)   To [understand] that $a$ is F is to [understand] that $a$ is G
($ii_u$)  To [understand] that $a$ is not F is to [understand] that $a$ is not G
($iii_u$) To [understand] that $a$ is F and H is to [understand] that $a$ is G and H
($iv_u$)  To [understand] that $(x)x$ is F is to [understand] that $(x)x$ is G

Putting principles (i) and (iv) together, and relying upon the definition of "or" in terms of "and" and "not" we derive:

(C) If F is s.s.i. with G, then "$(x)x$ is either F and G or neither F nor G" is s.s.i. with "$(x)x$ is either F and F or neither F nor F"

All we have done is create a complex extensional sentence (extensional because the predicates remain in positions where coextensive ones may be substituted *salva veritate*) which, because of our principles of conservation, must be s.s.i. with each other. And this is entirely in accordance with what we would expect. Similarly however, from (i$_u$) to (iv$_u$), we derive:

(C$_u$)   If F is s.s.i. with G, then to [understand] that $(x)x$ is either F and G or neither F nor G, is to [understand] that $(x)x$ is either F and F or neither F nor F

The difficulty is that it is not at all clear that this is true. For where "G" is a predicate which provides an analysis, or explicatory synonym, of "F", it would be natural to allow an activity of saying that everything is either both F and G or neither F nor G which *isn't* identical with, nor truly reported as, the activity of saying that everything is both F and F or neither F nor F.

For example, "$x$ is a widow" is s.s.i. with "$x$ is a woman who was once married, whose husband died while married to her, and who has not subsequently remarried", yet there seems to be an activity of wondering whether all and only widows are women who, etc., which is not truly reported as merely wondering whether all and only widows are widows. Indeed, presented with the identity most people will spend some time wondering whether all and only widows *are* women who, etc.—this is the point of deriving that particular consequence of the principles; this wonderment may be only a prelude to seeing that the co-extension holds, but it is a possible thing to do, and something a good deal more pointful, more relevant to rational acceptance of the identity, than puzzling about the trivial tautology.

Naturally the suggestion that (C$_u$) may be false will arouse opposition. There are indeed far-reaching consequences if it is false, for if so the notion of simple semantic identity will not enable us to construct truth-conditions for sentences incorporating propositional attitude operators; correspondingly facts about such sentences may not directly tell us anything about simple semantic identity. We would thus need to abandon or modify the enormous tradition which allows us to establish difference of "sense" between two terms by merely arguing that the information, understanding, or doubt that $\alpha$ is distinct from the information, understanding, or doubt that $\beta$, where these expressions differ by the substitution of one term for the other in extensional contexts. But is there anything in itself surprising in the falsity of (C$_u$)? On the contrary, its defence would seem to depend upon the view that we invariably know that s.s.i. items which we understand are s.s.i., but it is not at all clear that we do invariably know this.

Dummett, talking of Frege's argument for saying that the sense of a name cannot just consist in its having the reference which it does, sees it as dependent upon the "compelling principle" that "if someone knows the senses of two words, and the two words have the same sense, he must know that they have the same sense" ([1973] p. 95). But why should our understandings be thus flattered? "A grasp of the sense of a word is manifested by the employment of sentences containing the word" (p. 682), but then our linguist could quite possibly observe simple semantic identities, guaranteed by the most exhaustive study of competent native practice, yet whose uncovery comes as a complete surprise to the speakers. The investigation which is supposed to reveal the simple semantic identities of a language will not, therefore, guarantee the "compelling principle": indeed it would seem to make it plain that it could be false.

It will come naturally to many philosophers to offer a linguistic solution of the difficulty. This would mean two things. Firstly, $(C_u)$ is accepted, so that anybody who is strictly and literally wondering whether all and only widows are women who were once married, etc. is strictly and literally wondering whether all and only widows are widows. Since nobody sensible ever does that, the solution also demands that a person who appears to be wondering whether all and only widows are women who were once married, etc., is really doubting something whose truth-conditions involve mentioning words rather than using them. By turning the thought into one about a purely linguistic matter the problem is solved, for of course there is no difficulty at all in separating a propositional attitude to a view about a particular word from one to a view about a different, yet synonymous, word or group of words—the very subject matter is different. And if this route is followed then the concept of sameness of "sense" is at first sight secure from the paradox of analysis, for we have no real lack of substitution in propositional attitude contexts; all we have is a case where people are inclined to misrepresent what they have the attitude towards. However, this move is dangerously liberal. For until we have some control over when we are allowed the linguistic diagnosis, we will never be able to use different behaviour in propositional attitude contexts as a guide to difference of sense, since a defender of the synonymy will merely reply that the difference is only apparent, and to be given a linguistic diagnosis. Thus Scheffler argues that Church's move into language at a similar point could just as well be adopted to reinstate the view that all necessary propositions are identical. (Scheffler [1955]; Church [1954]). We have, it is true, the concept of simple semantic identity, which can be used to evade this consequence, but so long as it is unclear what is to control the possibility of rewriting awkward cases as mentioning words rather than using them, it will be unclear what is the point of evading consequences such as this.

The real objection to the linguistic diagnosis is that, whatever it represents me as really wondering about, it must retain the fact that I, unlike a foreigner, know the sense of the word "widow": I know what it means. And also, since $(C_u)$ is accepted, I am said to know that all and only widows are women who were once married, etc., for I know that all and only widows are widows, and taken strictly these are the same piece of knowledge. But if I know these things it is not easy to see what linguistic fact I can be represented as wondering about. For instance, a foreigner may certainly wonder whether "widow" means all and only women who were once married, etc., but I, who know the sense of the word, and who know that all and only widows are women who were once married, etc., would seem to have nothing left to ponder. The reason I do have something left to ponder is precisely that the Dummett principle is false: I can be aware of the sense of each of a pair of simple semantically identical terms, yet unaware that they have the same sense. But then the retreat to mentioning words loses its apparent initial advantage over a solution which preserves the evident fact that the thing I am really wondering about is displayed by using words rather than mentioning them.

The notion of simple semantic identity was supposed not only to relate predicates to the features in virtue of which they were applied, but also to yield whatever it is in virtue of which a proper name contributes to the truth-conditions of sentences incorporating it. Particularly since the work of Kripke there is renewed interest in the possibility of a direct semantic account: a proper name may serve to introduce the thing for which it stands as the bearer of the predicate, and the truth of what is asserted is purely a matter of how it is with *that thing*. In particular it is not a matter of how it is with a thing satisfying a description or cluster of descriptions, even if they served to introduce the name in the first place. With this account of the contribution of a proper name co-referential names become simply semantically identical. It has always been seen as a decisive objection to this that they need not substitute in propositional attitude contexts. Thus if we suppose "Chomolungma" to be the name of a particular mountain identifiable from the north, and "Everest" to be the name of some mountain seen from the south, a man might wonder whether Chomolungma is Everest, and not wonder whether Everest is Everest, yet the two terms may refer to the same mountain, and the two sentences be made up, in this theory, from s.s.i. components in an identical way.

Instead of taking this as refuting the described theory of proper names we can again question why simple semantic identity should be expected to license intersubstitutability in attitude contexts. To suppose that it must would be to legislate that a language cannot contain a term which (i) makes such a contribution to the truth-conditions of sentences *and* (ii) is yet applied by speakers to a thing *because* they see that thing as having some feature. But this is certainly possible. For the *because* in the second condition may be entirely causal: the name can be applied because of some feature of its bearer without that feature playing any role in its meaning. A good example of this comes with demonstratives: a conjurer can correctly describe his audience by saying "They don't know that *this* is the same thing as *this*"—showing some object under different aspects. But a direct semantic account of the demonstrative is obviously right. So if I apply "Chomolungma" to a mountain because it has particular features seen from the north, and "Everest" because it has others seen from the south, I may well be ignorant that Chomolungma is Everest, and this will be because of my ignorance that the two sets of features apply to one mountain. But this doesn't give any sort of argument that the proper name serves, semantically, to sum up those features, and other arguments into which we are not here entering, may make it extremely unlikely that it does so.

Where, then, are we left if we insist on the separation of simple semantic identity on the one hand and objects of the understanding on the other? Certainly not with an overall rejection of intensional notions, for as I have already argued the theory of meaning which the epistemology of meaning licenses can and must use intensional criteria to individuate the contribution of predicates and of some referential devices. But the other problem, of individuating objects of the understanding (or, in more modern dress, giving truth-

conditions for sentences using propositional attitude constructions)
is apparently as dark as ever. The only suggestion I would venture
about it is this. The theoretical problem of lack of substitutivity is
concealed in practice for two reasons: firstly because it is usually,
though contingently, true that people are aware of identity of
meaning between items if it obtains and if they understand them
both; secondly because it is not in practice often important if we
misreport them through importing an identity of which they are not
aware. Where neither condition obtains it will be important that a
report of what someone [understands] reproduces the linguistic
structure of the sentence which he would use to express his [under-
standing]; to differ by even trivial abbreviation or difference of
semantic structure can, as our difficulty with $(C_u)$ shows, give a false
report of the person. There can be little point in chasing up a limit
to the frailty of our grasp of identities, just as there is little point
in chasing up a limit to the degree to which we can be unaware of
trivial consequences of things we believe. So if we need an ideal of
strict reportage it will have to incorporate a linguistic criterion;
the report should be composed in identical ways out of intensionally
identical parts. This is the requirement of Carnap's concept of
intensional isomorphism, and it still seems to be the best suggestion
in the field. Yet even this does not meet the difficulty of lack of
substitutivity of "Chomolungma" and "Everest" in the sentence
"X [understands] that Everest is Everest", for on a direct semantic
account the substitution preserves intensional isomorphism. I have
already remarked why the loss of substitutivity arises, and why it
seems to me not to refute a direct semantic account. If these points
are accepted they strongly suggest a further criterion of "psychological isomorphism": a true report needs to consider more even than
the simple semantic identity of components, but also whether the
epistemology of their application matches the epistemology of the
application of the components in the reported person's expression of
his thought. It is perhaps not surprising that psychology matters in
what are, after all, reports of psychological states, but it does enforce
the separation of criteria of semantic identity on the one hand, and
criteria of identity of objects of the understanding on the other.

# Bibliographical Index

Ackermann, R. [1967] *Introduction to Many-Valued Logics*. Routledge & Kegan Paul, 1967. 33

Anscombe, G. E. M. [1958] *An Introduction to Wittgenstein's Tractatus*. Hutchinson, 1958. 111

Austin, J. L. [1962] *How to Do Things with Words*. Oxford University Press, 1962. 140

Belnap, N. D. [1961] "Tonk, Plonk, and Plink", *Analysis*, 1961–2, and in *Philosophical Logic*, ed. P. F. Strawson. Oxford University Press, 1967. 44

Bennett, J. F. [1965] "Substance, Reality and Primary Qualities", *American Philosophical Quarterly*, 1965. 22

[1966] *Kant's Analytic*. Cambridge University Press, 1967. 63

[1971] *Locke, Berkeley, Hume*, Oxford University Press, 1971. 22

[1973] "The Meaning-Nominalist Strategy", in *Foundations of Language*, 1973. 169

Brouwer, L. E. J. [1952] "Historical Background, Principles and Methods of Intuitionism", *South African Journal of Science*, 1952. 34

Campbell, C. A. [1958] "Contradiction: 'Law' or 'Convention'?", *Analysis*, 1957–8. 42

Carnap, R. [1937] *The Logical Syntax of Language*, Harcourt, Brace, 1937. 42

[1947] *Meaning and Necessity*. University of Chicago Press, 1947. 103, 104

[1956] *Meaning and Necessity*. 2nd ed., University of Chicago Press, 1956. 184

Church, A. [1946] Review of papers by Max Black and Morton White, pp. 132–3, *Journal of Symbolic Logic*, 1946. 104

[1954] "Intensional Isomorphism and Identity of Belief", *Philosophical Studies*, 1954. 203.

Cohen, L. J. [1971] "Some Remarks on Grice's Views about the Logical Particles of Natural Language", in *Pragmatics of Natural Languages*, ed. Y. Bar-Hillel. Reidel, 1971. 133, 134–43, 150, 151, 152, 153, 165

206

Davidson, D. [1968] "On Saying That", in Davidson and Hintikka
[1969]. 126

[1969] "The Individuation of Events", in *Essays in Honor of Carl Hempel*,
ed. N. Rescher. Reidel, 1969. 131

Davidson, D. and Hintikka, J. [1969] *Words and Objections: Essays in the
Work of W. V. Quine*. Reidel, 1969.

Dummett, M. A. E. [1959a] "Truth", *Proceedings of the Aristotelian Society*,
1958–9, and in *Truth*, ed. G. Pitcher. Prentice-Hall, 1964. 34

[1959b] "Wittgenstein's Philosophy of Mathematics", *Philosophical
Review*, 1959. 11

[1973] *Frege: Philosophy of Language*, Duckworth, 1973. 90, 104, 112,
131, 146, 147, 151, 202

Farber, M. [1942] "Logical Systems and the Principles of Logic",
*Philosophy of Science*, 1942. 34

Feyerabend, P. K. [1962] "Explanation, Reduction and Empiricism", in
*Minnesota Studies in the Philosophy of Science*, vol. II, ed. H. Feigl and
G. Maxwell. University of Minnesota Press, 1962. 43

[1963] "How to be a good Empiricist", in *The Delaware Seminar in the
Philosophy of Science*, vol. II. Interscience, 1963, and in *Philosophy of
Science*, ed. P. H. Nidditch. Oxford University Press, 1968. 43

Føllesdal, D. [1965] "Quantification into Causal Contexts", in *Boston
Studies in the Philosophy of Science*, vol. II, ed. R. S. Cohen and M.
Wartofsky. Humanities Press, 1965; reprinted in *Reference and
Modality*, ed. L. Linsky. Oxford University Press, 1971. 88

Van Fraassen, B. C. [1966] "Singular Terms, Truth-Value Gaps, and
Free Logic", *Journal of Philosophy*, 1966. 37

[1968] "Presupposition, Implication, and Self-Reference", *Journal of
Philosophy*, 1968. 37

[1969] "Presuppositions, Supervaluations and Free Logic", in *The
Logical Way of Doing Things*, ed. K. Lambert. Yale University Press,
1969. 37

Frege, G. [1892] "Uber Sinn und Bedeutung", *Zeitschrift für Philosophie
und Philosophische Kritik*, 1892; translated as "On Sense and Reference" in *Philosophical Writings of Gottlob Frege*, Blackwell, 1952. 100

[1918] "The Thought: A Logical Enquiry", in *Essays on Frege*, ed.
E. D. Klemke. University of Illinois Press, 1968. 119

Fremlin, C. [1938] "Must we always Think in Propositions?", *Analysis*,
1937–8. 42

Gasking, D. A. T. [1938–9] "Mr. Williams on the A Priori", *Analysis*,
1938–9. 7

Geach, P. [1972] *Logic Matters*. Blackwell, 1972. 111, 184

Grandy, R. E. [1972] "A Definition of Truth for Theories with Intensional Definite Description Operators", *Journal of Philosophical Logic*,
1972. 116

Grice, H. P. [1961] *The Causal Theory of Perception*, Proceedings of The Aristotelian Society Supplementary Volume, 1961. 133

[1969a] "Vacuous Names", in Davidson and Hintikka [1969]. 161

[1969b] "Utterer's Meaning and Intentions", *Philosophical Review*, 1969. 155

Haack, S. [1974] *Deviant Logic*. Cambridge University Press, 1974. 55

Hackstaff, L. [1966] *Systems of Formal Logic*. Reidel, 1966. 36

Hare, R. M. [1952] *The Language of Morals*. Oxford University Press, 1952. 144

[1970] "Meaning and Speech Acts", *Philosophical Review*, 1970. 151

[1971] *Practical Inferences*. Macmillan, 1971. 144

Harman, G. [1969] "An Introduction to 'Translation and Meaning', Chapter Two of *Word and Object*", in Davidson and Hintikka [1969]. 195

Hintikka, J. [1962] *Knowledge and Belief*. Cornell University Press, 1962. 96

[1963] "The Modes of Modality", *Acta Philosophica Fennica*, 1963. 77

Kaplan, D. [1969] "Quantifying In", in Davidson and Hintikka [1969]; reprinted in *Reference and Modality*, ed. L. Linsky. Oxford University Press, 1971. 64, 95, 96

[1973] "Bob and Carol and Ted and Alice", in *Approaches to Natural Language*, ed. J. Hintikka *et al*. Reidel, 1973. 118

Kirk, R. [1973] "Underdetermination of Theory and Indeterminacy of Translation", *Analysis*, 1972–3. 192

Kripke, S. [1972a] "Identity and Necessity", in *Identity and Individuation*, ed. J. Munitz. New York University Press, 1972. 89, 90, 109, 110, 113

[1972b] "Naming and Necessity", in *Semantics of Natural Languages*, ed. D. Davidson and G. Harman. Reidel, 1972. 89

Lambert, K. and van Fraassen, B. C. [1972] *Derivation and Counterexample*. Dickenson, 1972. 116

Lewis, C. I. [1932] "Alternative Systems of Logic", *Monist*, 1932. 45

Lewis, D. K. [1969] *Convention*. Harvard University Press, 1969. 169 nn, 171, 172

Linsky, L. [1969] "Reference, Essentialism, and Modality", *Journal of Philosophy*, 1969; reprinted in *Reference and Modality*, ed. L. Linsky. Oxford University Press, 1971. 100

Locke, J. [1690] *An Essay Concerning Human Understanding*, ed. A. S. Pringle Pattison. Oxford University Press, 1924. 22

Mackie, J. L. [1973] *Truth, Probability, and Paradox*. Oxford University Press, 1973. 133n, 142, 144, 145, 148–9, 160, 177

Marcus, R. B. [1961] "Modalities and Intensional Languages", *Synthèse*, 1961. 111

Mates, B. [1950] "Synonymity", *University of California Publications in Philosophy*, No. 25, 1950. 200

Mill, J. S. [1843] *A System of Logic*. Longmans, 1872. 111

Prior, A. N. [1960] "The Runabout Inference Ticket", *Analysis*, 1960–1,
and in *Philosophical Logic*, ed. P. F. Strawson. Oxford University
Press, 1967. 44

   [1964] "Conjunction and Contonktion Revisited", *Analysis*, 1963–4. 44

   [1971] *Objects of Thought*. Oxford University Press, 1971. 99

Putnam, H. [1957] "Three Valued Logic", *Philosophical Studies*, 1957. 44

   [1962] "The Analytic and the Synthetic", in *Minnesota Studies in the
Philosophy of Science*, vol. III, ed. H. Feigl and G. Maxwell. Holt,
Rinehart & Winston, 1962. 40, 44

   [1969] "Is Logic Empirical?" in *Boston Studies in the Philosophy of Science*,
vol. v, ed. M. Wartofsky and R. S. Cohen, Reidel, 1969. 34, 43, 44,
55

Quine, W. V. O. [1936] "Truth by Convention", first published in 1936,
in *Philosophical Essays for A. N. Whitehead*, ed. O. H. Lee; also in *The
Ways of Paradox*, Random House, 1966. 9

   [1943] "Notes on Existence and Necessity", *Journal of Philosophy*, 1943.
57

   [1951] "Two Dogmas of Empiricism", *Philosophical Review*, 1951, and in
*From a Logical Point of View*. Harper Torchbooks, 1953. 47

   [1953a] "The Problem of Meaning in Linguistics", in *From a Logical
Point of View*. Harper Torchbooks, 1953. 47

   [1953b] "Three Grades of Modal Involvement", *Proceedings of the XIth
International Congress of Philosophy*, vol. XIV. North-Holland, 1953;
reprinted in *The Ways of Paradox*. Random House, 1966. 63, 111

   [1956] "Quantifiers and Propositional Attitudes", *Journal of Philosophy*,
1956; reprinted in *The Ways of Paradox*. Random House, 1966. 63

   [1959] "Meaning and Translation", in *On Translation*, ed. R. A.
Brower. Harvard University Press, 1959, and in *The Structure of Language*, ed. J. A. Fodor and J. J. Katz. Prentice-Hall, 1964. 47

   [1960a] "Carnap and Logical Truth", *Synthèse*, 1960, and in *The Philosophy of Rudolph Carnap*, ed. P. Schilpp. Open Court, 1963, and in *The
Ways of Paradox*. Random House, 1966. 39, 43, 46

   [1960b] *Word and Object*. Wiley, 1960. 46, 47, 48, 50, 53, 55, 88, 189

   [1968a] "Epistemology Naturalised", in *Ontological Relativity and Other
Essays*. Columbia University Press, 1969. 189

   [1968b] "Ontological Relativity", *Journal of Philosophy*, 1968, and in
*Ontological Relativity*. Columbia University Press, 1969. 47, 48, 195

   [1970a] "Grades of Theoreticity", in *Experience and Theory*, ed. L. Foster
and J. W. Swanson. Duckworth, 1970. 48

   [1970b] "On the Reasons for the Indeterminacy of Translation",
*Journal of Philosophy*, 1970. 49, 99, 189, 191, 194

   [1970c] *Philosophy of Logic*. Prentice-Hall, 1970. 46, 50, 52, 53, 55, 126

Ramsey [1925] "The Foundations of Mathematics", in *The Foundations of
Mathematics*, Routledge & Kegan Paul, 1931. 10

Reeves, A. [1973] "Concerning Rabbits", *Philosophical Studies*, 1973. 196

Rescher, N. [1966] *The Logic of Commands*. Routledge & Kegan Paul, 1966. 146

    [1969] *Many-Valued Logic*. McGraw Hill, 1969. 34, 38

Russell, B. [1905] "On Denoting", *Mind*, 1905. 91, 96, 111

    [1910] "On the Nature of Truth and Falsehood", *Philosophical Essays*. Allen & Unwin, 1910. 64

    [1911] "Knowledge by Acquaintance and Description", *Proceedings of the Aristotelian Society*, 1910–11. 96

    [1919] "The Philosophy of Logical Atomism (Lecture IV)", *The Monist*, 1919; reprinted in *Logic and Knowledge*, ed. George Marsh. Allen & Unwin, 1956. 65

Scheffler, I. [1955] "On Synonymy and Indirect Discourse", *Philosophy of Science*, 1955. 203

Schiffer, S. [1972] *Meaning*. Oxford University Press, 1972. 155, 172

Scott, D. S. [1967] "Existence and Description in Formal Logic", in *Bertrand Russell: Philosopher of the Century*, ed. R. Schoenmann. Allen & Unwin, 1967. 116

Shapere, D. [1966] "Meaning and Scientific Change", in *Mind and Cosmos*, ed. R. Colodny. University of Pittsburg Press, 1966. 43

Smiley, T. J. [1959] "Entailment and Deducibility", *Proceedings of the Aristotelian Society*, 1958–9. 42

    [1960] "Sense without Denotation", *Analysis*, 1959–60. 54

Stevenson, J. T. [1961] "Roundabout the Runabout Inference Ticket", *Analysis*, 1960–1, and in *Readings on Logic*, ed. I. M. Copi and J. A. Gould. Macmillan, 1972. 44

Strawson, P. F. [1952] *Introduction to Logical Theory*. Methuen, 1952. 45

    [1964a] "Identifying Reference and Truth Values", *Theoria*, 1964. 118

    [1964b] "Intention and Convention in Speech Acts", *Philosophical Review*, 1964. 155

Tarski, A. [1936] "Der Wahrheitsbegriff in den formalisierten Sprachen", *Studia Philosophica*, 1936; translated as "The Concept of Truth in Formalized Languages", in A. Tarski, *Logic, Semantics, and Metamathematics*. Oxford University Press, 1956. 59

Wallace, J. [1970] "On the Frame of Reference", *Synthèse*, 1970; reprinted in *Semantics of Natural Languages*, ed. D. Davidson and G. Harman. Reidel, 1972. 84, 85, 87

Wiggins, D. R. P. [1968] "On Being in the Same Place at the Same Time", *Philosophical Review*, 1968. 131

Wittgenstein, L. [1953] *Philosophical Investigations*. Blackwell, 1953. 190